D1555262

5/19/14
#85.00

Critical Approaches to Children's Literature
Series Editors: **Kerry Mallan** and **Clare Bradford**

Critical Approaches to Children's Literature is an innovative series concerned with the best contemporary scholarship and criticism on children's and young adult literature, film, and media texts. The series addresses new and developing areas of children's literature research as well as bringing contemporary perspectives to historical texts. The series has a distinctive take on scholarship, delivering quality works of criticism written in an accessible style for a range of readers, both academic and professional. The series is invaluable for undergraduate students in children's literature as well as advanced students and established scholars.

Published titles include:

Cherie Allan
PLAYING WITH PICTUREBOOKS
Postmodernism and the Postmodernesque

Clare Bradford, Kerry Mallan, John Stephens & Robyn McCallum
NEW WORLD ORDERS IN CONTEMPORARY CHILDREN'S LITERATURE
Utopian Transformations

Margaret Mackey
NARRATIVE PLEASURES IN YOUNG ADULT NOVELS, FILMS AND VIDEO GAMES
Critical Approaches to Children's Literature

Andrew O'Malley
CHILDREN'S LITERATURE, POPULAR CULTURE AND, *ROBINSON CRUSOE*

Christopher Parkes
CHILDREN'S LITERATURE AND CAPITALISM
Fictions of Social Mobility in Britain, 1850–1914

Michelle Smith
EMPIRE IN BRITISH GIRLS' LITERATURE AND CULTURE
Imperial Girls, 1880–1915

Forthcoming titles:

Elizabeth Bullen
CLASS IN CONTEMPORARY CHILDREN'S LITERATURE

Pamela Knights
READING BALLET AND PERFORMANCE NARRATIVES FOR CHILDREN

Kate McInally
DESIRING GIRLS IN YOUNG ADULT FICTION

Susan Napier
MIYAZAKI HAYO AND THE USES OF ENCHANTMENT

Critical Approaches to Children's Literature
Series Standing Order ISBN 978–0–230–22786–6 (hardback)
978–0–230–22787–3 (paperback)
(*outside North America only*)

You can receive future titles in this series as they are published by placing a standing order. Please contact your bookseller or, in case of difficulty, write to us at the address below with your name and address, the title of the series and the ISBN quoted above.

Customer Services Department, Macmillan Distribution Ltd, Houndmills, Basingstoke, Hampshire RG21 6XS, England

Playing with Picturebooks

Postmodernism and the Postmodernesque

Cherie Allan

PN
1009
.A1
A415
2012

First published 2012 by
PALGRAVE MACMILLAN

Palgrave Macmillan in the UK is an imprint of Macmillan Publishers Limited,
registered in England, company number 785998, of Houndmills, Basingstoke,
Hampshire RG21 6XS.

Palgrave Macmillan in the US is a division of St Martin's Press LLC,
175 Fifth Avenue, New York, NY 10010.

Palgrave Macmillan is the global academic imprint of the above companies
and has companies and representatives throughout the world.

Palgrave® and Macmillan® are registered trademarks in the United States,
the United Kingdom, Europe and other countries.

ISBN 978–0–230–31949–3

This book is printed on paper suitable for recycling and made from fully
managed and sustained forest sources. Logging, pulping and manufacturing
processes are expected to conform to the environmental regulations of the
country of origin.

A catalogue record for this book is available from the British Library.

A catalog record for this book is available from the Library of Congress.

10 9 8 7 6 5 4 3 2 1
21 20 19 18 17 16 15 14 13 12

Transferred to Digital Printing in 2014

For Chris

Contents

List of Figures	viii
Series Preface	ix
Acknowledgements	x
Introduction: Looking Back	1
1 Looking Beneath the Surface	27
2 Destabilising Modes of Representation	56
3 Disturbing the Air of Reality	79
4 Interrogating Representations of the Past	95
5 Problematising Unity through Ex-centricity and Difference	123
6 Towards the Postmodernesque Picturebook	140
(In)Conclusion: Looking Forward	170
Notes	175
Bibliography	181
Index	195

List of Figures

1.1 'Little Red Running Shorts' illustration from *The Stinky Cheese Man and Other Fairly Stupid Tales* by Jon Scieszka, illustrated by Lane Smith. Illustration © 1992 by Lane Smith. Used by permission of Viking Children's Books, a Division of Penguin Young Readers Group. All rights reserved   45

2.1 Illustration from *Black and White* by David Macaulay. Copyright © 1990 by David Macaulay. Reprinted by permission of Houghton Mifflin Harcourt Publishing Company. All rights reserved   67

4.1 Illustration copyright © 1992 by William Kent Monkman from *A Coyote Columbus Story*, text copyright © 1992 by Thomas King. First published in Canada by Groundwood Books Ltd. www.groundwoodbooks.com   107

5.1 Image reproduced with permission from *The Lost Thing* by Shaun Tan, Lothian Children's Books, an imprint of Hachette Australia 2000   136

Series Preface

The *Critical Approaches to Children's Literature* series was initiated in 2008 by Kerry Mallan and Clare Bradford. The aim of the series is to identify and publish the best contemporary scholarship and criticism on children's and young adult literature, film and media texts. The series is open to theoretically informed scholarship covering a wide range of critical perspectives on historical and contemporary texts from diverse national and cultural settings. Critical Approaches aims to make a significant contribution to the expanding field of children's literature research by publishing quality books that promote informed discussion and debate about the production and reception of children's literature and its criticism.

Kerry Mallan and Clare Bradford

Acknowledgements

I would like to acknowledge and thank a number of people who were instrumental in supporting me on this journey. It is impossible to adequately express my gratitude to Kerry Mallan for her intellectual rigour and guidance as well as her unwavering support throughout this project. I also thank my colleagues at Queensland University of Technology who have continually offered their support to me. Particular thanks go to Annette Patterson, Amy Cross and Michelle Dicinoski. I also wish to express my gratitude to the members of the Critical Dialogues group, especially Michael Dezuanni, Ruth Greenaway, Erica Hateley, Jo Lampert, Geraldine Massey, Peter Mountney and Anna Whateley. I also acknowledge the professional support received from Ben Doyle, Monica Kendall and the team at Palgrave Macmillan.

On a personal note, completing this book would have been a more difficult enterprise without the continuing love and support from Chris, Brownyn, Caitlin and the two Camerons, as well as other interested family and friends, and for this I thank them.

Introduction: Looking Back

> To attempt to reject postmodernism entirely is to endeavour to stand outside one's age, to remove oneself from its everyday life and its cultural and intellectual currents. (Geyh, 2003, p. 6)

> [W]riters and illustrators of picturebooks over the last thirty years have been doing no more than responding to the tenor of the times, either consciously or unconsciously importing the approaches, techniques and sensibilities of postmodernism into their work. (Lewis, 2001, p. 87)

When the Little Red Hen in *The Stinky Cheese Man and Other Fairly Stupid Tales* (Scieszka and Smith, 1992) comes across a blank page in the story she asks: 'Why is that page blank?' She attempts to bring order to the narrative with cries of: 'Where is that lazy narrator? Where is that lazy illustrator? Where is that lazy author?' This iteration draws attention to the traditional constructors of a conventional picturebook narrative and points the finger squarely at those the Little Red Hen deems responsible for the fact that this book does not conform to the structure of conventional narratives. The narrator has lost control of some of the characters and the author and illustrator contradict each other on any number of occasions. Little Red Hen is becoming increasingly strident as she fears the loss of order and coherence within the narrative. She can perhaps be regarded in the light of a 'priest' who, according to Geyh's (2003) definition,

1

represents traditional literary scholars who pass on and interpret the 'sacred texts' and see themselves as 'keepers of the flame of culture'. In the above context Little Red Hen is insistent on keeping, not necessarily to the sacred texts themselves, but to the sacred *processes* of narrative, particularly that of the authority of the Author. She attempts to stand outside her age by loudly objecting to the influence of postmodernism on the narrative in which she has found herself.

Postmodern picturebooks are cultural texts which reflect the tenor of their times. As such, in keeping with the sentiments expressed in the first epigraph above, they are significant texts reflecting cultural and intellectual currents and thus worthy of our attention. Consequently, it is important to take into consideration the cultural contexts that have contributed to the evolving nature of the postmodern picturebook. Perry Nodelman (1992) suggests that the models of imaginative play and storytelling familiar to children today include products of popular culture such as video games, TV cartoons, toys and movies, and it is these products which help shape the ways in which children approach picturebooks. Throughout this book, therefore, it is appropriate to keep in mind these cultural factors as it traces the influence of postmodernism on the picturebook and approaches the question of what constitutes a postmodern picturebook. These cultural perspectives and differences play an important role in developing an understanding, not only of how readers approach these texts, but also of the cultural contexts in which the texts are produced.

In the ensuing chapters it will become evident that children's literature displays elements of postmodernism, albeit of a particular style. What, then, are the prevailing circumstances that create favourable conditions for postmodern writing for children? This is particularly pertinent as, until recently, conventional wisdom on children's literature identified its main objective as the enculturation of children into the dominant liberal humanist society.[1] For instance, Sipe and Pantaleo (2008) posit that, historically, children's literature has reflected societal values, attitudes and historical knowledge. Stephens (1996) suggests that children's literature and culture can also be 'radically pluralistic and interdisciplinary', thereby making the field readily available to current cultural influences. Consequently, it is hardly surprising, as indicated in the second epigraph to this chapter, that postmodern influences have been brought to bear on the form and structure of children's narrative as well as on its thematic concerns.

The cultural environment in which children's literature has been written over the past 30 or so years, according to Featherstone (2007), has become much more democratised, whereby cultural tastes and leisure practices have been overhauled to cater to wider audiences with an emphasis on the spectacular, the popular, the pleasurable and the immediately accessible. Such taste and leisure practices are epitomised by shopping malls, theme parks and holiday resorts where consumers accept the hyperreality of such places for what they are, namely a mediated experience. Meanwhile, cities today are postmodern sites of consumption that are saturated with signs and images. No longer is society driven by the metanarratives of progress, science and religion but is given over to playfulness and pleasure, hyperreality and image resulting in new metanarratives such as consumerism (discussed in detail in Chapter 6). The current phase of cultural declassification both inside and outside of the academy has produced an interest in popular culture and postmodernism (Featherstone, 2007). This interest is reflected in postmodern picturebooks. For example, *The Jolly Postman* (Ahlberg and Ahlberg, 1986) celebrates popular culture through its many intertextual references, not only to other fairy tales but also to other genres such as catalogues, letters, party invitations and newspapers. *Willy's Pictures* by Anthony Browne (2001) blurs the boundaries between high and popular art through the appropriation of famous classic paintings such as *St George and the Dragon* (Raphael) and *The Straw Mannequin* (Goya) onto which he imposes something of his own dreams and fears. *Who's Afraid of the Big Bad Book?* (Lauren Child, 2003) makes popular cultural references to the 'Just Right' breakfast cereal and features a cameo appearance by Agnetha and Benny of the former ABBA group.

The children's literature field is highly competitive and new writers need to carve out their own cultural space in the marketplace especially considering the vast array of media from film, television, computer games, DVDs and websites available to young people. These commodities compete with books for consumers' attention and it results in authors and illustrators forced to find new ways of telling stories, to 'defamiliarise' their narrative strategies in order to compete. Deborah Stevenson (1994, p. 32) argues that although popular art infuses easily into picturebooks, it is 'television, film and music video, far more than books, [that] are the messengers of postmodern culture to young people'. Certainly the cultural dynamic driving popular culture at the current time is the prevalence of the image. Within this visual culture, available technologies readily allow reproduction and appropriation which, in turn, enable writers and illustrators to draw attention to issues of representation and intertextuality, especially through pastiche and collage. Stevenson (1994) suggests that postmodern picturebooks such as *The Stinky Cheese Man and Other Fairly Stupid Tales* adopt 'postliterate' strategies more in common with the media than with books, and perhaps this is where a measure of their popularity lies, although the concept is probably now best represented by the term multiliteracies.[2] Picturebooks, with their dual codes of written and visual texts, are ideally located to appeal to a postmodern audience. The receivers of postmodern picturebooks (primarily children although their appeal to older readers must also be acknowledged) belong to what Elizabeth Freeman (2005) refers to as the iPod[3] generation. This generation is not overwhelmed or alienated by the technologies of today but readily accepts them as regular elements of their everyday lives. In response to Fredric Jameson's (1991) comments on the Westin Bonaventure Hotel in Los Angeles as an alien space, Geyh (2003, pp. 9–10) suggests that younger generations would not agree as: 'Their sensibilities, forged amid the hyperspeeds of Playstations, MTV fast-cut editing, and hip-hop sampling and fragmentation, find such supersaturated hyperspaces quite congenial.' It is to this audience that postmodern picturebooks appeal – little wonder that many of these readers find the fragmentation, non-linearity and playfulness familiar strategies.

In order to arrive at some understanding of postmodern picturebooks from which to proceed, it is necessary to examine the movement of postmodernism and trace its influence on literature in general and picturebooks specifically. The remainder of this Introduction outlines the concept of postmodernism and its effects on literature, as well as the changing modes of postmodern fiction. It then considers what makes a so-called postmodern picturebook 'postmodern' by attending to the conditions that have contributed to the emergence of this type of text and the research that it has generated. Finally, the chapter examines shifts in the direction of postmodern fiction and questions whether the influence of postmodernism in literature is in decline, and identifies a new classification of the postmodern picturebook, the postmodernesque.

Origins of postmodernism

The term *postmodernism* first entered scholarship in the late 1950s and indications suggest that British historian Arnold Toynbee,[4] in his *A Study of History* (1947), was one of the first recorded scholars to use the term, albeit to characterise a dramatic break in Western history (Best and Kellner, 1991). This notion of a radical break with modernism is also supported by other commentators such as Arthur Berger (2003), who notes that around 1960 there was a 'seismic shift' in our sensibilities from modernism to postmodernism and that this change began to be reflected in the work of architects, writers and artists. Christopher Butler (2002, p. 5), writing of the movement from modernism to postmodernism, claims that post-World War II: 'we can sense a break with [...] the modernist period' and adds: 'a new climate of ideas has arisen and brought with it a new sensibility'. He does warn, however, that there is no single line of development to be found in this shift from modernism to postmodernism, rather that a multiplicity of connections and disruptions constitute the shift.

Further support for this notion of a break came with Jean-François Lyotard's (1984, p. xxiv) declaration that the *postmodern* is an 'incredulity toward metanarratives' which reinforces the notion of a break with modernism. These grand or metanarratives are, as Berger (2003, p. ix) explains: 'the overarching philosophical beliefs that used to give people notions of what is important and how to live'. These myths by which we once legitimised knowledge and practice include Christianity, Science, Democracy, Communism and Progress (Keep et al., 2001). Terry Eagleton (1996) agrees that postmodernism signals disillusionment with these metanarratives or 'fond hopes' of modernism. He argues that such metanarratives have been historically discredited and are little more than dangerous illusions that have contributed to totalitarian politics. This disillusionment with the metanarratives of the modernist period is reflected in postmodern literature, including postmodern picturebooks, which interrogates the dominant discourses of liberal humanist societies. Ihab Hassan (2001,

p. 6), meanwhile, argues that it was not until the late 1960s and early 1970s that postmodernism began to signify a distinct development in American culture, signalling 'a critical modification, if not an actual end, of modernism'. While Berger and Butler write of a definite break from modernism, the break cannot be attributed to a single event or cause. Rather, it can be more reasonably conceived as the result of the combined effects of a number of factors, including disillusionment with the ideals of modernism, which led not to a utopian society, as hoped, but contributed to the totalitarian regimes of Europe in the lead up to World War II. It may be difficult to determine an exact timeframe for the emergence of postmodernism but it is generally accepted that its influence began to be noticed in the wake of World War II, and its influence continues, albeit arguably somewhat reduced. It is equally difficult to say exactly what was meant by the term *postmodernism* in the 1960s and what it means today.

Terminology

Few terms have been subjected to such intense debate as has *postmodernism*. One of the major difficulties in coming to an understanding of postmodernism and its effects on postmodern picturebooks has been the often-indiscriminate use of the term and its excessive use by the media. This term has been subjected to intense debate thereby making consensus on its meaning difficult to achieve. As Linda Hutcheon (1988, p. 3) says: 'Of all terms *postmodernism* must be the most over- and under-defined' and indeed, any attempt to encapsulate it in an all-encompassing definition is not an easy task. There are, as Stierstorfer (2003, p. 2) notes: 'too many divergent views [...] too many departures [...] and too many definitions of what postmodernism is or has been [... which does not] allow for a smoothly consistent argument'. The ambiguity and confusion may best be explained by the notion that there is not one, but many, versions of postmodernism depending on the viewpoint of the particular writer of any given commentary. Perhaps Tim Woods (1999) best sums it up when he observes that the term postmodernism has acquired a semantic instability or a shifting meaning that shadows and echoes its own notes of indeterminacy and insecurity.

The ambiguity of the precise usage of 'post' has also contributed to the ongoing debate surrounding the meaning of *postmodernism*.

Jameson (1991, p. 1), in a similar manner to those mentioned earlier, argues that the existence of postmodernism depends on the 'hypothesis of some radical break' from the modernist movement; that is post-modern.[5] However, a number of commentators see its usage as denoting 'not modern', indicating postmodernism's supposed antagonism towards all things modernist; while yet others see it as beyond modernism, indicating a link with and continuity of modernity. Perhaps Charles Jencks' (1991, p. 6) declaration that 'postmodernism has the essential double meaning: the continuation of modernism and its transcendence' comes closest to an acceptable position on this particular point. There are also questions surrounding the confusion between postmodernism and postmodernity. Linda Hutcheon (1989) notes a tendency for some (including Jameson) to conflate the terms but insists that while they are inextricably related they are, nevertheless, separate concepts. David Lyon (1999) defines postmodernity as the condition of society resulting from a loss of faith in the metanarratives of the Enlightenment period. Hassan (2001), too, argues that while postmodernism refers to the cultural sphere, postmodernity refers to what he calls the geopolitical scheme. He adds that postmodernity is a world process, sometimes labelled postcolonialism (in its widest sense), and features aspects of globalisation and localisation. Perhaps Bran Nicol's (2009, p. 2) explanation provides the greatest clarity by suggesting that there are three derivatives – 'postmodernity', 'postmodernism' and 'postmodern'. He explains:

> 'Postmodern' is an adjective that refers both to a particular period in literary and perhaps cultural history [...] and to a set of aesthetic styles and principles which characterize literary production in this period [1950s to 1990s ...] and which are shaped by the context of postmodernism and postmodernity. Where 'postmodernity' refers to the way the world has changed in this period, due to developments in the political, social, economic, and media spheres, 'postmodernism' (and the related adjective 'postmodernist') refers to a set of ideas developed from philosophy and theory and related to aesthetic production.[6]

Throughout this book, I use *postmodernity* to refer to the political and socio-economic organisation of society and *postmodernism* to refer to the cultural practices associated with said society.

In an effort to endow the term *postmodernism* with a sense of meaning while at the same time avoiding totalisations such as 'postmodern age' or 'postmodern culture', postmodernism, according to Hassan (2001, p. 9), is, among other things, one way 'we view the world in which we live, a filter through which we view history, interpret reality, see ourselves' in relation to society and to others. Further, it can be regarded as a rejection of many, if not most, of the cultural certainties on which life in the West has been structured over the previous two centuries (Sim, 2005). This rejection resulted in a developing scepticism primarily towards the authority, received wisdom, and cultural and political customs of the Enlightenment period. Such scepticism continues to affect all aspects of life and is expressed through changes in everything from architecture, literature, fashion and the media to how we view the political and cultural practices of dominant social groups. Woods (1999) argues that despite the fairly indiscriminate use of the word 'postmodernism' (discussed above), particularly in relation to cultural production, it is possible to distinguish two specific uses of the term. Firstly, he suggests it is used in reference to the contemporary cultural context as a whole, and secondly, as a set of characteristics which are evident in a group of texts. To accept the second category in a broader context than simply 'literature' we would need to embrace the broadest possible meaning of the word 'text' to include works of art, music, architecture and so on. Ursula Heise (1997), in contrast to Woods' fairly narrow designations, provides a more comprehensive list of commonly accepted usages of the term postmodernism: she includes a chronological period, a particular style found in some contemporary artworks and literary texts, a specific way of thinking theoretically about issues such as language, knowledge and identity, and, more latterly, a property of social structures at the end of the twentieth century and/or a change in the values of certain societies. Heise adds the warning that different interpretations of these basic meanings further add to the complexity of the term. Many commentators (including myself) would designate the latter two meanings to be more aligned with *postmodernity* (as defined previously) than with postmodernism.

As I trace the influence of postmodernism on picturebooks, my emphasis is on postmodernism as it applies to a particular cultural context as well as to a set of characteristics that pertain to a particular group of texts, so-called postmodern picturebooks. At the same time

I recognise the multitude of guises in which postmodernism is held. I also acknowledge that this particular cultural context exists within a chronological period (although the boundaries of this period are fluid, as briefly outlined above) and that this context and the subsequent texts resulting from such a context are products of the social (as well as economic and political) structures referred to by Heise (and others) above.

Characteristics of postmodern fiction

What exactly do these categories mean in relation to the literature of postmodernism? One of the major impulses of postmodern literature is its challenge to realist fiction: both the ideologies embedded within realist texts and how various narrative strategies and devices of realist fiction present these attitudes and values as 'natural'. This results in texts which, in both the broad cultural context and more specifically in relation to the texts a postmodern culture produces, exhibit, according to Lyon (1999, p. 10): 'blurring of boundaries between high and low culture; the collapse of hierarchies of knowledge, taste and opinion; and an interest in the local rather than the universal'. Eagleton (1996, p. 201), on the other hand, describes the typical postmodern work of art as 'arbitrary, eclectic, hybrid, decentred, fluid, discontinuous, pastiche-like'. Eagleton adds that postmodernist form (including that of narrative) tends to be ironic, indulges in playfulness and pleasure, and points to its status as a construct, its intertextual origins and its parodic recycling of other works. Postmodern narratives consistently draw attention to the conventions and structures of narrative itself. Readers are constantly reminded that the very (postmodern) process in which they are engaged is not so much clarifying the world for them, as the realists had proposed, as much as immersing them in the problem of representation. *The Stinky Cheese Man and Other Fairly Stupid Tales* is designed from the very first page to draw attention to the book's own awareness of its constructedness. This is made evident by the narrator who shouts at the Little Red Hen: 'You can't tell your story right here. This is the end paper.' Rather than projecting certainty, postmodern texts focus on difference, creating conditions in which distinct cultural boundaries and certainties are questioned. This uncertainty is reflected in particular children's texts that resist the traditional narrative consolations of resolution and certainty; instead they often offer indeterminacy and lack of closure.

In philosophy there has been a departure from the belief in one true reality to a conviction that it is impossible to accurately represent 'reality' in all its guises and that texts only ever present different versions of reality or, as some writers have flippantly stated: 'Reality isn't what it used to be' (Crook et al., 1992, p. 32). Keep et al. (2001), meanwhile, suggest that postmodernism, rather than not believing in 'truth', sees truth and meaning as being historically constructed and, therefore, is intent on exposing the means by which this construction is hidden and naturalised. In a related comment Butler (2002) proposes that postmodernism is strongly opposed to the dominant ideologies that help maintain the status quo of any given society. However, I argue that rather than being 'strongly opposed' to these dominant ideologies, postmodernists object more to the fact that these dominant ideologies are often naturalised through practice and are, therefore, more likely to unwittingly be accepted as natural rather than recognised as constructed. Consequently, postmodern fiction often works to 'lay bare' the hidden nature of particular ideologies. A common example in children's literature, particularly of past decades, is the exposure of the patriarchal societies in which the female voice is not often heard. For instance, *Piggybook* (1986) by Anthony Browne is the story of the Piggott family, Mum, Dad and two sons. Mrs Piggott, as well as having a job, does all the housework until one day when she walks out and leaves a note which states: 'You are pigs.' The men folk of the Piggott family examine their behaviour and changes are made. Babette Cole's parody of the fairy-tale genre in the picturebook *Princess Smartypants* (1986), discussed in more detail in Chapter 1, also draws attention to such naturalised practices. This interrogation of naturalised ideologies with regards to gender, although not without its own difficulties, has also expanded in other texts to include areas of race, ethnicity and sexuality among others.

In its attempts to unsettle realist fiction's claims of representing *real* life, postmodern philosophy and literature foreground issues concerning the ontological status of fictional worlds and texts. Ontology is a branch of metaphysics concerned with the nature of being. Philosophical takes on postmodernism incorporate the study of the nature of being, existence and reality. McHale (1987), writing in relation to fiction, describes ontology as a theoretical description of a universe: *a* universe rather than *the* universe; thereby allowing description of *any* universe (real or fictional for example). He implies, potentially, a *plurality* of universes and raises existential questions such as: 'what is a world?' and 'what kinds of worlds are they?' While McHale concedes that it is possible to interrogate a postmodernist text with regards to its epistemological implications, he claims that it is more imperative to address its ontological concerns. He sees a shift from dominant problems of *knowing* to problems of *modes of being* – from the epistemological dominant associated with modernist fiction to the *ontological* dominant of postmodern literature. This attention to *modes of being* in relation to worlds ('impossible' as well as 'possible' worlds) requires asking questions such as: What is the mode of existence of particular worlds and how are they structured? How are particular worlds constituted and how do they differ, one from another?[7] Further, what happens when different kinds of worlds are placed in conflict or when boundaries are violated? In order to interrogate aspects of realist fiction, postmodern texts utilise strategies which foreground not only the ontological status of a world (or worlds) projected within a text, but also the ontology of the literary text itself (McHale, 1987). For instance, the picturebook *Come Away from the Water, Shirley* (Burningham, 1977) projects a number of different worlds. The primary world or *diegetic* level (McHale, 1987) appears to be situated in the present time in which a small girl, Shirley, is at the beach with her parents. A further world, on a *hypodiegetic level*, is constructed through the girl's imagination in which she is held captive on a pirate's ship. The differences between this hypodiegetic (secondary) level and those of the diegetic (primary) level are reinforced through separation by the book's gutter as well as differences in colour and media, although slippages also occur when a dog wanders along the beach and is drawn into Shirley's imaginary or hypodiegetic world.

Through the projection and often collision of different worlds, postmodern fiction foregrounds boundaries between worlds, and destabilises the ontological status of the central ontological world of a text. This creates fragmentation, indeterminacy and/or ambiguity within the texts. Ann Grieve (1993) suggests that this ontological plurality and/or instability is also a governing dynamic of much postmodern children's fiction. Cheryl McMillan (2002) agrees that, in postmodern children's literature, the epistemological concerns of modernism have been replaced by the ontological concerns of postmodernism. This results in a change from perceiving oneself at the centre of the world (a common trait of characters/focalisers in conventional children's literature) to wondering to which of the many worlds 'I' belong and where are the boundaries of said worlds. Whether the shift has been as all encompassing in children's literature as this suggests remains uncertain, especially as children are still concerned with perceiving themselves at the centre of their world. This continues to be reflected in many postmodern, as well as conventional, picturebooks. Perhaps McHale's statement that some postmodern texts raise both epistemological and ontological concerns is more in line with children's literature as they are, as stated above, attempting to define their world(s). These issues concerning ontology are examined in more detail in Chapter 3.

Along with an interest in cultural and social assumptions such as 'origins and ends, unity and totalizations [...] and [...] representations and truth' (Hutcheon, 1988, p. 89), the postmodern enterprise has initiated a renewed interest in history. Contrary to some claims, postmodernists do not maintain that the past does not exist, rather they question how we can know that past history as it can only ever be known through its texts. Nicol (2009), for instance, points to the existence of 'an unbridgeable gap' between the real past and historiography's representation of it. In a similar vein, Alun Munslow (1997, p. 1) calls for 'a rethink of the historical enterprise' and later (p. 89) asserts that history can no longer legitimately be viewed as simply or merely a matter of the discovery of *the* story of the past. Keith Jenkins (1991, p. 4) writes of 'histories rather than history'. Although his work received greater attention from literary theorists than from historiographers, Hayden White (1976) was one of the first theorists to draw attention to the similarities between literary practices and those of historiography.[8] Thus, it is a history mediated through language which 'has its own forms of terminological determinism, represented by the figures of speech without which discourse itself is impossible' (White, 1976, p. 134). Building on the work of White (among others), Keith Jenkins (1991, p. 21) argues that: 'history *per se* is an ideological construct (which) means that it is constantly being reworked and re-ordered by all those who are variously affected by power relationships'. In other words, as De Certeau (1975) asserts, the act of telling about the past, of writing history, turns the 'given' into a 'construction' and thus must be treated as such.

In contesting attempts to represent the past, postmodern narrative highlights the similarities between fiction and historiography. Jenkins (Munslow, 2003, p. xiv) maintains that history is first and foremost a literary narrative *about* the past. This aligns with Hutcheon's (1988) assertion that history as a narrative account is unavoidably figurative, allegorical and fictive, and always already textualised, always already interpreted. In other words, both historiography and fiction are forms of narrative and function as signifying systems. Therefore any meanings drawn from such systems will always be constructed and thus, provisional. So, too, with historical fiction, of which Jameson (1991, p. 25) argues: 'The historical novel can no longer set out to represent the historical past; it can only "represent" our ideas and stereotypes about the past.' Postmodern historical fiction, or *historiographic metafiction* as Hutcheon (1988) labels it, seeks to interrogate and problematise conventional representations of an historical past. Historiographic metafiction is fiction which uses metafictional strategies to draw attention to history as a construction and question its ability to accurately represent that past. This is not to say that significance cannot be derived from history, rather that we should not readily accept all that history presents. These discussions around historical knowledge are taken up in more detail in Chapter 4.

Criticism of postmodernism

The cultural phenomenon of postmodernism has attracted a great deal of criticism from a range of theorists and commentators. One of the major criticisms levelled at it is that, as an enterprise, postmodernism is dominated by white, middle-class, heterosexual, Western male theorists, authors and academics. Homi Bhabha (1994) argues that a wide range of people, including women, the colonised, bearers of policed sexualities and other minority groups, are not readily given a voice under postmodernism. In the case of women, Meaghan Morris (2002) points out that while many women (Hélène Cixous, Luce Irigaray and Donna Haraway for example) have engaged with, even shaped, aspects of the postmodernism debate, they have been excluded from the critical canon because they do not *explicitly* address the questions of postmodernism nor write within the theo-retical parameters set by male theorists.

Postmodernism has also been criticised for lacking scholarship. Richard Bernstein (1992) is critical of postmodernists' methods and asks: 'critique in the name of what?' He argues that the very grammar of critique requires a standard or measure, some basis for critique, and in his opinion postmodernists fail to provide such a measure. Furthermore, Niall Lucy (1997, p. 17) suggests that a certain version of postmodernism might conclude that there is nothing 'below' the surface of any text, that 'there is only a "play" of textual surfaces [...] instead of meaning-to-say there is only meaning-to-play'. Spencer (2005) concedes that terms used in reference to postmodernism by critics – nihilistic, subjectivist, amoral, fragmentary, arbitrary, defeatist, wilful – could be seen to support this claim. Such claims led Jameson[9] (1991) to label postmodernism as a 'depthless culture'. Bertens (2001) argues that there are two ways of looking at this. In the first instance, postmodern fiction could be seen as liberating as it effectively undermines all metanarratives as well as the beliefs and values associated with those metanarratives. Conversely, postmodern fiction also undermines itself by exposing its own fictionality and refusing to answer the questions it poses. And yet, Bertens goes on to say, through its use of intertextuality it indirectly affirms traditional texts and perspectives, tacitly endorsing the political status quo in the world outside of the text.

Ironically, postmodernism, despite its antagonism towards total-ising schemes (evidenced by Lyotard's declaration of 'incredulity toward metanarratives', mentioned earlier in this chapter), has, itself, been accused of being a metanarrative. Klaus Jensen claims: 'Postmodernism is itself a grand narrative, announcing the death of another grand narrative in its rearview mirror' (cited in Cobley, 2001). Yet, as already discussed, postmodernism is not a unified endeavour in which writers have formed a consistent whole. Furthermore, intellectuals working in areas pertaining to postmodernism come to the topic from a wide variety of cultural and political orientations. Spencer (2005) argues that postmodernism's multiplicity of compet-ing definitions, its spirit of dissent, and its mood of ambivalence and uncertainty make it difficult to uphold claims of postmodernism as metanarrative. Bryan Turner (2000) says 'postmodernism makes commitment to a single grand narrative unlikely'. My position is that postmodernism rejects totalisations and resists being labelled yet another metanarrative.

The (im)possibility of postmodern fiction for children

One of the challenges in writing this book, as indicated above, has been to provide any clear understanding of postmodernism and postmodern literature. To then transpose any tentative definitions arrived at onto children's literature presents further difficulties. While it may share a number of characteristics with other forms of postmodern literature, the postmodernism of children's literature does not always conform to the postmodernism of adult fiction. This stems, in part, from the particular nature of children's literature in as much as it is written *by* adults *for* children with all the attendant constraints this might suggest.[10] Stephens (1992) observes that writing for children generally aims to foster (dominant) socio-cultural values, with the most pervasive theme in children's literature being the transition to a maturing social awareness. He adds that: 'children's fiction belongs firmly within the domain of cultural practices which exist for the purpose of socializing their target audience' (p. 8). Clare Bradford (1996) argues that children's texts function as agents of socialisation particularly as they inscribe ideologies concerning social and cultural norms. Considering the nature of conventional children's literature thus described, it is hardly surprising that other writers struggle with defining postmodern children's literature. According to McMillan (2002) postmodern children's literature is likely to be a *representative* type of postmodernism, drawing from and reflecting certain influences that suit its form and purposes, while implicitly refuting the theoretical trends that seem irrelevant (or deemed inappropriate?) to its direction.

Exactly what constitutes a postmodern picturebook is a debate still vigorously contested. In fact, the label has been bandied about quite freely, often with little thought to what is meant by the term *postmodern picturebook*. A number of commentators have attempted to provide some parameters by which a postmodern picturebook may be defined. David Lewis (2001), for instance, is not convinced that such an artefact exists, arguing that most so-called postmodern picturebooks are merely metafictive.[11] Lawrence Sipe and Sylvia Pantaleo (2008) also grapple with this dilemma, claiming that not only is it difficult to list the specific characteristics that are necessary for a book to be classified postmodern, but that such a list creates a binary of postmodern/not postmodern. In order to avoid such a binary which is 'antithetical to the spirit of postmodernism' they propose a continuum of postmodern characteristics on which picturebooks are located according to the number of characteristics or qualities of postmodernism they utilise. Nevertheless, I suggest that such quantitative measures are also antithetical to the spirit of postmodernism. Sipe and Pantaleo fall into their own binary trap by attempting to distinguish between texts with a 'few attributes of the postmodern picturebook' and those with many such characteristics. They then classify the latter as 'truly postmodern' thereby reinscribing the very binary they were hoping to avoid.

My own usage of postmodern in relation to postmodern picturebooks takes as its model Hutcheon's (1988) designation of postmodern fiction as those texts that *both* subvert the strategies and devices of conventional narrative *and* interrogate dominant discourses of liberal humanism. While these dual characteristics raise the texts above the 'merely metafictive' it is necessary to acknowledge that the postmodern picturebook requires different considerations and different approaches from, for example, a postmodern novel for adults. For instance, Nodelman (2008) disagrees with Dresang's (1999) label of 'radical change' to describe recent texts for children which have departed from the traditional in children's literature. He claims that while they may seem to be open they inevitably lead towards conventional understandings and assumptions. As an example, Nodelman (2008) points to *Black and White* (Macaulay, 1990) and argues that its hypertextual techniques and multiple perspectives may mark it as postmodern, yet they represent a form of postmodernism peculiar to children's literature. This is a point which I discuss further in the analysis of a number of the focus texts. Nodelman contends that the characteristics postmodern children's literature shares with conventional children's texts remain as important as what differentiates them. This is the paradox of postmodern picturebooks – while influenced by postmodernism, as suggested by the second epigraph to this chapter, they often revert to a more conventional perspective. Given the difficulties of arriving at a consensual way of defining what constitutes a postmodern picturebook it may be more useful to refer to picturebooks *influenced by* postmodernism rather than speak of a definitive postmodern picturebook. However, the term *postmodern picturebook* is well established in the literary criticism of children's literature. Consequently, throughout this book, both considerations – postmodern influence and postmodern picturebooks – are utilised. In an endeavour to further contextualise the postmodern picturebook, I turn to Hassan (2001, p. 2), who argues that while we may be unable to define postmodernism we can 'approach it, surprising it from various angles, perhaps teasing it into a partial light'. He suggests that by looking at a lot of words relating to postmodernism it creates a *context* for postmodernism, if not a definition. The next section of this Introduction works with Hassan's notion of context rather than definition, and bears in mind the paradoxical nature of postmodern children's literature. It creates a context for the postmodern picturebook through an examination of the literature pertaining to postmodern picturebooks.

Influence of postmodernism on children's picturebooks

As previously indicated, the discipline of literary studies and the pro- duction of literature in the past 40 or 50 years have been preoccupied by questions relating to postmodernism. It is in this field of literary studies, according to Woods (1999), that the term 'postmodernism' has received the widest usage and provoked the most vexed debate. While this claim is certainly open to dispute (debate on the influence of postmodernism has also raged in areas as diverse as architecture, art, performance and, more recently, law, science and technology), it is in these areas of literary studies (including children's literature) and the production of narrative that the interest of this book lies. Questions about ontological plurality, multiple realities, naturalised ideologies and contested constructions of history are evident in many texts for adults but also emerge in playful ways in many exam- ples of postmodern picturebooks. These preoccupations indicate how children's writers and illustrators are very much a part of the cultural and intellectual milieux that postmodernism has engendered. In fact, children's literature has always responded to the changing social and cultural environments in which it is located, so it comes as no surprise that the utilisation of postmodern impulses in children's pic- turebooks emerged as early as 1963 with the publication of Maurice Sendak's *Where the Wild Things Are* and continued through the 1970s and 1980s with texts by authors and illustrators such as Burningham, Browne, the Ahlbergs and Sendak.[12]

Although adult literature experienced the most highly productive period of postmodern writing in the period from the 1960s to the 1980s, it wasn't until the 1990s that the postmodern picturebook flourished. This creative output saw the publication of such texts as *Black and White*, *The Stinky Cheese Man and Other Fairly Stupid Tales* and *Voices in the Park* (Browne, 1998). This impetus continued into the first decade of the new century with *The Three Pigs* (Wiesner, 2001), *Willy's Pictures* (Browne, 2001) and *Who's Afraid of the Big Bad Book?* (Child, 2003), to mention but a few. The first critical comments on the postmodern picturebook began to emerge in the early 1990s, with Lewis (1990), Grieve (1993) and Bradford (1993) all noting the utilisation of such metafictive strategies as excess, indeterminacy and boundary-breaking (Lewis), irony and self-reflexivity (Bradford), as well as questions of originality and ontological plurality (Grieve), thereby drawing parallels between these picturebooks and adult postmodern fiction. The 1990s and first decade of the twenty-first century have proven to be the most prolific period for production of the so-called postmodern picturebook accompanied by a great deal of academic interest and an increasing number of scholarly publications.

The influence of postmodern literary features on children's literature studies can be seen in picturebooks. The postmodern picturebook refuses to abide by conventions, employs a pastiche of styles and generally refuses to conform to a specific generic categorisation. Often this pastiche results in a playful approach to the construction of fiction, designed to enhance reading enjoyment as it challenges and teases readers to see the allusions, parody and other textual games at work between the covers (and *even* the cover) of the book. Juliet O'Connor (2004, unpaginated) suggests of the postmodern picturebook: 'prediction, expectation and resolution are challenged and the fictionality and structure of the picture book is questioned'. While all narratives contain gaps (elements of the plot not included or explained), many postmodern picturebooks deliberately draw attention to these gaps by refusing to disclose aspects of the narrative and/or use the illustrative text to contradict the written text. Such strategies can be seen as metafictive because they draw attention to the constructed nature of the text. In keeping with the postmodern rejection of absolutism many postmodern narratives are indeterminate; they refuse closure and/or a satisfying resolution. As Lewis (2001, pp. 93–4) suggests: 'Postmodern fiction is not interested in the traditional satisfactions and consolations of story, but it is interested in the nature of fiction and the processes of storytelling, and employs metafictive devices to undermine the unreflective and naïve reading of stories.' Thus postmodern texts deliberately work against traditional approaches to fiction. Despite the influence of postmodern approaches in text production, the majority of children's books still conform to a traditional modernist approach. Nevertheless, the influence of postmodernism on children's picturebooks is significant and warrants an investigation.

Whilst the playful nature of postmodern picturebooks may appeal to a wide range of ages it would seem that the majority remain aimed at children as the primary audience, although the acknowledged dual readership of picturebooks (adult and child) is a particular feature of postmodern picturebooks. Their appeal to an older readership (adolescents and adults alike) lies in their ironic and parodic nature, yet they still retain their appeal for young children through overt playfulness. For example, in *The Stinky Cheese Man and Other Fairly Stupid Tales* the author and illustrator take obvious delight in playing with the nursery rhyme genre and the role of the narrator, as illustrated when the narrator exhorts the reader: 'I know. I know. The page is upside down [...] If you really want to read it you can stand on your head.'

The changing postmodern literary landscape

Discussions concerning postmodernism's declining influence on the arts have increasingly turned the focus more on what lies beyond postmodernism. John Barth's 1967 'Literature of Exhaustion' essay (Barth 1984) suggests that all literary trends or movements follow a cycle of resistance – acceptance – decline and reach a point of exhaustion when the particular strategies and themes of the movement become clichéd. Butler (2002) argues that during the twentieth century the rise of (any) radical ideas was generally followed by disillusionment then modification. He indicates that this sequence is already the case with postmodernism: 'it [postmodernism] has already lasted as long as the high modernism of the period before the war'. Hassan (2001) suggests that while postmodernism grew and then died, its spectre still haunts much of the Western world because postmodernism has become a way we view the world. In a related comment, Barry Lewis (2005) claims that postmodern writing dominated (adult) literature between 1960 and 1990, bookmarked by the assassination of President Kennedy and the declaration of a *fatwa* on Salman Rushdie for his novel *The Satanic Verses* (1988). These dates, together with the comments of Hassan and Lewis, suggest that the period of postmodern writing in adult fiction finished some 20 years ago. Hutcheon (2002) takes a somewhat different approach but arrives at a similar conclusion. She argues that the postmodern phenomenon has now become fully institutionalised: it has its own canonised texts, anthologies and readers as well as dictionaries and histories, and this, effectively, makes it a 'thing of the past'.[13]

A number of commentators, including Robert McLaughlin (2004), along with Barry Lewis (2005) and Alan Kirby (2010), are already referring to emerging writers as 'post-postmodernists'. Rachel Adams (2007), however, cautions that it is too early to assign names to any emerging trends and, indeed, this particular neologism (post-postmodernism) is awkward and does not indicate direction, merely moment-in-time. Stierstorfer (2003, p. 1) argues that postmodernism is entering a period of stock-taking and that the long-running dispute on what constitutes postmodernism is in the process of being archived. Postmodernism appears to be approaching the end of its influence over literature and the arts, and new directions are emerging. As yet, there is no consensus on what lies beyond postmodernism; however, one particular direction which seems to come out of some of the areas of concern examined by postmodern literature is that of identity politics. While so-called 'classic postmodern' (Hassan, 2001) adult texts (those of the 1960s and 1970s perhaps) interrogated dominant ideologies of a liberal humanist society, including issues surrounding those on the margins of society or 'ex-centrics', increasingly such issues have been taken up by a relatively recent emphasis on cultural politics or 'literature of others beyond straight, white males', as McLaughlin (2004, p. 61) phrases it. Steven Connor (2004, pp. 11–12) suggests: 'postmodern discourse may now be entering a new phase of productive dissipation, in which some of the very cultural themes and phenomena that it has made its concerns are now themselves achieving a kind of autonomy'. Areas achieving autonomy by creating their own discourses include postcolonial, queer, post-feminist, autobiographical and post-human fiction, and could be seen to be taking over the role of postmodern literature in this regard. Connor (2004) claims that by the 1990s the *post* of postmodernism had achieved a level of autonomy which perhaps heralds postmodernism's transcendence from its links to modernism (as suggested by Jencks) and ushers in a new period of postmodernism.

This period of autonomy is also reflected in the picturebooks produced as a result of these changes. Adams (2007) claims that currently this is a period of transition, while Hoberek (2007) suggests it is a 'lull' between distinct periods where there are texts being produced that could be labelled postmodern while others have moved outside that category, yet still retain aspects of it. Alan Gilbert (2006, pp. 82–3) posits that as literature moves out of the era of postmodernism there is the possibility for a more substantial pluralism. He warns however: '[O]ut of an aesthetics of fragmentation arises the potential to create a culture of heterogeneity. The key is not to have this new pluralism splinter into irreconcilable differences.' To what extent these, or any other trends, become a dominant or recognisable mode in literature remains to be seen, remembering that postmodern literature, even at its height, was not the only, or even the dominant, literary trend.

As well as a possible demise of postmodernism and its influence over the fiction being produced, there is also some evidence of the emergence of a literature of exhaustion (after Barth, see above) in which some postmodern texts seem to employ a 'bag of tricks' approach (Hassan, 2001) in their attempts to achieve playfulness and self-reflexivity. These trends are also evident in a number of picturebooks such as *Do Not Open This Book!* (Muntean and Lemaitre, 2006), *An Undone Fairy Tale* (Lendler and Martin, 2005) and *Cindy-ella* (Champion and Singleton, 2008). Both *An Undone Fairy Tale* and *Do Not Open This Book!* rely on direct address to urge readers not to open the book and/or turn the page. In the former text the story has not yet been written, while the illustrations for the latter are incomplete. Despite the use of metafictive strategies such as direct address, changing fonts and illustrative styles, the texts do not progress much beyond the initial joke of, for instance: 'Do not turn the page.' *Cindy-ella*, on the other hand, is a revisioning of the traditional tale (Cinderella) into an Australian setting in which its Ockerism[14] produces a sexist tale more offensive than humorous. Hassan (2001, p. 5) accuses cultural postmodernism of having 'metastazized into sterile, campy, kitschy, jokey, dead-end games or sheer media stunts' and, certainly, these picturebooks seem to fall into some of these categories. This 'bag of tricks' approach is, perhaps, an indication that the nature of postmodern fiction is undergoing changes such that it may no longer be postmodern and, in some cases, it may have reached its use-by date. Indeed, Kirby (2010) takes an extreme position by arguing that the only place where the postmodern is extant is in children's cartoons such as *Shrek* and *The Incredibles*, and even then only as a concession to the parents who are obliged to sit through these with their children. This attitude, however, ignores the rich culture of children's picturebooks. Geyh (2003, p. 2), meanwhile, asserts that even as the postmodern era is perhaps drawing to a close 'we are still as puzzled and perplexed as we were in the beginning'. This suggests that despite its decline, or possible exhaustion, there is still much work to be done within the study of postmodernism to achieve an understanding of it as an enterprise and a way of knowing the world through its literature and other cultural artefacts.

Parallel to a debate on the influence of postmodernism, discussed above, a number of commentators – including Hassan (2001), Geyh (2003), Connor (2004), McLaughlin (2004), Adams (2007) and Hoberek (2007) – have noted recently the changing nature of postmodernism over the years between the 1960s and the present day. Hassan (2001, p. 1) notes: 'postmodernism has changed, I have changed, the world has changed [... it] will shift and slide continually with time, particularly in an age of ideological conflict and media hype'. Accordingly, as postmodernism has changed so, too, has the literature emanating from these changing cultural conditions. One of the main changes to have affected postmodern fiction and, subsequently, be reflected in recent postmodern picturebooks, is the advent of the age of mass media including television and electronic media such as the Internet (see Heise, 1997; Hassan, 2001; Geyh, 2003). McLaughlin (2004, pp. 64–5 after Wallace) suggests the shifts in postmodern fiction have occurred because television has co-opted the role of postmodernism in such areas as irony and self-referentiality, and consequently the techniques that were means of subversion for the early postmodernists have now become part of the mainstream. While some forms of mass media, particularly television, have been with us for many years, the past 20 years have seen an exponential growth in the influence of the media over our lives, resulting in, according to Geyh (2003, p. 4): 'a proliferation of an all-pervasive media culture which has spawned a "society of spectacle" (after Guy de Bord) in which everything [...] is turned into a representation'. Added to this, Connor (2004) claims that the media has also led to the 'immediatization' (a play on both 'immediate' and 'media') of contemporary society, which has been driven, to a large extent, by access to technology, particularly television and the Internet. Related to this media culture is the advent of a world of consumer technology and consumption which is, in turn, associated with the development of a post-industrial society[15] and the rise of a global economy.

Where once postmodern texts were concerned with challenging the dominant ideologies of liberal humanist societies, increasingly they have turned their attention to the ideologies and practices of postmodernism and the conditions of postmodernity. Woods (1999) writes of adult literature of the 1980s by so-called generation X or 'brat-pack' novelists,[16] who produced a different type of writing which did not make recognisably radical narrative disruptions, yet still maintained the postmodern label. Woods (1999) describes these texts as: 'not so much postmodern novels as novels about postmodern existence'. Nicol (2009, p. 197) describes their writing as presenting: 'an accurate portrayal of the morally bankrupt, consumerist, celebrity-obsessed culture of the late twentieth-century North America'. Geyh (2003) suggests that today, postmodern literature functions as a site which critiques effects of postmodernism, particularly in its political and cultural forms such as those of globalisation, mass media and consumer consumption. Increasingly, these trends are reflected in a range of postmodern picturebooks published in the first decade of the twenty-first century.

The emergence of postmodernesque picturebooks

Just as adult postmodern fiction is experiencing a shift, so, too, is this shift becoming evident in children's literature. While a number of postmodern picturebooks written after the turn of this century continues to interrogate both the process of writing and the dominant attitudes and values inherent in much conventional children's fiction, many of the picturebooks emerging in most recent times have turned to an examination of the effects of postmodernism upon social, political and economic structures. It may be that postmodern children's fiction, which was the experimental literature of the years 1980–2000, is now moving away from challenging the dominant ideologies of the day as explained above. The shifts in emphasis in adult literature are beginning to be reflected in some of the postmodern picturebooks published in recent years. Such texts, examined in Chapter 6, include: *In the City* (Harvey, 2007), *The Empty City* (Megarrity and Oxlade, 2007), *The Short and Incredibly Happy Life of Riley* (Thompson and Lissiat, 2005), *Il Libro piu corto del mondo* (Cox, 2002) and *The Race of the Century* (Downard, 2008). In a similar manner to the adult texts described by Woods, these picturebooks use some metafictive strategies but are often fairly linear and generally achieve some sort of resolution. They do, however, consider aspects of postmodernity and the postmodern condition.

Therefore, rather than persist with the label *postmodern* in relation to these particular texts I offer instead *postmodernesque*. This differentiation is not merely cosmetic or convenient. Instead, it is motivated by the need to differentiate between the picturebooks produced as a result of the cultural conditions prevailing during the latter part of the twentieth century and those picturebooks being produced in the early years of the twenty-first century. Of course there will be crossover texts (*The Lost Thing* for example has elements of modernism, postmodernism and the postmodernesque); however, by utilising a new term, I aim to bring a degree of clarity to the issues surrounding current debates over what exactly constitutes a postmodern picturebook. My coining of the term *postmodernesque* draws upon the term *carnivalesque* and is used in a similar manner but with a postmodern inflection. Carnivalesque texts are those that have emerged from the carnival literature, as identified by Bakhtin (1968), and based on the work of Rabelais. Just as elements of the carnivalesque were carried over into literature, postmodernesque picturebooks have emerged from the postmodern tradition and yet exhibit a sufficient shift in direction to warrant a separate designation. These texts draw attention to aspects of postmodernity, including globalisation and its attendant components of mass media and consumerism. Chapter 6 will further differentiate between postmodern and postmodernesque picturebooks.

Structure of the book

In coming to a tentative understanding of what a postmodern pic-turebook might look like I refer again to Hutcheon's understanding that a postmodern work of fiction generally contains both disruptions to the conventions of narrative and interrogations of the dominant discourses of liberal humanism. This understanding influenced the structure of the book in so much as Chapters 1 and 2 examine disruptions to a number of conventions of narrative particularly applicable to children's literature, including narrative frames, point of view and representation. Chapters 3, 4 and 5 interrogate a number of discourses of the dominant liberal humanist mode of being – including raising questions about the ways in which reality (Chapter 3), history (Chapter 4) and unity (Chapter 5) are represented in fiction. Finally, Chapter 6 signals a break; rather than interrogate aspects of liberal humanism, these postmodernesque texts (as outlined above) interrogate aspects of postmodernity.

The selection of texts used in the book is drawn largely from the 1990s, which represents the most prolific period of postmodernism's influence on children's literature (as discussed earlier). I also include a number of texts from the late 1980s and the early years of the new millennium. Postmodernesque texts are almost exclusively drawn from texts written after the turn of the twenty-first century, indicating the shift (outlined above) which has taken place within postmodernism. A particular challenge to the selection process centres on the small collection of available texts and the extent to which these texts have already been, extensively in some cases, analysed by other writers in the field. Yet, the position from which I am examining these texts allows for new perspectives to be considered. Postmodernism is regarded as a phenomenon of the Western world (although that no longer holds as discretely as it once did) and as such all texts are from Western regions, particularly North America, the United Kingdom, Europe and Australasia. During the selection process I initially attempted to restrict the use of each text to one chapter. However, taking into consideration the small pool of available texts and their suitability for specific purposes, I have used a number of texts throughout, while other picturebooks have been used for a particular section, whereas yet others have only been referred to as examples of a specific point at a particular place in the discussion. For instance, *The Red Tree* (Tan, 2001) has only been briefly mentioned whereas *The Stinky Cheese Man and Other Fairly Stupid Tales* features extensively.

The postmodern picturebook is not a static category of children's texts but rather a dynamic form responding to the changing social, cultural and political conditions in which it is produced, as becomes evident in the following chapters. The shape, form and content of the postmodern picturebook will continue to develop and change as other diverse cultural, social and political influences are brought to bear upon it. Grieve (1993, p. 24) suggests 'A theory of the post-modern picture book offers a new critical discourse for exploring how literature can continually shape and reshape itself.' This book contributes to this ongoing critical discourse, particularly through its examination of the shifts in postmodernism that have manifested over recent years and its recognition of the emergence of the post-modernesque picturebook.

1
Looking Beneath the Surface

> Different codes and layers of meaning below the
> surface of a classic realist text are on open display
> in a postmodern text, which exhibit the fact that it
> is not natural, finished and seamless but rather is
> constructed, open, fragmented and plural. (Travis,
> 1998, p. 47)

One of the major characteristics of postmodern literature is its challenge to realist fiction. The challenge is two-fold: to the ideologies
embedded within realist texts and to the apparent 'naturalness' of
the various narrative strategies. The major concern of this chapter
is to examine these challenges by considering how various narrative
processes that are often 'below the surface', as Travis phrases it, are
made overt in postmodern picturebooks. As the discussion demonstrates, this overtness is achieved largely through the employment
of a range of metafictive strategies which, as Hutcheon (1988) notes,
self-consciously comment on their own narrative and linguistic characteristics. This self-reflexivity is a dominant subject of postmodern
fiction, and is also a defining feature of metafiction. As Waugh (1984)
notes, metafiction refers to self-reflexive fiction which intentionally draws attention to its status as fiction and, in so doing, poses
questions about the relationship between fiction and the reality it
purports to represent. In the first section of this chapter, I discuss
metafictive strategies drawing on a number of postmodern picturebooks to illustrate their use. The second section examines several
picturebooks in more detail, illustrating further how these strategies

are incorporated into texts to offer different points of view and multiple 'truths'.

Metafictional strategies foreground the ways in which meaning is constructed, highlight the texts' own processes of production and reception, and disrupt the codes and conventions of 'realist' fiction. It must be remembered, however, that rarely are metafictive devices used in isolation in texts, and that the most common application is for a number of strategies to be employed together (Stephens and Watson, 1994). Whilst the application of metafictive strategies in the adult novel has a long history,[1] the utilisation of metafictive strategies in children's literature (picturebooks in particular) is fairly recent. The appearance of metafictive strategies in children's literature was first acknowledged in the 1960s where its utilisation mirrored that of mainstream literature. Initial reactions to this use of metafiction in children's literature were mixed. For example, upon publication in 1963 of *Where the Wild Things Are* by Maurice Sendak, it was criticised for its apparent endorsement of Max's 'bad' behaviour but also for its typographical experimentation and conflicting spatio-temporalities. However, this initial resistance gradually turned to acceptance and, in some circles, celebration (Stephens, 1992) and the book is now considered a classic children's picturebook.

In examining the use of metafictive strategies in children's literature[2] I draw upon Robyn McCallum's (1996) view that when fiction draws attention to its status as text, it does so in order to reflect upon processes through which narrative fictions are constructed, read and made sense of while simultaneously posing questions about the relationships between the interpretation and representation of fiction and reality. Stephens (1992, p. 124) makes a similar point of children's texts that 'employ textual strategies which undermine the illusion of fictionality by drawing attention to the nature of text as text'. For instance, in Lauren Child's picturebook *Who's Afraid of the Big Bad Book?* the narrator comments: 'At long last, he came to an enormous door. It was difficult to open because the illustrator had drawn the handle much too high.' Such self-conscious strategies bring to readers' attention the processes through which the fictive worlds are constructed and the 'realities' they represent. As Patricia Waugh (1984, p. 6) explains, such metafictional strategies in constructing a fictional illusion are also 'laying bare' that illusion.

Waugh (1984) argues that attention to metafictive strategies is necessary for examining the narrative *processes* that are disrupted by postmodern narrative. It is through these processes that texts select, organise, narrate and represent the events and characters of the story world. Such processes include the use of particular narrative conventions (such as the orientation–complication–resolution structure of stories) as well as the utilisation of various strategies (intertextuality, parody and so on) and devices (metaphor, metonym). As suggested in the epigraph above, picturebooks that have been influenced by the approaches of postmodernism make obvious 'codes and layers of meaning' of narrative which tend to present realist fiction as 'natural, finished and seamless' rather than the 'constructed, open, fragmented and plural' nature of postmodern fiction. In making explicit the conventions and strategies of realist fiction through metafictive devices, postmodern picturebooks playfully create uncertainty, fragmentation and ambiguity within their narratives, rather than offer readers the certainty, coherence and resolution of more conventional 'realist' picturebooks.

The playfulness of postmodern picturebooks is noted by John Stephens (1992), who sees the readers cast in the role of 'author's playmate'. Kerry Mallan (2002a, p. 34), too, notes the playful function of the postmodern picturebook and suggests that the process of reading 'takes on a game-like quality (as the) reader moves towards (but may never reach) the fulfilment of desire'. These comments accord with David Lewis' (2001) claim that because the implied reader of picturebooks is in a state of 'perpetual becoming' this concept of play is more acceptable to her/him. And, indeed, the picturebook with its dual semiotic codes invites readers and critics to engage in playful games: with play used in both senses of the word as a sense of enjoyment as well as possibilities of interpretation (Geyh, 2003). Both Bradford (1993) and McCallum (1996) consider this postmodernist notion of 'play' as being central to how picturebooks entice readers to interpret the visual and verbal texts and to also consider the playful relationship between the two. As McCallum (1996, p. 398) argues, the linguistic and narrative games authors and illustrators play as they exploit the visual and verbal codes of the picturebook genre provide a heightened sense of the status of fiction as play: a common metafictive strategy. Other aspects of play are noted by Nikolajeva (2008b), who suggests that in postmodern picturebooks playfulness is often expressed through the materiality of the text as artefact. The postmodern picturebook therefore engages readers on two levels: the subversive and the playful, through the codes of both the written text and the illustrations. The irony is, of course, that this playfulness has a serious purpose in that it draws attention to the ideologies of the text and its own metafictive constructedness, and thereby positions readers to pay close attention to the text.

This preliminary discussion of the often playful subversion of various textual strategies is intended to highlight how these strategies draw attention to the conventions themselves. However, there is often a fine line between 'realistic' and 'postmodern' picturebooks. Waugh (1984, p. 18) notes a similar fine line between realist fiction and postmodern fiction: 'very often realistic conventions supply the "control" in metafictional texts, the norm against which the experimental strategies can foreground themselves'. And certainly the postmodern picturebooks under discussion in this book do largely adhere to the conventions of realist fiction but take delight in disrupting particular strategies which then serves to draw attention to them as textual strategies. This self-consciousness contributes to a paradox of postmodern fiction that Hutcheon (1988) observes: while seemingly subversive, postmodernism works from within the very systems it is challenging; it is both complicitous with and critical of prevailing norms. In this it shares similarities with the postmodern picturebook which, while resistant, often reverts to a perspective which conforms to that of conventional children's literature. The paradox of postmodern fiction that Hutcheon notes above is intended to challenge realism's lack of transparency, and, in so doing, Lewis (2001) suggests, postmodern fiction prevents the glossing over of the incoherencies and contradictions of fiction, thereby revealing narrative for what it is: a construction, an illusion of a real world.

Traditionally, authors of realist fiction attempt to position readers by retaining control over stories through the utilisation of conventional narrative codes and/or structural elements of narrative, including, in the case of picturebooks, codes and elements of the illustrative text. This constructedness has become naturalised, or taken for granted, as a result of the conventions and devices of narrative being internalised through cultural immersion to the point where they are (largely) invisible to community members (Derrien, 2005). The following section now turns to examine generally how, through the utilisation of metafictive strategies in postmodern picturebooks, the conventions and devices of fiction are 'laid bare'.

Fiction stripped bare

Perhaps the most readily recognised metafictive strategy is *intertextuality* whereby, in its simplest form, one text alludes to another. However, intertextuality operates on a much wider scale than mere allusion or parody and on a number of different levels. Kristeva (1986, after Bakhtin) argues that a literary work is not simply the product of a single author, but of its relationships with other texts and to the structures of language itself. Further expansion of the term intertextuality came with Barthes'[3] claim that the influence of an individual author on a text is subsidiary to language and cultural influences. Barthes (1981, p. 39) posits that a text is a tissue of past citations in which '[b]its of code, formulae, rhyming models, fragments of social language, etc. pass into a text and are redistributed within it'. Postmodern picturebooks delight in drawing attention to these past citations and literary precedents.

Intertextuality foregrounds the postmodern theory of common discursive property which involves a reconsideration of the idea of origin and originality. Bakhtin (1981, p. 280) agrees, and claims that '[w]hether they are conscious of it or not, artists are profoundly affected by their social and cultural milieux and by the texts and other creative works that already exist'. It is only by utilising prior discourses (intertextual references) that any text derives meaning and significance, thus confirming the 'inevitable intertextuality of all writing' (Hutcheon, 1988, p. 126). When a story begins with 'Once upon a time' readers are, consciously or unconsciously, already positioned by their previous experiences of fairy-tale texts (including popular cultural texts such as Disney film productions of fairy tales). While many of these intertextual relationships operate in a 'naturalised' way, increasingly texts deliberately draw attention to these links by self-consciously including references to intertexts or pretexts. This self-reflexivity has contributed to something of an evolution of the term whereby intertextuality in postmodern fiction has come to be regarded not only as a theoretical stance as posited by Kristeva, but also as a conscious narrative strategy to be applied in the pursuit of parody and/or allusion to particular intertexts and pretexts. Fuery and Mansfield (2000, pp. 66–9) argue that where texts overtly exploit an awareness of their literary precedents they do so in order to: 'call on one another to problematise and challenge the cultural meanings with which they have become connected', thereby endowing this usage of intertextuality (that is, as a deliberate strategy) with a measure of influence.

Parody is a particular form of intertextuality. Hutcheon (1984) suggests that parodic art is both a deviation from and inclusion of the convention with itself as the background material. This understanding results in her definition of parody as 'Repetition, with critical distance' (1985, p. 6) which acknowledges parody's sense of continuity through the pretext but also marks 'difference rather than similarity'. One of the most popular genres to be parodied in children's picturebooks is the fairy tale. Parodies of original tales often are used to question 'naturalised' social conventions embedded within the original stories. Babette Cole's picturebooks, *Princess Smartypants* (1986) and *Prince Cinders* (1992), for example, playfully and humorously interrogate traditional gender roles. *Princess Smartypants* parodies a number of elements of the traditional fairy tale, including the rich and beautiful princess, suitors all clamouring for her hand, the setting of tasks to achieve the hand of the princess and, finally, what appears to be the ideal suitor. However, the princess rejects his proposal and so: 'she lived happily ever after' after all. Prince Cinders, on the other hand, is a weedy Prince who wins the hand of his Princess by default. This use of parody is discussed in further detail in ensuing chapters in relation to a number of fairy tales, including: *The Frog Prince Continued* (Scieszka and Johnson, 1991), *The Stinky Cheese Man and Other Fairly Stupid Tales* (Scieszka and Smith, 1992), *Beware of the Storybook Wolves* (Child, 2000c), *Who's Afraid of the Big Bad Book?* (Child, 2003), *Wait! No Paint!* (Whatley, 2001) and *The Three Pigs* (Wiesner, 2001). Parody can be problematic in children's literature, however, especially as it relies on readers having some knowledge of the pretext for the parody to be completely effective. For instance, in Tohby Riddle's *The Great Escape from City Zoo* (1997), in which four animals escape from a zoo and unsuccessfully attempt to live on the outside, there is a visual reference to the Beatles and the cover of their Abbey Road album. While this may appeal to adult readers, such a reference to pop icons of the 1960s and 1970s might be missed by younger generations. Interestingly, despite these possible difficulties, parody is a surprisingly prevalent mode in children's picturebooks. Other metafictive disruptions, besides intertextuality and parody, occur through frame-breaking.

Writing on adult fiction, Hutcheon (1984) contends that narrative disruption and discontinuity in texts using metafictive strategies bring readers to an understanding of the use of narrative codes and conventions by disturbing comfortable habits associated with the act of reading. This is particularly evident in the use of *frame-breaking* as a metafictive strategy. Frames here refer to the structures around which narratives are generally organised, including genre, beginnings and endings, spatio-temporality and so on. Frame-breaking is used to 'lay bare' or self-consciously draw attention to these organisational structures and include stories within stories as well as characters who (literally) step in and out of the narrative frame. The outer or overarching frame generally represents 'reality' but, when broken, readers are left to grapple with an alternative reality (or realities), constructed around an alternative frame in which time and space may be suspended or proceed differently. This began in the 1960s with *Where the Wild Things Are* and continued in the 1980s with, for example, *The Story of a Little Mouse Trapped in a Book* (Felix, 1988) and then, perhaps, ran rampant in the 1990s with examples such as *The Stinky Cheese Man and Other Fairly Stupid Tales* (1992), *Black and White* (1990) and *Voices in the Park* (1998). In the 'noughties' the use of frame-breaking strategies continued, with examples such as *Wolves* (Gravett, 2006), *Who's Afraid of the Big Bad Book?* (2003) and *The Three Pigs* (2001). Several of these books are examined in more detail in later sections and chapters; for now, they are intended to illustrate the way postmodern picturebooks continue to experiment with their dual modes of signification which provide increased opportunities for frame-breaking and narrative disruption.

Narrative disruptions also create indeterminacy, ambiguity and lack of closure. These are often achieved through the employment of what Iser (1978) terms textual gaps. Lewis maintains that while all stories are built on gaps, postmodern picturebooks deliberately extend these gaps, and the dual codes of picturebooks provide many opportunities to reinforce or widen such gaps. The picturebook *Granpa* (Burningham, 1984) plays with narrative and temporal linearity through the presentation of parallel narratives separated by the gutter. A small girl regularly comes to stay for the day at her grandfather's house. The text relies almost exclusively on the illustrations to transmit the story as the only written text consists of seemingly disjointed and fragmentary comments by the grandfather and his granddaughter as they spend time together over an undefined period of time. While the recto page appears to be current story time, although that is by no means certain, the verso at times seems to represent Granpa's memories, creating a situation where he is simultaneously living in a number of pasts as well as in the present. At other times the illustrations appear to be the granddaughter's imagination at play whereby she projects a number of possible futures into the present (Allan, 2006). Readers' attempts to construct a single, logical and chronological narrative are frustrated and interpretative certainty is denied.

Yet another form of disruption to the literary codes of narration is *metalepsis*. Metalepsis is the transgression of logical and hierarchical relations between different levels of narration (Genette, 1980, pp. 234–5). This occurs in *The Story of a Little Mouse Trapped in a Book* (Felix, 1988). The trapped mouse nibbles at the page in order to free herself then folds a page into a paper plane on which she makes her escape. The mouse becomes both character and authorial agent and so disrupts the conventional hierarchy of relations between character, narrator and author. Other examples of metaleptic disruption to the narration of the primary or diegetic level of the story occur in *The Three Pigs* (discussed later in this chapter) whereby the third-person narration is gradually usurped by the speech balloons of the pigs and their companions. So, too, in *Wait! No Paint!*, although in this story it is the illustrator who creates the metaleptic disruption to the third-person narration by, initially, spilling orange juice on a page of the book (see Chapter 3). These metaleptic disruptions create shifts in who has 'control' over the narrative which, in turn, has implications for the particular points of view being presented to readers.

Through the two systems of signification, picturebooks lend themselves to the construction of what Bakhtin (1981) terms 'dialogic' narratives. Dialogism is achieved through multi-stranded and/ or polyphonic stories which incorporate a broad range of human voices, some of which may be authorised while others seek to undermine or subvert this authority. Picturebooks are predisposed to dialogic exchanges, as Nodelman (1988, p. 153) explains: 'through the words, pictures, and the interaction between the two, picturebooks have the potential to contain at least three stories; the one told by the words, the one implied by the pictures, and the one that results from the combination of the two'. Postmodern picturebooks self-consciously exploit this potentiality to create multiple narratives. Multiple narratives contain a number of (usually) interconnected strands which use shifts in temporal or spatial relationships to differentiate between these strands (McCallum, 1996). These narratives invite readers to view the text from a range of positions, offering a number of, often competing, discourses rather than privileging one particular discourse at the expense of all others, associated with what Barthes sees as the more 'readerly' texts of conventional narratives. This recognition of the dialogic characteristic of language is not metafictive in itself. However, by deliberately exploiting its characteristics to draw readers' attention to the dialogic nature of 'voice', it becomes self-consciously metafictive. Polyphonic picturebooks often require repeated readings in order to determine significance. They are deliberately constructed to offer multiple meanings (polysemic) rather than containing one, authorised meaning. These meanings often remain unstable, resisting total recuperation or resolution and allowing readers to consider a number of possible viewpoints rather than accept a single perspective, as becomes evident in the final section of this chapter.

Conventional notions of *time and space* also require reconsideration in postmodern picturebooks. In realist texts readers are positioned temporally and spatially within the fictional world about which they are reading and willingly enter. As Cobley (2001, p. 3) notes: 'narrative is a particular form of representation implementing signs; [...] necessarily bound up with sequence, space and time'. While there may be some shifts in timeframes, such as analepsis and prolepsis,[4] the sequencing of conventional narrative is generally linear. Bakhtin (1981, p. 243) coined the phrase *chronotope* to refer to the spatio-temporal matrix on which conventional narratives are built: 'A literary work's artistic unity in relationship to an actual reality is defined by its chronotope.' However, where once time and space were regarded as 'fixed and inflexible, categorical and absolute' (Goldstone, 2008, p. 124), no longer can the concept of chronotope adequately account for the spatio-temporal aspects of postmodern narrative. Instead, Paul Smethurst's (2000) concept of the *postmodern chronotope* is more appropriate. According to Smethurst, the postmodern chronotope has a two-fold function: it recognises that postmodern fiction destabilises realist notions of both space and time, as well as acknowledges a shift in emphasis from time (modernism) to space (postmodernism) within the time–space matrix. Postmodern narratives frequently employ disruptions to time and space as strategies for subverting the fictiveness of the text and commenting on its relation to the narrative representations of 'reality'. In *Where the Wild Things Are* Max sails off over a 'year and a day' and yet when he returns home his supper is 'still hot', which raises questions as to how long he was gone, if at all, and where the action of the text took place. These disruptions often occur through interconnected narratives which are differentiated by shifts in temporal and spatial relationships, as becomes evident in later discussions of *Voices in the Park* and *Black and White*, to name but two examples. We can no longer speak of space as a defined geographical location particularly as the influence of technology extends the narrative possibilities of both space and time. Postmodern picturebooks, through their verbal and visual texts, construct a multi-dimensional spatio-temporality that includes setting, imagination, memory, intertextuality, cyberspace and often the physical space of the book as artefact.

Typographic and formatting experimentation, as well as the appropriation of peritextual elements of the text, serve to remind readers of the status of the book as artefact. Many of the picturebooks examined in this volume employ changing font size and colour, unusual page layouts, pages that appear torn, nibbled or folded. These formatting innovations highlight these normally 'invisible' elements of a work of fiction. The materiality of the book is also made explicit in constructed, interactive and participatory picturebooks which deliberately draw attention to the book's format as text. Readers are expected to actively engage with the physical aspects of the book as part of the reading process. These texts foreground the nature of the book as an artefact that can be handled and manipulated. *Little Mouse's (Emily Gravett's) Big Book of Fears* (Gravett, 2007), as well as having a self-reflexive title, contains flaps to be lifted and a folded map which has to be removed from its pocket and unfolded in order to be read. Such devices operate metafictively; their very interactivity draws the attention of readers away from the illusion of the fictive world of the narrative to the material substance of the book itself.

Other picturebooks exploit the elements of a literary work (author's name, a title, preface, illustrations and a dedication) known as the *peritext*. Genette (1997) maintains that while these features remain subordinate to the body of the text they nevertheless have the ability to create an 'implicit context' which defines or modifies the text's meaning and may affect the reception and consumption of the primary text through the positioning of its readers. When Jack, the narrator of *The Stinky Cheese Man and Other Fairly Stupid Tales*, realising the dedication page is upside down, declares: 'Who reads this stuff anyhow?' our attention is immediately and self-reflexively pointed towards that very 'stuff'. In fact, Jack looks over his shoulder and invites the reader to become an active participant, or playmate, in the text by saying: 'If you really want to read it – you can always stand on your head.'

Further examination of *The Stinky Cheese Man and Other Fairly Stupid Tales* reveals the Little Red Hen has outraged the narrator, Jack, by using the endpapers on which to begin her story. Jack announces the arrival of the title page: 'Here comes the Title Page!' After this proclamation, the title page literally states its self-evident status as the 'Title Page', while the actual title is added as an afterthought, in parentheses, at the bottom of the page. The Table of Contents falls as a curtain on the Chicken Lickin' story, while on the back page the Little Red Hen demands: 'Who is this ISBN guy?' Embedded within the bibliographical details is a note informing a discerning reader that the illustrations are rendered in oil and vinegar, playfully drawing attention to these editorial details as well as parodying the discourse of 'food as art'. As Grieve (1998) notes, the dust cover of the book also parodies the advertising industry and the restriction of the conventional page restriction to 32 pages: 'Only $16.00' and has '56 action-packed pages [and] 75% more than those old 32 page Brand X books. New! Improved! Funny!' For Grieve, *The Stinky Cheese Man and Other Fairly Stupid Tales* is the ultimate exercise in metafiction to the point where it parodies metafiction itself. By drawing readers' attention to these peritextual elements through such visible means, any 'implicit context' which may have been otherwise created is playfully undermined, particularly when the blurb on the back cover informs the reader that the book contains: 'Over fifty pages of nonsense [...] Blah, blah, blah.' Postmodern picturebooks playfully engage with such peritextual elements in order to draw attention to the possible construction of implicit contexts and positioning of readers through the peritext.

As this section has shown, the employment of one, or more commonly several, metafictive strategies breaks readers' immersion in the narrative by drawing attention to its status as a text, and the processes of its fictional construction. Metafictive strategies also provide a means to reassess a narrative and its inherent ideologies or attitudes from a more critical or detached position. One of the most significant strategies through which the inherent ideologies of a text are promoted is narrative point of view (Stephens, 1992). The following section examines, in detail, narrative point of view with respect to a number of picturebooks, some of which have already been discussed briefly. The purpose is to explore how sample texts disrupt the authority of the narrator usually evident in realist texts, particularly children's fiction.

Who is telling the 'truth'?

In conventional children's literature the subject positions made available to children are, according to Stephens (1992), often restricted and restrictive and most often reinforce the ideologies of dominant cultural discourses. Because of familiarity with these discourses, readers may be unconsciously interpellated by the ideological stance of the text, particularly through point of view. Point of view is presented primarily through the voice of the narrator(s) and/or the focaliser(s). In the case of picturebooks, narrative point of view is also extended through the illustrative text. Conventionally, narrative point of view in realist texts is achieved primarily by offering a particular position, or 'truth', adopted by the narrator and reinforced through the illustrative text. Belsey (2002) maintains that classic realism is structured in such a way as to organise the disparate voices and languages of a story into a *hierarchy of voices* with one voice being dominant. This hierarchy works to establish the 'truth' of the story, often privileging a single discourse, while all other discourses remain subordinate. This address presents events from a specific and integrated point of view. Point of view is achieved primarily through the strategies of narration and focalisation that limit the play of meaning by installing a single position from which the scene is meaningful. In *conventional* children's literature (works that are not considered 'postmodern' or 'metafictive'), much of the authority of the text is exerted through the utilisation of a third-person (often omniscient) narrator with the voice of an adult (or an adult voice that purports to be that of a child), while the action of the plot is focalised through one or more characters with a 'child's' voice (Nikolajeva, 2003). Stephens (1992) maintains that conventional children's texts utilising a third-person narrator or focalised through one character results in the projection of restricted positions from which engagement with the text is directed. McCallum (1996) argues that this strategy is often used in children's literature in order to promote a dominant interpretive stance. The following discussion begins with an early picturebook by Anthony Browne, *A Walk in the Park* (1977), to see how a hierarchy of voices and a restrictive reader positioning are established. This text provides a contrast to subsequent examples which are more polyphonic, offering multiple positions from which to read the text.

A Walk in the Park relates the details of two families, the Smythes (Mother, son Charles and dog Victoria) and the Smiths (Father, daughter Smudge and dog Albert) on a visit to the park. The events of this outing are told through a third-person, omniscient narrator offering a single position from which to view the characters: 'While the dogs played, Smudge and Charles edged nearer and nearer to each other. Mr. Smith and Mrs. Smythe looked the other way.' Similarly, the illustrative text offers a fixed, middle viewpoint on each of the pages which basically confirms the single point of view offered by the written text. Doonan (1999) notes that Browne's illustrative style in relation to the characters in *A Walk in the Park* is dispassionate, particularly as the characters are most often shown in profile with little visible emotion on their faces. Such restricted access to the characters works to increase reliance on the narrator in constructing a point of view. The picturebook contains a number of what Moss (1992, p. 60) labels 'incongruent and absurd images', such as Tarzan swinging through the trees[5] and a man walking a pig, which serve to distract attention from the written text and create an element of playfulness. Despite such playfulness, this picturebook offers a fairly limited perspective with little scope for construction of significance beyond that offered by the implied author through the third-person narrator. The codes and conventions of storytelling, particularly point of view, usually remain implicit and, therefore, relatively invisible in works of realist fiction.

Postmodern picturebooks disrupt the construction of a dominant voice which presents seemingly objective or naturalised 'truths' or 'textual authority' (Kaplan, 2003, p. 37). When different points of view co-exist in a text, rather than a single authorial position, Bakhtin's ideas concerning polyphony (multi-stranded narratives) and heteroglossia[6] (a collection of competing, often antagonistic, voices) are useful for understanding the dialogic interrelationship between the text's 'truths'. A further strategy common in this regard is the device of metalepsis that was discussed previously. Commonly referred to as frame-breaking, metalepsis blurs the lines between fiction and reality, and is apparent when disruptions occur at different levels of narration. A third strategy is intertextuality and/or parody. The following discussion examines how narrative point of view is challenged through these three metafictive devices in: *Voices in the Park*, *The Stinky Cheese Man and other Fairly Stupid Tales* and *The Three Pigs*. The disruption to the construction of a dominant voice through polyphony, for example, is evident from an examination of *Voices in the Park*, a sequel to *A Walk in the Park*.

As its similar title suggest, *Voices in the Park* (Browne, 1998) chronicles the same day spent in the park by the same two families first encountered in *A Walk in the Park*. However, the families are now drawn as zoomorphic figures rather than as humans. *Voices in the Park* provides multiple points of view from which the text can be viewed. There are four first-person narrators (polyphony), who create shifting points of view, with each narrator performing the role of principal focalising character of their particular segment. These focalised accounts work in conjunction with the points of view offered by the illustrations. The polyphony of different focalisers or 'voices', each narrating the events from their point of view, disrupts a single narrative voice or 'truth'. Each focaliser presents her/his own, first-person point of view, which addresses an implicit 'you', and gives the text its title *Voices in the Park*. Readers, too, are required to participate as there is not one monologic discourse running through the text, but multiple, seemingly valid voices or discourses. The most pervasive strategy for effecting the illusion of realism, according to Stephens (1992), is the use of first-person narration where the narrator and principal focaliser are the same. Readers are positioned to share this view and thus may undergo textual subjection. However, the multiple first-person narrators in *Voices in the Park* avoid any 'textual subjection' as readers actively shift between narrators, and the illusion of 'realism' is openly shattered.

The layout of the text supports multiple voices. The text is divided into four separate sections each presented in a different font and sequentially entitled 'First Voice', 'Second Voice' and so on. The four voices are differentiated, not only by age, gender and class, but also by changing seasons. The different seasons associated with each character contribute to the construction of a postmodern chronotope in which time and place are not in accordance. While Belsey (2002) warns that polyphony does not necessarily guarantee recognition of the plurality of voices, the postmodern picturebook usually makes this polyphony explicit, thereby drawing attention to the strategy rather than concealing its use. The distinctly separate sections in *Voices in the Park* used for each voice, along with the use of characteristic fonts and changing use of colour, make obvious the text's polyphonic approach. The iterations serve to confirm aspects of the afternoon in the park, but also highlight inconsistencies, while its parodic undermining of parental and class values and attitudes functions interrogatively. According to Kristeva (1969), the use of polyphony in fiction deflects the critical focus from the author to the production of the text.[7] While realist texts may also contain a number of voices, it is usually the authorial, narrating voice (Belsey's privileged voice) which guides interpretation of the other voices out of which the story is woven. Conversely, texts influenced by postmodernism such as *Voices in the Park* enable active participation in the construction of the significance of the text from a range of voices. By giving characters an opportunity to tell their own version of events, access is provided to their motivations ('It's so boring') and their emotions ('I felt really, really happy'), something not available to readers of *A Walk in the Park*. This dialogic interrelatedness or interplay of different voices and perspectives allows the points of view provided to be considered – one against the other. The iterations in *Voices in the Park* provide ample opportunities for this.

Different points of view of a similar scene are offered in the depiction of the Smythe family leaving the park. Their departure is first witnessed in the final illustration of 'First Voice' as told by Mrs Smythe. It consists of a full-page view of the park through the open gates as mother and child (Charles) and dog (Victoria) walk left to right in the direction of their home. Mrs Smythe has her considerable nose

in the air implying outraged indignation over Charles' disobedience
in leaving her side to play with Smudge. Charles is almost totally
obscured from view behind his mother's bodily frame, metonymically conveying her dominance over him. A trail of autumn leaves
follows the trio as they walk out of the double gates of the park into
the early evening. In the background a bush has burst into spontane-
ous combustion, a further symbolic indication of the power of Mrs
Smythe's indignation and outrage. Their exit is also documented in
the closing illustration in 'Third Voice' (Charles). A full-page scene
with the family group in the middle distance captures them in an
earlier moment while they are still inside the park. The statue to
their right is a zoomorphic version of Cupid, and his arrow is being
directed towards Charles, who is looking back over his shoulder, presumably towards Smudge. Interestingly, the lampposts depict more
conventional lampshades rather than those of earlier illustrations
that resembled Charles' mother's hat. The absence of Mrs Smythe's
hat suggests that Charles' experiences in the park with Smudge may
have tempered the dominance of his mother over him. However, the
verbal text tentatively suggests, 'Maybe Smudge will be there next
time?', indicating that Charles has little agency over his life and can
only *hope* to meet with his new friend again.

Smudge's description of the Smythe family's departure in 'Fourth
Voice' is foreshadowed by her statement: 'Then his mum called
him and he had to go. He looked sad.' The accompanying full-page
spread shows a close-up of the trio just about to go out through the
gates of the park. Mrs Smythe is the dominant figure, signified not
only in size but through the bold colours of her clothes. The motif
of her hat is repeated on the gate tops echoing Smudge's opinion of
Mrs Smythe's dominance over her son. The resultant construction of
different points of view is influenced by the combined effects of the
illustrative and written texts. Both Charles' and Smudge's versions
of the departure from the park show Mrs Smythe with her hand on
Charles' shoulder forming a transactional vector between mother
and son, reinforcing the bond between them. How readers view
this relationship may change as they progress through the text, or
through their repeated readings.

Narrative voices are not enclosed or deaf to one another. According
to Bakhtin (1984), they call back and forth to each other, and are
reflected in one another. In 'Third Voice', readers not only are

presented with Charles' version of events in which he seems to tolerate his mother's dominance, but may also recall Mrs Smythe's concern for Charles' safety ('You get some frightful types in the park these days!') in 'First Voice'. These details offer different interpretations. On the one hand, Mrs Smythe's arm on her son as they leave the park could be viewed as guiding, protective or even, remembering Charles' timidity, comforting. The expression on Charles' face as he looks back over his shoulder is too difficult to read at that distance, but the verbal text (quoted above) suggests a slight optimism. On the other hand, Smudge's account ('Fourth Voice') that 'He looked sad' and the now clearly visible expression on Charles' face as one of sadness, reinforces Smudge's point of view. Mrs Smythe's arm on Charles' shoulder, in this instance, may now be seen as domineering and assertive. This is the penultimate illustration of the book and is, perhaps, the lasting image of the relationship between Mrs Smythe and her son that readers take from the text. These differences result in a number of positions being provided from which to assess this one incident rather than a single reading offered in the pretext, *A Walk in the Park*. The utilisation of a number of focalisers, combined with the points of view offered by the illustrative text, encourages resistance to a dominant reading of *Voices in the Park* and to view the text from a number of different positions. This interplay of different voices and perspectives, discernible in *Voices in the Park*, and used to disrupt the projection of a dominant point of view, is also evident in *The Stinky Cheese Man and Other Fairly Stupid Tales* (Scieszka and Smith, 1992) in which a host of characters parades through the pages, each vying for attention while they create narrative mayhem.

The Stinky Cheese Man and Other Fairly Stupid Tales actively draws attention to the role of the narrator through playfulness and parody, and, in doing so, subverts the narration at a number of levels. The text masquerades as a collection of fairy tales, and Jack, the narrator, acts as its Master of Ceremonies. In writing of the presence of the narrator in (realist) texts, Todorov (1973) claims that the role is for the most part invisible, apprehended largely through the discourse. The narrator of *Stinky Cheese Man and Other Fairly Stupid Tales*, however, makes no attempt to disguise his presence and defiantly proclaims his function: 'I'm Jack. I'm the narrator.' He resorts to cajolery in his attempts to orchestrate the reception of the tales through direct address ('Just turn the page very quietly'), as well as editorial

asides ('Is that great or what?') in an attempt to direct readers' attention and influence their reception of his tales. His visibility is ensured
through the visual text where he is represented as a caricature, an
elfin-like figure dancing on the margins of the illustrations. This use
of an intrusive, and at times abusive, narrator serves as a structuring
device, which provides the overarching frame of the book by link-
ing the tales within the collection. It also provides opportunities
for a number of the characters to overtly challenge the narrator's
conventional authority. Hutcheon (1984) argues that such authorial
intrusion in texts that employ metafictive strategies serves as a self-
reflexive device for commenting on the storytelling processes which,
in turn, creates narrative distance from the textual world. McHale
(1987, p. 197) would argue that it destroys the illusory reality of the
fictional world while still leaving, if not *the* real world, at least *a* real
world. Rather than presenting a text which privileges a single, dominant discourse, Scieszka and Smith playfully create a heteroglossia of
competing, sometimes antagonistic voices, points of view and possible meanings which allow textual space for the active construction
of significance from within the voices that compete for attention.

The struggle for authority over the narrative between the narrator and some of the characters is made explicit in this text when a
number of characters step outside the frames of their own tales to
argue, harangue or bully Jack in order to express indignation (Little
Red Running Shorts), promote their particular story (Little Red Hen)
or appropriate a number of other people's stories for their own purpose (Giant). This frame-breaking, or metalepsis, transgresses the logical and hierarchical relations between different levels of narration.
If a character, for instance, becomes both character and authorial
agent s/he disrupts the conventional hierarchy of relations between
character, narrator and author or implied author, which then undermines the authority of the narrator and provides alternative points
of view from the authorised version. This occurs between Jack, Little
Red Running Shorts and Wolf.

At one point, Jack gets carried away with his role as narrator and
gives a brief summary of one of the stories – 'Little Red Running
Shorts'. However, both Little Red Running Shorts and her companion, Wolf, are indignant that the narrator has usurped their roles as
narrators of their own stories by presenting their story from his (the
narrator's) point of view. They refuse to retell their tale and readers

Figure 1.1 'Little Red Running Shorts' illustration from *The Stinky Cheese Man and Other Fairly Stupid Tales* by Jon Scieszka and Lane Smith (1992)

are left with the narrator's third-person perspective rather than a first-person telling from the main characters involved. Jack's action oversteps the boundaries between the world *in which* one tells, and the world *of which* one tells (Genette, 1980). This notion of who tells/speaks is subverted by the illustrative text (see Figure 1.1) where white silhouettes replace the characters, literally reflecting the written text where Little Red Running Shorts and Wolf leave with the parting words: 'We're out of here.' The white space indicates not only their absence from the story (because they have walked out on the narrator), but also their abdication from any responsibility for telling the tale and the particular point of view presented. However, despite their absence from the narrative, their absence–presence is still evident in the silhouettes, which suggest a further frame-breaking between present and not present.

Further examination of the visual text shows that Little Red Running Shorts is obviously indignant whereas Wolf's casual wave back towards Jack suggests a certain degree of ambivalence that is typical of postmodern fiction. However, their solidarity is evident as they march off to the left, back from whence they came – against the left-to-right flow of conventional Western reading – as the narrator pleads with them to return. Jack's pleading however has more to do with his awareness of the departure from the fiction-making process. He protests that the story should be three pages long (so far he has managed one page of written text and one page of illustrative text). Consequently, upon turning the page, readers are confronted by a blank page that serves as a comment on how the characters have seized control of the storytelling process and refused to cooperate in its construction. Such examples of metalepsis not only destabilise the ontological status of the fictional worlds but invite questions about authority, power and freedom within narratives. In this instance, the narrator Jack, who traditionally would have considerable power in the storytelling process, has his authority challenged by the characters (Little Red Running Shorts and Wolf) who exercise their freedom to leave. When Jack cries after them: 'What do I do when we turn the page?' he signals his loss of authority over the text and draws attention to the predicament in which Little Red Hen now finds herself.

Little Red Hen's querulous tone when she confronts the blank page left by the absence of part of the story of 'Little Red Running Shorts' reflects her confusion and draws readers' attention to the fact that this book does not conform to the codes of conventional narratives: she asks: 'Why is that page blank?' As detailed in the Introduction to this book, Little Red Hen attempts to bring order to the narrative by accusing the narrator, author and illustrator (those who conventionally would have authority over the text) of being lazy. This subversion of narrative convention highlights the constructedness of picturebook narratives and the possible ways in which a postmodern perspective disrupts their codes. Another character, the Giant, also challenges the primacy of Jack's authority over the story by direct intervention, stating in uppercase letters, 'I WILL READ MY STORY NOW.' Jack's only comment is 'And he did', suggesting passive acceptance of this metaleptic seizing of power over the narrative by the Giant. While children's texts such as picturebooks are generally more structured, *The Stinky Cheese Man and Other Fairly Stupid Tales* represents a heteroglossia of competing, often antagonistic, voices in which Jack, the narrator, struggles to be heard and seen; ideas are presented and challenged and any notion of synthesis is playfully resisted.

The accompanying illustration to the 'Giant Story' displays a number of fairy-tale books strewn at the base of the large bean stalk with pages torn out. These metonymically convey the disruption to conventional fairy tales, as well as anticipate the following pages in which the Giant constructs his own story; a subsequent illustration shows the Giant using tiny scissors to cut from a book. Readers may gather from this that the Giant is literally constructing his story from pretexts. Such a reliance on past texts underscores the point about originality in which Grieve (1993, after Foucault) suggests that through intertextuality the postmodern theory of common discursive property is foregrounded and requires a reconsideration of the idea of originality of the text. The Giant's action can also be interpreted through Hutcheon's (1988, p. 126) notion that a truly original work would have no meaning for readers and it is only by utilising prior discourses that any text derives meaning and significance, thus the inevitable intertextuality of all writing. And indeed, when the page is turned and attempts are made to read the Giant's story, it becomes evident that while it is a jumble of conventional phrases appropriated from any number of 'prior discourses', through familiarity with such fairy tales, it *is* possible to make some sense of it: 'The End [...] the evil stepmother said "I'll huff and I'll puff" [...] give you three wishes [...] Once upon a time' and so on. This is similar to Waugh's (1984, p. 24) analysis of B.S. Johnson's 'A Few Selected Sentences' which she describes as:

> [A] series of fragments taken from a wide variety of discursive practices [...] which, although resisting final totalisation, can be arranged into a number of conventional narratives. The fragments rely on readers' knowledge of the conventions of stories.

The Giant's story does not conform to the beginning–middle–end sequence of a conventional narrative. Rather it reflects the nonconformity of *The Stinky Cheese Man and Other Fairly Stupid Tales* itself.

Perhaps the most playfully subversive aspect of the Giant's story, aside from his attempts to usurp Jack's authority as narrator, is that it includes many of the Proppian elements of a fairy tale; it relies on readers to reconstruct the semblance of a tale out of the fragments despite its disrupted sequence.[8] The illustration accompanying the Giant's story contains many visual references to a large number of fairy-tale characters and objects (Cinderella's slipper, Aladdin's lamp, a black bird in a pie, alphabet letters, a witch and a rose). These examples serve as signifiers of both individual fairy tales and universal fairy-tale motifs. The images also include the Ginger Bread Man, the pretext upon which the approximated tale of *The Stinky Cheese Man* story is based. Just as the Giant has cut and pasted his story, so too is the accompanying illustration a collage of shapes, images and symbols seemingly drawn from the annuls of fairy-tale illustration. These self-reflexive repetitions are a pastiche of styles and media reflecting the fragmentation of postmodern art with little attempt at synthesis and which results in varying degrees of ambiguity or, at best, ambivalence rather than any authoritative textual meaning.

The Three Pigs (Wiesner, 2001) picturebook uses metalepsis and parody but also incorporates a carnivalesque aesthetic in its revisioning of the familiar folk tale. A carnivalesque approach to the retellings provides for 'the suspension of all hierarchical rank, privileges, norms and prohibitions' (Bakhtin, 1968, p. 75), which allows the interrogation of the patriarchal and hierarchical discourses of the fairy tales. The text begins traditionally and deceptively enough with the archetypal wolf stalking the three pigs as they build their own homes (as a first step towards independence) but rapidly turns to parody. The initial narration is from a third-person narrator in a fairy-tale register: 'Once upon a time there were three pigs.' Expectation is soon disrupted, however, when the wolf huffs and puffs so strongly that the first pig is blown out of the picture frame into what can only be described as narrative limbo – he is neither in the story frame nor has he disappeared from readers' view. This metaleptic violation of the boundary of the primary fictional world (that is, the world of the original folk tale to which the wolf and three pigs belong) creates uncertainty as to the exact ontological or 'truth' status of the space into which they have escaped, thereby drawing attention to it. At this point the third-person narration of *The Three Pigs* is disrupted by the characters' own voices, delivered by way of speech bubbles. This signals a break from the structuring frame of the original story: 'Hey! He blew me right out of the story!' While the wolf is trying to figure out what has happened, the porcine playmates are depicted folding a page of the book into a paper plane before making good their escape (a strategy noted previously in *The Story of a Little Mouse Trapped in a Book*). Not only have the pigs usurped the role of the narrator through the use of direct speech but they have also seized an element of the text (a page) through which to effect their escape and advance the story.

The comical effect produced by this metalepsis not only allows the pigs access to a number of peripheral worlds (a medieval tale and the 'Hey diddle, diddle' nursery rhyme), but also produces different levels of narration, which result in a struggle for control over the story and, consequently, the point of view offered. This is clearly evident through an examination of the visual text in which the third-person narration doggedly continues with its original trajectory despite the disruption caused by the pigs' escape which results in a contradiction between the written and illustrative texts. The usually authoritative third-person narration continues to run parallel to the direct-speech bubbles employed by the pigs but recedes to the background as pages become folded, discarded and ignored, thus lessening its power over the storytelling process. After a romp through a storybook labyrinth the pigs eventually gather up the pages of their tale and reconstruct their story space and thus effect a return to the primary diegetic level established at the beginning of the story. While the text also returns to third-person narration towards the end of the story, the characters actively reconstruct scattered letters to form the words of the text and are thus afforded an agential role by creating their own version of the old tale. The text also characterises those aspects of the carnivalesque aesthetic which seek to 'mock and challenge authoritative figures and structures of the adult world' (Stephens, 1992, p. 122). The wolf as predator and the prince (from the medieval tale) as conqueror are no longer afforded the rank and privileges which they have come to expect as their due, but are left bewildered by the unexpected turn of events. This bewilderment is evident in the visual text where the prince is pictured scratching his head at the disappearance of the dragon from the story space of the medieval tale. The wolf, towards the end of the book, is pictured on his back, reeling from the thrust of the dragon's head as it intervenes at the moment the wolf is about to attack the pigs. The wolf is not used to being at the mercy of others and its subservient position with its legs in the air and surprised expression on its face convey the bewilderment it feels as the storyline of the traditional tale is turned on its head. The text also mocks and challenges the conventional structures of narrative. The parody undermines the authority of the traditional narration, and most notably inverts the traditional hierarchy of voices, allowing space for alternative points of view (such as that of the pigs and the ancillary characters, the dragon and the cat). Ironically, it is the lowly pigs and their companions who now exercise control over the (re)construction of the narratives. Thus the original point of view promoting a Protestant work ethic, presented by the third-person narrator, has been subverted and alternative points of view have been offered. Further points of view are offered through the use of perspective in the visual text.

While the notion of 'who speaks' is a primary consideration in the construction of points of view in a narrative, so too is 'who sees', which determines perceptual point of view (Stephens, 1992). This is achieved through manipulating the perspective in the visual text that, in turn, contributes to the construction of a variety of positions from which viewers observe each scene which creates a particular attitude towards the narrative at each specific juncture (Stephens, 1992). Just as polyphony and heteroglossia contribute to changing points of view so too does the presentation of multiple perspectives in the visual text. Multiple perspectives are conveyed in *The Three Pigs*, the weight of which is carried through the visual text. Readers are rarely allowed to remain as mere observers; rather they are invited to become 'active participants' (Kress and van Leeuwen, 2006) allied with the wolf as he stares eagerly into the house of sticks in anticipation of the pork dinner within. However, with a shift from the wolf's perspective to that of the pig's position, readers 'become' the frightened pig, intimidated by the image of a howling predator at his door, or at least this is the role readers may be willing to take on as part of the textual game. (The idea of reader identification with the perceptual point of view of the characters is a common feature that texts for small children often exploit.) Readers are later positioned in a subordinate role, by witnessing the pigs flying overhead from a ground-level viewing position. Finally, readers are implicated in the actual construction of the new narrative from the moment the first pig, in extreme close-up, peers out at the implied audience and comments: 'I think ... someone's out there.' This draws readers into the ontological universe of the text, becoming 'insiders', as suggested by Goldstone (2008, p. 119). In the final scene, the open interior space of the home invites a readerly sense of being there with the pigs and their friends, a positioning that seems preferable to being located on the hillside with the lonely wolf.

These shifting points of view in the visual text, especially the close-ups (Kress and van Leeuwen, 2006), demand the active engagement of readers in contrast to many conventional texts for children which assign them a more passive role. These perspectives work to position readers to empathise, rather than identify, with the pigs and their companions. This seems to concur with Stephens' (1992) claim that subject positions constructed in interrogative texts tend to discourage simple identification with subject positions of the characters which allows for greater flexibility. Rather than the construction of a fixed point of view, readers are encouraged to view the narrative from a range of positions that contributes to the uncertainty, fragmentation and ambiguity characteristic of postmodern fiction.

The use of polyphony, heteroglossia, parody and metalepsis as well as shifting perspectives does not, of itself, guarantee that a hierarchy of voices, resulting in a dominant point of view, will not be established. While the preceding discussion examined a number of postmodern influences on the construction of the focus picturebooks, *Voices in the Park* and *The Three Pigs* are not without their inconsistencies with regards to their 'postmodern' approaches. This is evident in conflicting critical comments on the texts. For instance, in reference to *Voices in the Park*, Frank Serafini (2005, p. 50) suggests: 'the voices represent a polyphonic narrative where no one perspective is privileged over the others'. Conversely, Andrea Schwenke-Wyile (2006) implies there is a hierarchy, maintaining that the voices are presented in order from least to most sympathetic. While the written text is conventionally regarded as subjective, the illustrative text is seen as objective (Schwenke-Wyile, 2006). Thus, when the visual text, through its use of changing seasons, differing fonts, composition and colour, seems to present some of the characters more favourably than others, it does so with some measure of authority. The illustrative text, therefore, acts in the manner of a third-person narration despite a first-person narrator in the written text. This can result in differing points of view between the written and visual texts, creating narrative tension. To return to *Voices in the Park*, a reading of 'Fourth Voice', for instance, could imply that Smudge's account *is* privileged and, therefore, treated by readers as having a higher truth value.

The vibrant colours and luxuriant growth of the visual text of 'Fourth Voice' are accompanied by a bold, informal font and the brilliant sunlight of summer. The visual text, with its extravagance of bright colours and dislocated shapes in the form of giant fruits, is accompanied by the informal register adopted by Smudge: 'Dad had been really fed up.' The appeal to the senses of this riot of colour evokes a degree of empathy with the character of Smudge. This is further enhanced by Smudge's developing attitude towards Charles whom she initially dismisses as 'a bit of a wimp', but then admits that 'he's okay'. No such leeway is granted to Mrs Smythe, however, who is dismissed as a 'silly twit' and portrayed unsympathetically in the visual text, while Mr Smith only appears in the first illustration of 'Fourth Voice' as the family arrives at the park. The illustrative text of 'Fourth Voice' shows the children at play. Smudge's verbal text adds to this impression: 'We both burst out laughing' and 'I felt really, really happy.' The full-page illustration of the children and dogs leaping about on the bandstand presents an image of freedom and fun through its sense of movement and use of bright primary colours. However, the *joie de vivre* emanating from the illustrative text of 'Fourth Voice' is somewhat tempered by a wistful note that creeps into the written text. This is evident from the first encounter with Smudge's 'voice' when she admits that: 'I was pleased when he said we could take Albert to the park' and seems to be confirmed by her declaration that she felt 'really, really happy', suggesting that it is not always the case. Additionally, the tender way Smudge treats the flower given to her by Charles suggests that this friendly gesture is a rare event; it may be that it is more often Smudge who is caring for others, namely her father. This all works to present Smudge's account as having a high level of truth value or modality. By contrast, both Mrs Smythe and Charles are portrayed as unreliable narrators: Mrs Smythe in 'First Voice' claims 'some scruffy mongrel' chased

Victoria over the park but the visual text shows that it is Victoria that is chasing Albert. Also, Charles claims to have 'showed Smudge the way' when climbing trees but the visual text shows Smudge at the top with Charles clinging to a branch below. Mr Smith, on the other hand, is seen as self-absorbed and fairly non-communicative. Nevertheless, despite the privileging of 'Fourth Voice', it is the fifth voice which seems to be shown in the most positive light.

The fifth 'voice', told largely through the illustrative text and consequently somewhat overlooked by most commentators, is that of the dogs that race through the park uninhibited by considerations of class or gender and may well represent, whether intentionally or not, the 'voice' of the implied author. In *Voices in the Park*, however, this is achieved almost entirely through the illustrative text and readers are left to determine the social implications of the dogs' free and easy manner in contrast to the initial awkwardness between Charles and Smudge and the frostiness of Mrs Smythe and indifference of Mr Smith. Ultimately, readers are positioned by the 'accumulated details and perspectives' (Schwenke-Wyile, 2006, p. 187) of each of the 'voices' and are forced to view each new (re)telling in the light of the previous 'voices'.

While *Voices in the Park* provides different positions from which the text can be viewed it also needs to be recognised that all texts carry with them inherent ideological traces and, as detailed above, *Voices in the Park* is no exception. *The Three Pigs* has evidence of what Beverley Pennell calls (1996, p. 5) 'ideological drift' whereby 'the overt, or explicit, ideology of the text may be subverted by its covert, or implicit, ideology'. At the level of implicit ideology, *The Three Pigs* reinscribes a liberal humanist view. The picturebook certainly embraces a number of postmodern influences, including breaking of frames and indeterminacy, as well as multiple spatio-temporalities and ontological layers. In the end, though, the text appears to privilege the liberal humanist qualities of cooperation, compromise and joint decision-making. These characteristics are foregrounded in a number of scenes: when the pigs rescue the dragon from the medieval tale; when the pigs along with the dragon and the cat jointly make the decision to return to the original tale; and in the cooperation of the characters in the construction of the final words of the text. This reversion to a liberal humanist perspective accords with the tendency, discussed in the Introduction, of children's postmodern literature to be a particular type of postmodernism in its attempts to foster socio-cultural values in order to enculturate children into the prevailing ways of the society in which they live. In doing so, however, it may undermine the postmodernist influences otherwise evident in the text.

The Stinky Cheese Man and Other Fairly Stupid Tales, on the other hand, comes much closer to providing a more genuinely egalitarian approach to its narrating voices. Lewis (2001, p. 100) claims *The Stinky Cheese Man and Other Fairly Stupid Tales* (at the time) as the only 'true' postmodern picturebook. While this label has been debated in the Introduction, this picturebook does seem to exhibit all the characteristics detailed by Sloboda (1997, pp. 112–13), writing on Barthelme's postmodern novel *Snow White*, as being postmodern. Sloboda points to the juxtapositioning of random thoughts and fragments which suspend characters' notion of certainty and progression, and promotes alternative interpretations, perceptions and concepts of knowledge and different aspects of 'being-in-the-world'. This description could also serve as a comment on *The Stinky Cheese Man and Other Fairly Stupid Tales* in which the text rejects synthesis, both textual and ideological, and resists resolution. Margaret Mackey (2008, p. 114) argues that *The Stinky Cheese Man and Other Fairly Stupid Tales* is designed to be read as mayhem and uproar, while Stevenson (1994, p. 32) posits that the text, through the comment in the introduction, 'won't tell you anything'. These different comments point to a multiplicity of meaning (through postmodern excess) rather than meaninglessness.

The focus picturebooks under analysis in this first chapter, through the utilisation of a range of metafictive strategies, highlight the fact that fictional texts are not 'natural, finished and seamless' but are, in fact, 'constructed, open, fragmented and plural' as suggested in the epigraph. These texts provide multiple positions from which to view the texts through shifting points of view presented both verbally and visually. However, it would seem that a number of picturebooks, although influenced by postmodernism, may inadvertently reinscribe liberal humanist ideals or inadvertently privilege a particular position. This appears to be the case in *The Three Pigs* and *Voices in the Park*. *The Stinky Cheese Man and Other Fairly Stupid Tales*, on the other hand, appears to delight in drawing attention to the limited points of view and/or authority available to narrators and focalisers of a text thereby seeming to advocate, in accordance with the character of postmodernism, the need to treat all points of view offered as provisional. As this chapter has discussed, postmodern texts frequently draw attention to how realist texts construct versions of reality through the utilisation of the codes and conventions of narrative such as narration and point of view. Other positions from which to view the texts are provided by destabilising the conventional modes of representation, examined in Chapter 2.

2
Destabilising Modes of Representation

> Metafictional texts show that literary fiction can
> never imitate or 'represent' the world but always
> imitates or 'represents' the discourses which in turn
> construct that world. (Waugh, 1984, p. 100)

In recent years, problems of representation have come to dominate contemporary critical theory and this is increasingly reflected in the fiction itself, as Waugh notes in the epigraph above. Hutcheon (1989) maintains that all cultural forms of representation – literary, visual and aural – are ideologically grounded, they structure how we see ourselves and how we construct notions of self and the societies in which we live. She further argues that representation (in narratives) cannot be avoided but it can be studied to show how it legitimates certain kinds of knowledge, and, therefore, certain kinds of power. This chapter examines the nature of narrative representation and the multiple ways in which postmodern picturebooks foreground representational strategies. All narratives are representations. According to Moon (2001), these representations are simplified models of reality influenced by the conventions, beliefs and values of the society in which they are produced. They emerge from habitual ways of thinking about or acting in the world. Realist texts artificially construct their fictional worlds in terms of particular ideologies while presenting these as transparently natural and external. Ommundsen (1993) argues that reading such realist texts is reassuring because they echo the cultural conventions that are familiar to their audience. However, readers need to be aware of the constructedness of such texts, especially as they are value-laden and often present a simplified world which can descend into overworked formulas and stereotypes (Moon, 2001). Readers may become immersed in the text and therefore may lack any awareness that the text is a representation.

Postmodern fiction, including postmodern picturebooks, draws readers' attention to the text as representation or construct by 'laying bare' this construction through the utilisation of metafictive strategies, including intertextuality, indeterminacy and polyphony. Thus, Hutcheon (1989) argues, by both using and abusing general conventions and specific forms of representation, postmodern texts work to denaturalise them. Through the latter part of the twentieth century and into the current one, postmodern texts have drawn readers' attention to how conventional narrative codes construct 'real' and imaginary worlds, presenting them as natural and external (Waugh, 1984). An examination of the multiple ways in which metafictive strategies are used to denaturalise forms of representation follows.

Many commentators have noted with respect to contemporary Western society's consumerist, multi-mediated culture that representations have become more significant than the real (Baudrillard, 1983; Berger, 2003). Postmodernism's contestation of mimetic (imitative) representation accords with Jean Baudrillard's (1983, p. 148) claim that the image has become more important than the 'real' thing that the image captures, and that reality has been replaced by hyperreality: 'It is reality itself that is hyperrealist.' Berger (2003) notes that representations of the real have become stand-ins for actual, lived experience. What is real then becomes judged against cinematic-video productions that usurp reality in such a way that reality pales in comparison to the blockbuster account. However, this has become so much a part of postmodernity that Featherstone (2007) contends that today's tourists (or 'post-tourists' as he calls them) happily accept the montage world and hyperreality of many tourist destinations (for example, Las Vegas and Disney World) for what they are. Turner (1991, pp. 3–4) agrees that we live in a media-dominated world of images and simulations of reality and suggests: 'this world of signs has undermined our sense of reality and dissolved our sense that there are fixed structures and stable boundaries, that anything has meaning'. These considerations of the unstable boundaries between reality and representation are evident in the picturebook *I Will Not Ever NEVER Eat a Tomato* (Child, 2000a).

In the picturebook, Charlie attempts to encourage his little sister Lola to eat various foods including peas, potatoes and tomatoes. Lola resists his attempts and Charlie is required to resort to subterfuge by substituting make-believe names for the real ones. Carrots become 'orange twiglets from Jupiter', peas become 'green drops from Greenland' and mashed potatoes become 'cloud fluff from Mt. Fuji'. By changing the signifier Charlie makes the food seem more appealing and allows Lola to taste the food without appearing to back down from her adamant stance: 'I will not ever Never eat a'. While the illustrations are predominantly rendered in pencil and crayon, photographs of actual peas, carrots and tomatoes are incorporated into the text to represent the various foodstuffs. This contrast in modality between the pencil and crayon drawings and the photographs portrays the foodstuffs as hyperreal and imbues them with a sense of 'otherness'. Lola plays along with the game but lets Charlie know that she is aware it *is* a game when she renames tomatoes 'moonsquirters' then slyly asks: 'You didn't think they were tomatoes, did you Charlie?' Lola thereby names the object or signified while appearing to deny its actuality or 'realness'. This play with both signifiers and hyperrealism raises questions about the nature of representation by blurring the boundaries between reality, hyperreality and representation. The linguistic play at work here is similar to Hutcheon's (1988) argument that postmodern art does not deny the simulacrisation of mass culture, but problematises the whole notion of the representation of reality. Lola's naming of the tomato a 'moonsquirter', and her further comment to Charlie, demonstrate that she self-consciously acknowledges the latter's existence as representation, and therefore does not obliterate the referent altogether.

Playing with language and linguistic representation

The dominant feature of any narrative, especially with regards to representation, is language. Derrida's (1976, p. 158) declaration that 'there is nothing outside of the text' expresses the notion that in relations between humans and the world there is nothing that is not conditioned by the structure and practice of language and textuality. While narratives rely on language to construct representations of the world, language is nevertheless an arbitrary system of signs where the only relationship between the signifier and signified is based on convention. As Derrida (1976) argues through his theory of *différance*, any meanings constructed through language are provisional and subject to transformation over time. Postmodern picturebooks seek to draw attention to this arbitrary nature of language, often through playfulness. The instability of language in children's literature is playfully referenced, for instance, through the utilisation of puns which involve incongruity of meaning that results in breaches of coherence (Collins, 2002). This instability of language is alluded to in the visual text of both *The Three Pigs* (Wiesner, 2001) and *The Red Tree* (Tan, 2001). In *The Three Pigs* this occurs when the dragon's head scatters the words of the picturebook's text and the pigs reconstruct the written text from the scattered letters to form the conclusion of the story (noted in the previous chapter). In *The Red Tree* the protagonist holds up a megaphone in an attempt to communicate but the words tumble out of the megaphone as a jumble of letters rather than as any form of meaningful communication. These examples allude to the constructed and unstable nature of language, and any attempt to draw significance (meaning) from a text needs to bear this in mind. One of the ways in which postmodern children's literature demonstrates the arbitrary relationship between the signifier and signified is through wordplay that includes, in some cases, the creation of an invented language.

Two picturebooks, *Ooh-la-la (Max in Love)* (Kalman, 1991) and *Baloney (Henry P.)* (Scieszka and Smith, 2001), foreground language gaps and utilise invented languages in their representations of the intratextual world. *Ooh-la-la (Max in Love)* exploits the semiotic instability of language creating a playful, yet sophisticated, text that draws attention to the very language from which the text is constructed. Max Stravinsky is a 'millionaire poet dog' on a visit to Paris, during which he falls in love with both the city and a dalmation called Crepes Suzette. The text is a playful romp through Paris (or *'Paree'*). In writing on this picturebook, Schwenke-Wyile (2006, p. 183), comments: '[it] consists of games connected to graphic games connected to visual games connected to literary games, all of which play with forms of representation'. One particular game involves the interrogation of the minimal differences between signifiers. In relation to the elements of a linguistic system, Saussure (1959, p. 117) argues: 'Their most precise characteristic is being what the others are not.' Thus the whole language system is based on minimal differences.

While the arbitrariness between the sign and its referent applies to the *fundamental* relationship between words and their referents, in actual practice those relationships have, through usage, become a matter of convention (Bertens, 2001). These minimal differences are playfully highlighted through rhyming pattern and homophonic pun in *Ooh-la-la (Max in Love)* during a phone conversation between Mimi and Jacques:

'Listen.
Zouzou called Loulou,
Loulou called Coco,
Coco called Kiki and
Kiki called me me.' [Mimi]

This example supports Bertens' (2001) point that the differential principle not only works to distinguish words from each other ('Zouzou' from 'Loulou'), it simultaneously distinguishes *meanings* from each other ('me me' from 'Mimi') as a change in the signifier, no matter how minimal, indicates a new signified.

This emphasis on difference results in a series of seemingly nonsense poems Max spots in the street. For instance, the line 'An Antelope cant elope with a cantaloupe' is an indirect reference to the arbitrariness of language. The signifiers *antelope* and *cantaloupe* may look similar, nevertheless one is an animal and the other a fruit, therefore making it (biologically) impossible for them to elope. Furthermore, the words *cant elope* also look remarkably similar (almost but not quite anagrams) to both *antelope* and *cantaloupe*. Other absurdities include the statement: 'The door, she knocked', light-heartedly referring to the French language's convention of assigning masculine or feminine articles to a noun. (The door, *la porte*, is feminine and so 'she knocked'). The playfulness is extended through to the notion of the door knocking – certainly there was a knocking noise emanating from the door, but it was a person knocking on the door. Such playfulness acknowledges inconsistencies in how we express ourselves. The absurdity of language is further highlighted through the sentence: 'I was awakened by a k-k-k-knocking at the door.' The repetition of the 'k' sound imitates the sound of knocking but in the pronunciation of the word 'knocking' the 'k' remains silent. The size of the letter 'k' also increases as the knocking becomes louder. Such foregrounding of the linguistic medium creates tension between its function with regards to reference and the text's compositional playfulness.

Play with shifts in meaning is extensive in this text. Much of the play is doubly encoded through French–English interchanges and metaphorical and literal punning. When news of Max's arrival in Paris spreads, Mimi tells Jacques: 'He is the coolest cat, I mean the hottest dog.' This play with shifting signifiers ('cool', 'hot') continues as Max's French tutor arrives and expresses surprise that he is '*a chien. A dog!*' then comments that she has taught plenty of rats in her time. The use of 'rat' here of course is used to denote not another animal, but rather a person who deserts or betrays friends in their time of need, in other words, a cad. Furthermore, Max's comment on falling in love with Crepes: 'I was smitten. I was bitten,' relies on a play on the signifier 'bitten' to direct meaning. While it would normally signal to sink teeth into, cut or pierce, here it is used to suggest that one is affected, impressed or, in this case, fallen in love. The use of the term 'bitten' is particularly appropriate (and amusing) as both Crepes and Max are dogs. Besides providing humour, these usages point to the imperative that what a given element signifies within a culture depends on convention which can change with usage over time (Derrida, 1976). Thus, the relationship between signifier and signified is further destabilised highlighting the elusiveness of language and how we use it.

The picturebook, as noted above, also draws attention to the differences between languages, including, in this instance, differences between American-English and French. Following Saussure's and Derrida's work on semiotics, Fuery and Mansfield (2000) point out that there is no necessary reason why one particular combination of sounds or marks on the page is used to denote a specific concept. Rather than conduct an analysis of the signifier/signified relationship of structuralism, Jameson (1983) suggests that postmodernism places the signifier in the context of other signifiers which thus sees meaning (signification) emerging from signifier/signifier relations. As noted in previous examples, *Ooh-la-la* employs alternating signifiers in French (*chien*) and English (*dog*). The text also mixes French and English in the same sentence, such as when Fritz explains to Max that: 'the *chef* in a fit threw *escargot* on my *chapeau*'. Additionally, a number of the words used in English (*beret, chef, bus (autobus)* and *soufflé*) are in fact French in origin. Further play with language involves the use of *cliché* (*crème de la crème*, 'the rest they say is history') and slang ('beat', 'bushed', 'shack') which rely on cultural practice for their meanings. This play with signs is extended through the utilisation of an invented language in the picturebook *Baloney (Henry P.)*.

The use of invented languages has been a popular strategy throughout the history of children's literature: A.A. Milne, Lewis Carroll and Dr Seuss are familiar exponents. However, as Geoff Moss (1992) notes, postmodern (children's) writers utilise linguistic inventions to underline the construction of the world through language and to highlight the relationship between the signifier and signified as random and arbitrary. The picturebook *Baloney (Henry P.)* tells the story of the eponymous Henry P. Baloney, a small boy who is always late for school. On the occasion described in the text, Henry's teacher demands an explanation for his tardiness otherwise he must face the consequences. While endeavouring to provide a plausible excuse, Henry tells a long-winded tale involving *zimulis*, *pordos*, *battunas* and *razzas* and other seemingly invented names. The dual codes of words and pictures enable readers to make assumptions about the meanings of the invented words, reinforcing the contention that the visual text has the capacity to narrow the signification of the verbal text. For instance, when Henry refers to his 'trusty *zimulis*' the illustrative text clearly shows a pencil. The pictorial code of the text is that of a science-fiction story complete with rockets, planets and launch pads, allowing readers to embrace the apparently invented language with its unfamiliar words as being appropriate to the genre.

In order to highlight the arbitrary relationship between signifier and signified, the text provides a humorous moment in which Henry forgets the Astrosus word for 'thank you' and instead offers another Astrosus word which actually means 'doofbrain', which provokes the people of Astrosus. When Henry returns to Earth and offers his teacher an explanation for his absence, the teacher, with some irony, comments that the task for today is to write a tall story. The implication being that Henry's excuse for being late is a tall story, in itself full of exaggeration and invention. The tall tale is flagged by the title *Baloney (Henry P.)* and the endpapers which feature BALONEY[1] in large uppercase letters on what looks like a black, starry sky. An Afterword at the end of the text claims that the message (the story) is a transmission received from outer space and comes with a decoder, which seems to suggest that all the words are equally alien to those from outer space. It turns out that the seemingly invented words are in fact actual words from a range of Earth languages including Swahili, Finnish, Esperanto (itself an invented or constructed language) and Inuktitut. This playfulness points to the way in which language is embedded in culture. Any disorientation or failure to grasp meanings arises from a lack of knowledge and understanding of cultural location and practices. For instance, Henry's sense of self and how he sees and interprets the world, as well as the means by which he gives meaning to himself and his world, are constructed through language which is both real and constructed. The irony of the text is not so much that the words exist as other languages, but that these words are arbitrary anyway. Nevertheless, readers are positioned to see them as a quirky part of Henry's imagination. The strategies utilised by these two picturebooks playfully draw attention to the constructed and arbitrary nature of language, and, in so doing, highlight the difficulties of relying on language to construct representations of the world. Works of art, including fictional texts, are also organised and perceived through other structures and 'frames' (Waugh, 1984) besides language.

Playfully refusing to follow the rules of representation

Narrative framing structures such as genre expectations, linearity, spatio-temporalities and compositional details assist in the organisation and presentation of experience. John Frow (2002) argues that frames are often multiple and may supplement and/or narrow the kind of aesthetic space being presented within a work of art. Frow notes that frames for literary texts are particularly complex and include not only the structures mentioned above, but also paratextual elements such as book covers, title pages, publishing details as well as special framing effects (if the book is a collection and so on). He argues that one of the difficulties of the concept of 'frame' is its *invisibility* because it is culturally determined, and consequently such features of a text are generally taken for granted. Postmodern picturebooks, in order to expose and/or problematise narrative frames, utilise a number of frame-breaking devices that range from parody and inversion, through intertextuality and blurring of ontological levels, to playing with editorial conventions and literal frame-breaking in the visual text.

Conventional Western narratives tend to proceed in a linear fashion along the left to right trajectory of conventional Western reading, which incorporates the orientation–complication–resolution model. This convention is satirised in *Beware of the Storybook Wolves* (Child, 2000c) by Herb, the focalising character, who explains: 'The story got very nasty in the middle and everybody nearly came to a sticky end ... but, by the last page ... it had all turned out well and went happy-ever-afterly.' Through linear narrative structure and use of mimetic devices, fiction attempts to immerse readers in the story and convince them that what they are reading is a true reflection of the 'real' world. However, rather than constructing real reflections of life, fictions merely construct versions of reality which are partial, incomplete and fragmentary. And it is this aspect that the following postmodern picturebooks work to highlight, including their use of arbitrary beginnings and conclusions.

Most fictions utilise conventional narrative codes to signal the beginning of a story. Perhaps the most well-known phrase with which to signal the beginning of a particular type of narrative is the 'Once upon a time' convention adopted by traditional fairy tales. Such codes disguise the fact that these beginnings are in fact arbitrary. Jack, in *The Stinky Cheese Man and Other Fairly Stupid Tales*, self-consciously and playfully lays bare this notion of arbitrary beginnings by drawing readers' attention to the convention. Jack instructs Little Red Hen: 'You have to start with Once upon a time.' This introduction explicitly exposes knowledge of the convention, yet implicitly questions the convention. Each of the stories within the collection of 'fairly stupid tales' begins with '*Once upon a time*', in coloured, script font, which highlights the convention rather than masks its presence. The arbitrary nature of fictional beginnings is problematised in another picturebook, *Il Libro piu corto del mondo* (*The Shortest Book in the World*, Cox, 2002), which is discussed in more detail in Chapter 6. The spiral-binding of this text, with no identifiable title page or beginning, flaunts convention and leaves readers to determine where to begin. In fact, readers may start and finish at different places each time they read the text.

Convention also dictates that stories have a satisfactory conclusion in which loose ends are tied up and closure is achieved. This convention is particularly observed in children's literature where the accepted wisdom seems to be that children need resolution with, preferably, a satisfactory outcome (Rose, 1984; Lewis, 1990; Stephens, 1992). *The Stinky Cheese Man and Other Fairly Stupid Tales*, however, goes out of its way to ensure that readers are aware of such conventions of traditional narratives. Despite the disrupted opening and continual interruptions, the text does offer a conclusion, of sorts, to the overarching story. The Giant devours the Little Red Hen in a chicken sandwich and Jack takes advantage of the Giant's inattention to make his escape, concealed within the letters of THE END. Similarly, the vast majority of the inner tales achieve plausible (if at times unexpected) endings but also include the stock phrase 'The End' in coloured script in a similar manner to the 'Once upon a time' beginnings already discussed, thereby leaving readers in no doubt. Initially, readers may have been positioned to expect the 'happily ever after' ending of traditional fairy tales (the archetypal fictional ending according to Waugh), but are subtly reminded that these 'fairly stupid' tales do not conform to conventional fairy-tale endings.

The picturebook *The Frog Prince Continued* (Scieszka and Johnson, 1991) satirises this notion of the happily-ever-after conclusion to which most fairy tales adhere. It begins with an ending: 'The Princess kissed the frog. He turned into a prince. And they lived happily ever after ...'. The use of an ellipsis rather than a full stop draws attention to the view, raised by postmodern interrogations of fiction, that most narrative endings are arbitrary and provisional. This book underscores this point by suggesting that, in fact, the princess and frog prince were not living happily ever after. In fact they, like most newly weds, were experiencing difficulties adapting to life together. Exchanges such as: 'Stop sticking your tongue out like that' (Princess) and 'How come you never want to go down to the pond anymore?' (Prince) also playfully highlight differences that idealised fairy tales tend to gloss over. After one such exchange, the Prince rereads his story and discovers that it says 'right there at the end [...] "They lived happily ever after. The End." So he stayed in the castle and drove the Princess crazy.' Eventually, however, he realises that he needs to be a frog again so sets out to find a witch who can turn him back into a frog. He comes across a number of possible candidates from a variety of familiar fairy tales but with indifferent success, so he returns to the castle and his Princess, who berates him for his absence. The story continues: 'The Prince looked at the Princess who had believed him when no one else in the world had, the Princess who had actually kissed his slimy frog lips. The Princess who loved him.' As readers turn the page, however, this seemingly serious and conventional ending is again thwarted: '*The Prince kissed the Princess. They both turned into frogs. And hopped off happily ever after. The End.*' These self-reflexive endings serve as humorous asides upon the conventions of both representation and resolution: the latter previously regarded as essential for children's texts.

The picturebook *Black and White* (Macaulay, 1990) disrupts many of the conventional frames of narrative discussed above and is, therefore, full of ambiguities and indeterminacies which result in a representation of the recorded events of the narrative that is partial and incomplete. Any expectations of a conventional reading experience are immediately disrupted by the warning stamp on the title page. The stamp, itself a parody of the type of warning stamps seen on packets of cigarettes, for instance, warns that the text may contain several stories, but then again perhaps only one, and recommends 'careful inspection of both words and pictures'. Further disruption is experienced when readers, upon turning the page, are confronted by a double-page spread over which are four seemingly separate stories each with their own title, a border between them on each page and the gutter visually framing each as an individual tale (see Figure 2.1). This represents an example of what McHale (1987) calls a *split text* in which two or more texts are arranged in parallel and meant to be read, as far as possible, simultaneously. Rather than reading linearly as is the norm in a conventional picturebook, this disrupted format calls upon readers, already positioned by the warning stamp, to make decisions particularly with regards to the order in which the tales are to be read. This format forces readers to improvise an order of reading as well as create an increased awareness of the text as object, which then foregrounds difficulties with establishing any stability of the projected world(s) within the book.

The individual episodes of *Black and White* begin at different times and places within what appears to be one overarching story. While Stevenson (1994, p. 33) describes this text as 'a synchronous telling of four interrelated stories', there is evidence of a postmodern chronotope operating in which conventional spatio-temporalities do not

Figure 2.1 Illustration from *Black and White* by David Macaulay (1990)

apply. The initial temporal differences are slight: Story 1 ('Seeing Things') begins on the train with the boy in the very early hours of the morning; Story 2 ('Problem Parents') opens with a family at breakfast; Story 3 ('A Waiting Game') shows early morning commuters who include the parents from 'Problem Parents' who are waiting for the 8.13 am train; and Story 4 ('Udder Chaos') follows a prisoner making good his escape, presumably before the train passes that spot (given later developments). By the seventh opening, however, the disjunction between the timeframes of these tales is quite pronounced. In 'Seeing Things' the cows have just moved off the rail tracks (early morning) while the parents in 'Problem Parents' have arrived home from work (after 7 pm) and are busily folding a newspaper. Yet, in 'A Waiting Game' it is still morning and the commuters on the station platform have not begun to fold their newspapers. Meanwhile the escapee and several of the cows have hidden themselves in a choir. The timeframe of this episode is uncertain, and, to add to the ambiguity and indeterminacy, at times certain elements of one story migrate into another.

This disruption to the spatial frames of individual tales begins on the title pages of the separate stories when the escapee's knotted sheets pass down 'The Waiting Game' frame into that of 'Udder Chaos'. Thus, the escapee 'migrates' (to use McHale's term, 1987) from his original story world (presumably the gaol) into the space of 'Udder Chaos' from whence he effects his escape. On opening 11, the text of Story 1, written on torn paper from Story 3, floats into Story 2 and becomes the mail which has been 'ripped into a million pieces' by the father who is still in a jovial mood from the morning at the railway station. The train from Story 1 crosses the book's gutter on opening 13 to arrive at platform one of Story 3 and a cow pokes its nose across the page towards the door of Story 2. By the next opening, 14, all borders between the individual story strands are dissolved and the full double-page illustration is rendered in black and white ink which creates a unifying effect that reinforces the message on the warning stamp that the book may contain only one story. This apparent violation of the various boundaries between the individual worlds destabilises the status of the represented world(s) projected in the text and appears to construct a single reality. This use of framebreaking also blurs the boundaries between narrative levels, with characters or objects from one story appearing in another. However, opening 15, the penultimate illustration, reverts to the previous structure of four tales, each with its own media and borders, once again creating a multiplicity of possible worlds. The title of *Black and White* can be read ironically, as this text, like many postmodern picturebooks, does not deliver an uncomplicated or unified narrative. Furthermore, it draws attention to those aspects of narratives which are incomplete. Any sequential organisation belies the reality of the ways in which the narrative events may occur and, as discussed, such anomalies are foregrounded in a number of the picturebooks discussed in this chapter.

In a similar manner to the ending of *The Stinky Cheese Man and Other Fairly Stupid Tales* (detailed above) resolution is reached in the penultimate opening for each of the four individual stories from *Black and White*. The boy is met by his parents, the family heads for bed, with one parent asking about homework, suggesting a (welcome?) return to normality, the porter gets on with his work and the escapee makes his getaway, while the cows return to their paddock to be milked. However, the final illustration of a child's hand reaching in to pick up the (toy?) railway station violates the already unstable ontology of the narrative and questions the possibility of an achievable conclusion. Collins (2002) ties this illustration to the black and white photograph of a young boy in a model train engine which appears on the book jacket (peritext) where a picture of the author would normally reside. Collins makes the assumption that this is the author as a young boy and, from this, concludes that the episodes within the book all stem from the author as a young boy at play. It *could* be extrapolated from this that the interconnected events of the various narratives were played out in the young boy's imagination as he played with his train set on the living-room floor while waiting for his parents to arrive home from work. Then again, he may have invented aspects of the narrative in order to account for his parents' seemingly bizarre behaviour. In ontological terms, the final illustration suggests that the boy playing with his train represents the primary diegetic narrative to which the character belongs, while the other stories represent a number of hypodiegetic levels. Such strategies foreground the ontological instability of the text rather than its epistemological dimension.

Rather than encourage readers to construct their own personal resolutions, Meek (1988) suggests that readers need to learn to 'tolerate uncertainty'. Serafini (2005), meanwhile, insists that we take it further and 'entertain ambiguity'. Postmodernists would argue that some stories do not make available a possible ending and that perhaps readers need to accept this rather than attempt to achieve one. Bertens (2001) argues that in literary terms a text can never achieve *closure* because there is no final meaning; instead, the text remains a field of possibilities. In accordance with postmodernism's rejection of absolutism, picturebooks such as *Black and White*, influenced by postmodernism, play with this view and draw on Derrida's notion of deferral to provide a number of possible explanations rather than a definitive conclusion. Postmodern illustrators also playfully engage with methods of *visual* representation.

Playing with pictorial representation

When René Magritte in his work *La Trahison des images* (*The Treachery of Images*, 1928–29) produced his famous image – with the words *Ceci n'est pas une pipe* ('This is not a pipe') written below the painting of the pipe – he did so in order to provoke awareness of the representative nature of art. His point being: no matter how accurately an object is depicted in a work of art, the object is merely an image, marks on the paper, rather than an actual object. So, too, many illustrators of postmodern picturebooks draw attention, often through humour and irony, to the conventions of visual representation in order to create awareness of their constructedness. This is immediately evident from the cover of *El llibre dins el llibre dins el llibre* (Muller, 2002, *A Book in a Book in a Book*). The dust jacket creates the appearance of a gift, complete with wrapping paper and a blue ribbon tied in a bow. Part of the wrapping paper has been torn away to reveal the book 'inside'. This concept of making overt the act of representation is perhaps taken to extremes in the book *Zoom* (1995) by Istvan Banyai. *Zoom* contains no conventional written text and in order to construct any narrative readers must rely entirely on the visual text which contains iconographic text that does provide some further guidance. Readers are taken on a journey through a series of connected images each presented in such a way that they might think that the next image is the 'real' one. However, each turn of the page widens the angle of view revealing each image as a development of the previous image which, in turn, is yet another representation creating *mise-en-abyme* (a picture-within-a-picture-within-a-picture). Images include a rooster which in turn is revealed as one image from a picture of a toy farm featured on the back cover of a magazine, being held by a boy on a chair on an ocean liner, which in turn is revealed as a poster on the side of a bus, and so on. Finally, the 'real' image (a tribal chief in the Solomon Islands) is revealed, only to alert readers to the fact that it, too, is merely a representation.

Layers of representation are also utilised in the picturebook *Bad Day at Riverbend* (Van Allsburg, 1995), which tells the tale of a mysterious 'greasy slime' that progressively covers horses, people and the landscape of a typical North American western town. The manifestation of the slime coincides with the appearance of a strange light in the west. The illustrative text is predominantly black pen outlines except for the multi-coloured slime. The final pages, however, unveil a realistic-looking hand holding a crayon which intrudes onto the page from the lower right – a position of the unknown, according to Kress and van Leeuwen (2006). On the following page, a child in a cowgirl/boy hat sits at a desk working on a 99 cent colouring-in book. Each time the child sits down to work on her/his colouring-in s/he opens the book and turns on a desk light. This brings a new degree of understanding to the text and perhaps explains the source of the strange light in the story. Mackey (2008) suggests that the light represents the book being opened and closed: 'Then the light went out', which is also signalled by the black endpapers. While this is a plausible explanation it could also be caused by the child turning off the desk light.

The text consists of a number of different levels of representation. Firstly, there are the black line drawings signifying the town and townsfolk, which, with retrospective knowledge, are seen as outlines typical of a colouring book. Then there is the stick figure drawn in crayon by the child, feared by the sheriff and his posse, and yet every bit as realistic or acceptable as a representative member of the 'people' of Riverbend. The text playfully mocks the townspeople who find the stick figure (whom they designate, a 'skinny devil') scary and yet this stick figure is only a representation, as they, too, are mere representations. Goldstone (2001) suggests that the picturebook makes fun of itself. Perhaps it is more making fun of (or problematising) the notion of representation. Next, there is the illustration of the child and her/his room rendered in a much more realistic manner but, nevertheless, still a depiction. Finally, the photograph on the back cover provides

yet another level of representation. Mackey (2008), by way of explanation, points to the book's dedication 'To Sophia My Little Buckaroo' as
well as the photograph on the back cover (Genette's 'implicit context')
to suggest that this is the author's daughter (or niece, or friend). The
layers of representation pass from lowest modality (the stick figure)
through somewhat higher modality of the black ink figures of the
townsfolk to the quite realistic representation of the child at the desk
to finally the highest modality being the photograph of the young girl
(Sophia?) on the back cover. In grappling with these various levels of
representation any sense of reality is undermined.

The written text subtly alerts readers to the fictional status of the
town of Riverbend in the opening paragraph: 'Riverbend was a quiet
little town – just a couple dozen buildings alongside a dusty road
that led nowhere. Though the stagecoach occasionally rolled through
town, it never stopped because no one ever came to Riverbend and no
one ever left.' It is only after the discovery that Riverbend is a town
in a colouring-in book that the constructed nature of the town (and
the illustrations) and the significance of the opening lines quoted
above become evident. The result is playful despite the voice being
somewhat deadpan. Claudia Nelson (2006) argues that the child
resists adult authority by refusing to colour within the lines. However,
it could be viewed that the act of colouring is itself a self-reflexive
gesture, which draws attention to the work of the illustrator of the
text readers are viewing, particularly as the text interrogates modes of
representation. Postmodernism's approach to visual representation is
eclectic, as it draws on a range of artistic and literary strategies including parody, pastiche, collage, appropriation and quotation, among
others. These strategies can deliberately expose conventional methods
of representation as well as subtly underscore the notion that art lacks
all authority, originality and the mythological status of 'authorship'
(Foucault, 1973; Barthes, 1977; Grieve, 1993). Suzanne O'Sullivan
(2008) points out that collage, for instance, constructs new images
out of the remnants of others which then draw attention to the constructedness of visual texts. Pastiche operates in a similar way and is
often used in parody. A number of Lauren Child's picturebooks draw
attention to the conventions of illustration and make visible the act of
representation through mixing collage and hyperrealism.

Child's illustrative texts largely use watercolours but also collage
comprising magazine cut-outs, pieces of fabric and photographs – the

latter rendering a highly realistic representation. Susan Lehr (2008) argues that Child's illustrative techniques give her texts a scrapbook look. This system of mixing modes of representation is evident in the picturebook *My Uncle is a Hunkle Says Clarice Bean* (Child, 2000b). The story relates the events of a time when Uncle Ted came to babysit Clarice and her siblings. The illustrations are a combination of watercolours and cartoon-style drawings. Readers versed in the concept of illustrations accept these representations as conveying a textual reality despite a lower modality than other types of illustrative techniques. However, on a number of openings alongside these representations, photographs are also employed. For instance, on the third opening the illustrative text shows Uncle Ernie in a hospital bed by a window. While Uncle Ernie, the nurse and the hospital ward are all rendered in watercolours and ink, the view of the city through the window is what appears to be a photograph of an urban nightscape. This illustration accords with Baudrillard's (1983) point that postmodernism has contributed to a different sense of the real, namely the hyperreal, which problematises not only any concept of the real but also the very notion of artifice. The problematisation of representation is extended in this case as Child not only uses photographs, but also collage images constructed from magazine clippings and other materials which render the status of the photographs as uncertain. The juxtapositioning of the photographs (a supposed 'reality') alongside the watercolours (artistic representation) blurs the boundaries between reality and representation by drawing attention to the concept of representation and the modes that render something as 'real'. If readers accept the 'reality' of the representations they then must consider the 'photograph' as hyperreality.

Juxtapositioning between 'reality' and televised fictions further destabilises notions of representation. McHale (1987, p. 128) argues that television and movies threaten to overwhelm our primary, literal reality. He suggests that: 'If culture as a whole hovers between reality and televised fictions what could be more appropriate than for texts of the culture to hover between literal reality and a cinematic or television metaphor?' This hovering is evident on opening five in which Clarice (who is wearing a cowgirl outfit) and her Uncle are pictured in the foreground on the family couch watching westerns on television while eating eggs and beans. This scene is rendered in watercolours and ink while the entire background of this opening is what purports to be a photograph of a typical western desert landscape complete with mesas and buttes. Over to the right is Minal Cricket (Clarice's brother) who is tied to a cactus plant. The written text declares: 'I lassoed my brother. He wasn't too happy either.' There are a number of different fictional realities represented within the text, and the use of collage techniques, which include (re)constructed photographs alongside drawings, raises additional questions about the relations between these represented fictional realities and their exact status. While the primary projected world of the illustration is that of the living room in which Clarice, Uncle Ted and Minal Cricket are watching television, the world of the 'western' they are watching has been incorporated into this primary world, so that boundaries between diegetic levels and hypodiegetic worlds are increasingly blurred, particularly through the influence of mass media. McHale (1987, p. 128) argues that: 'miniature escape fantasies' provided by television and movies destabilise already unstable fictional realities and their representations. Clarice's absorption into the world of the 'western' and her ability to incorporate the mediated reality of the televised desert landscape into her reality (the living room) illustrate his point and highlight a further element of postmodern picturebooks, namely, their playful challenge to realist notions of character.

Disruption to the representations of character

A number of the focus picturebooks such as *Black and White* and *The Stinky Cheese Man and Other Fairly Stupid Tales* question, or create confusion around, the identity of a number of characters. This is in line with Christopher Butler's (2002) argument that recent fiction has seen a shift from the exploration of the psychology of character (as in modernism) to an examination of the inadequacy of the concept of character (postmodernism). Children's literature has traditionally carried a predominantly humanist message about the individual as a unified self with a central core of identity that is unique, rational and established. However, Bertens (2001) argues that postmodern texts do not treat characters as individuals in the same manner as those texts which convey humanist ideas about individuality.

A character is generally constructed in a narrative text not only through narration and description, but through the character's represented actions, speech and thought processes. A postmodern text uses such strategies as ambiguity, repetition and indeterminacy to undermine such stable constructions. For instance, a small boy features in three of the four stories told in *Black and White* (Macaulay, 1990). This repetition raises the possibility that these different characters are one and the same. In 'Seeing Things' the character through whom the events are focalised is a small boy undertaking his first train journey on his own. The second story, 'Problem Parents', features a small boy who is the brother of the first-person narrator, and in the fourth story, 'Udder Chaos', a small boy is one of the singers in the choir through which the escapee, along with the herd of cows, passes. And, as noted previously, the photograph of the author as a young boy on the back cover along with the final illustration that shows a small child at play could, quite plausibly, indicate that they are one and the same character. On the other hand, the differing spatio-temporal frames of the multiple stories could indicate that the boy is not one character but different characters. There is no resolution provided to the question of this identity, which is shown to be plural and uncertain, and leaves readers to consider the postmodern contention that identity is often destabilised and problematic. Bertens further argues that identity is made highly problematic in postmodern fiction in order to problematise the whole concept of a stable self. Postmodernists reject the concept of the individual that has prevailed in Western thought since the time of the Enlightenment. Rather than privilege the self, they see identity as constituted in interaction with what is outside of the self and is thus relational or social, rather than individual. Viewed in this way, identity is not fixed but rather *in process* and will never reach completion. Despite its seemingly restricted format and young audience, the picturebook, with its dual semiotic systems, provides sufficient scope for raising questions about identity and subjectivity.

This notion of the instability of identity also features in *The Stinky Cheese Man and Other Fairly Stupid Tales* (Scieszka and Smith, 1992) in which uncertainty surrounds the 'real' identity of the narrator, Jack. On the Introduction page Jack's address is listed as 'Up the Hill, Fairy Tale Forest', which implies that this is Jack of Jack and Jill fame. Furthermore, on the Dedication page, the visual text shows an impatient Jill, hands on hips, standing by the well at the top of the hill obviously waiting for Jack who is busily addressing the readers. However, the narrator's direct participation in the stories 'Jack's Bean

Problem' and 'Jack's Story' suggests that the narrator could well be the Jack of 'Jack and the Beanstalk'.[2] Jack appears as a shifting signifier, not necessarily anchored to any one text, but as flitting in and out of a number of fairy tales and dancing on the margins of others. Recognition of his double life (so to speak), rather than contribute to any sense of stability to the identity of this Jack, raises questions about the possibility of a stable identity, but in typical postmodern fashion chooses not to provide any resolution on the issue.

Postmodern fiction also questions whether characters are real people or textual constructions. A mimetic view sees characters as real people. For instance, in conventional children's literature writers often use mimetic devices to create characters as 'real' people with whom readers may align themselves. In such instances readers tend not to relate to them as literary creations nor as semiotic constructs, but as possible human beings (Marie-Laure Ryan, 1999). As a result, readers of conventional texts often align with particular characters, especially the focaliser(s), and any readings of the text are influenced by such alignments. A postmodern view, as I have previously noted, actively draws attention to the ontological status of characters. This tension (between character and construct) is evident in *The Stinky Cheese Man and Other Fairly Stupid Tales*. In the tale 'Little Red Running Shorts' the use of the lower case 'w' when the narrator Jack refers to the wolf is of significance. Jack uses 'wolf' as a signifier to denote a particular animal; however, that signifier is also laden with all the intertextual connotations associated with the wolf as predator, especially as depicted throughout the history of children's literature. This usage of a lower case 'w' by the narrator re-signifies the wolf from character to object/construct or embodiment. Little Red Running Shorts, however, addresses him as Wolf ('Let's go, Wolf'), the upper case 'W' indicating that this is the wolf's name, thereby demonstrating that she sees him as a character/person rather than as a construct. Uncertainty surrounds the ontological status of the wolf/Wolf and epitomises the conflict between the various ways in which readers may view characters in picturebooks. The white silhouettes in the visual text, referred to in Chapter 1 (see Figure 1.1), contribute to this opposition by representing both Little Red Running Shorts and Wolf as constructs easily removed from the illustration. This act visually reinforces Waugh's (1984, p. 56) statement that: 'Characters are absent because they are linguistic signs [...] literally signs on a page.'

It also resonates with Magritte's point about visual representation being marks on the page.

A different approach to the issue of identity is taken by another picturebook, *That Pesky Rat* (Child, 2002). Rather than raise concerns as to a character's exact identity or ontological status, this text reveals how a postmodern/poststructuralist view sees identity as constructed through interaction with the discourses of society as well as through their relations with others (intersubjectivity). The opening page reveals a brown rat who defines himself in terms of his physical characteristics, including having a 'pointy nose and beady eyes' as well as being 'brown and smelly'. He adds that he would like to be someone's pet because most of all he would like to have a name. Just as language constructs a subject's identity, the brown rat too would like to construct his new identity through naming. The brown rat is convinced he will achieve completeness by becoming a pet and acquiring a name. In defence of this stance, the brown rat regales readers with a list of his friends who are all pets with names and cosy houses in which to live. Each pet however is subjected to the demands of its owner and is required to perform a particular 'act'. For instance, Pierre the chinchilla has to endure being bathed, a rabbit called Nibbles has to perform in a circus act with his master on a trapeze and high wire, while Andrew, the Scottie dog, is required to wear a Tartan hat and coat on outings. Thus, the notion of the unitary and autonomous subject is both installed and then subverted. Each animal is installed (literally) as a pet then subverted when they are subjected to the will of their owners, who in turn are subjected to various cultural and social discourses, for example of health and hygiene, entertainment and so on.

In his quest to find an owner who would bestow a name upon him, the brown rat goes to the local pet shop and puts a notice in the window: 'Brown rat looking for owner.' Eventually a Mr Fortesque, who has bad eyesight, comes along and says: 'I'll take him [...] I've been looking for a brown cat for ages.' Putting aside the matter of his myopia, the language slippage reinforces the point that identity is never fixed and stable but provisional. There is a pause when Mrs Trill, the pet shop owner, and the brown rat look at Mr Fortesque and 'neither of us say a word'. This momentary suspension of language provides an opportunity for the brown rat to gain a measure of agency by accepting the necessity of becoming a cat in order to fulfil his desire of being a pet and having a name. Foucault (1973), however, might say that the rat repeats the social norms of 'catness' in order to make itself intelligible as the desired pet.

The final illustration shows Mr Fortesque and the brown rat happily settled in their home with Mr Fortesque saying: 'Well, Tiddles, who's a pretty kitty cat?' and the brown rat squeaks 'I am.' Almost in parentheses the brown rat adds: 'So what if I have to wear a little jumper.' Thus, the *I* (brown rat) becomes *I* (Tiddles the pet cat) in its relationship to *you* (Mr Fortesque) with the *I* and the *you* mutually defining each other (after Maurice Merleau-Ponty). It must be remembered that the brown rat has a completely different relationship, and thus identity, with his friends such as Pierre and Nibbles. While the ending appears to be happy, as the rat seems to have achieved his goals of becoming a pet and acquiring a name, this conclusion is provisional. Once the rat becomes used to his identity, in relation to Mr Fortesque as Tiddles the cat, he may eventually become dissatisfied or caught out, thus remaining *in process*. This reinforces the contention that identity is continuously (re)constituted through self-narrations. The narrative offers no indication of this future prospect but its conclusion confirms the illusory nature of a fixed identity – while Mr Fortesque has 'fixed' the rat's identity, the rat is cognisant of his need to play along with the illusion. Thus, the narrative strategy of characterisation evident in conventional texts is replaced by constructions of the self in postmodern texts, including postmodern picturebooks.

Postmodern texts deliberately and playfully draw attention to the conventions of representation and, consequently, undermine the represented discourses within the texts. It is commonly acknowledged that when readers become immersed in a realist text, any awareness of the text as a representation is often 'naturalised' and, as a result, readers may come to accept the particular representation as 'true' or 'real'. As is evident from the foregoing discussion, in picturebooks that are influenced by postmodernism the representative nature of narrative is often foregrounded, making it less likely for readers to be drawn into the 'naturalised' ideologies of the text. Postmodern picturebooks also question the ability of narrative to represent 'reality' with any degree of certainty.

3
Disturbing the Air of Reality

> The challenging of certainty, the asking of ques-
> tions, the revealing of fiction-making where we
> might have once accepted the existence of some
> absolute 'truth' – this is the project of postmodern-
> ism. (Hutcheon, 1988, p. 48)

Traditionally, there has been a perception that within stories from
the canon of children's literature there is some sort of inherent
'truth' waiting for readers to discover (Nodelman, 2008). Certainly,
children's literature tends to be dominated by discourses of liberal
humanism, and with its self-imposed function to socialise the child,
the texts often reinforce their own metanarratives which offer,
among other things, resolution and certainty. In its endeavours
to provide a measure of this resolution and certainty, children's
literature may appear to promote a version of 'real life' in which
seemingly inherent 'truths', such as a stable identity, are assumed
as self-evident facts, and ideals such as unity and consensus are
unquestioned norms. However, postmodern culture, as indicated
in the epigraph above, contests this. All texts, according to Butler
(2002), are constructed from language, and language's relationship to
reality is not a given as all language systems are cultural constructs
and are, therefore, inherently unreliable. This is equally the case with
canonical children's texts. From Derrida's (1976) perspective, language never offers direct contact with reality; it is not a transparent
medium, nor is it a window on the world. On the contrary, language
inserts itself *between* readers and the world. Waugh (1984) cautions

that realist texts artificially construct apparently 'real' and imaginary worlds in terms of particular ideologies while presenting these as 'natural' and 'external', which may position readers to accept these representations as true. Conversely, Eagleton (1986) argues that postmodern theory and practice argue that 'truth' is institutional as we always act and use language in the context of politico-discursive conditions. Postmodernism seeks to unmask the constructed nature of these 'truths', not by denying the 'truths' of reality and fiction, but by contesting them.

This chapter continues the previous chapter's discussion of metafiction and notions of representation, but focuses on the multiple ways in which a selection of postmodern picturebooks interrogates the discourses of reality by challenging statements of certainty, revealing fiction-making processes and refusing to accept any proposal of absolute 'truth'. In the process, rather than offering resolution and certainty, these texts create indeterminacy and ambiguity.

Crossing ontological worlds

The picturebook has a long tradition of representing the primary world of the child, her/his family and everyday environment. However, recently picturebooks have emerged which playfully engage with broader issues such as the slippage of boundaries between real and fictional worlds. This slippage involves notions of ontology, which McHale (1987, p. 27) describes as 'a theoretical description of *a* universe', 'its mode of being'. In questioning the conventional belief that narratives reflect or mirror the 'real' world, postmodern picturebooks draw attention to the fictional process of storytelling, the fictional world as construct and the text as artefact. These aspects of narrative are foregrounded by way of the construction of worlds and sub-worlds, through violations of the ontological boundaries between worlds, and by the use of intertextual references to further destabilise these worlds. McHale (1987) points out that the space of a fictional world is a construct just as the characters and objects which occupy that space are constructs. He proposes that in order to determine the ontology of a particular world a text may pose specific questions such as: How are particular worlds constituted? How do they differ, one from another?, and, What happens when different kinds of worlds are placed in confrontation or when boundaries are violated?

When John Gardner (1978) argues that fiction should not break the illusion or disturb the air of reality it has constructed, he appears to be reinforcing the conviction that particular 'truths' are contained within that represented reality. However, as Hutcheon (1988, p. 180) reminds us, realism is merely one 'particular way of ordering and understanding the world around us' and not the bearer of legitimate 'truths'. One way in which postmodernism disrupts the air of reality of conventional fiction is by foregrounding the ontological structure of texts and fictional worlds. The focus texts examined in this first section are *Wolves* (2006) by Emily Gravett and *Wait! No Paint!* (2001) by Bruce Whatley. *Wolves* constructs two separate ontological worlds: the first is a world of rabbits and the second a world of grey wolves. Through metafictive strategies such as metalepsis, intertextuality and disruption to the typographical elements of the text, a rabbit is absorbed into the ontology of the library book he is reading and placed at the mercy of a grey wolf. On the other hand, *Wait! No Paint!* initially constructs the ontological world of the folk tale, 'The Three Little Pigs'. Largely through metaleptic transgressions, the implied illustrator of the book violates the boundaries of this world by enacting changes to the original storyline. This results in the pigs and the wolf finding themselves in a world that looks remarkably like another folk tale, 'Goldilocks and the Three Bears'.

Wolves uses the metafictive device of *mise-en-abyme* (a book-within-a-book structure) to tell the story of a white rabbit who is so engrossed in his library book, similarly entitled 'Wolves' (by Emily Grrrabbit), that he fails to notice that he has entered the ontological space of this book, the world of the grey wolves about which he is reading. The rabbit inadvertently walks up the tail and along the back of one of the wolves then reappears on its nose just as the written text states an indisputable truth: 'Wolves mainly eat meat [...] They also enjoy smaller mammals, like beavers, voles and ...'. Upon turning the page readers are confronted by a badly ripped, red library book beside which is a scrap of paper bearing the word 'rabbits'. Even the most inexperienced readers might conclude that the wolf has eaten this somewhat dim-witted rabbit. The replication of the endpapers of the external book *Wolves* not only sets up a *mise-en-abyme* of the text but also signals that these narrative borders may be breached through metaleptic transgressions. The primary narrative is that of the rabbit's world, whereas the secondary narrative appears to be a non-fiction book that outlines the world of grey wolves. The contrasting dual ontologies of the rabbit's narrative world and the (embedded) world of the grey wolves would normally remain separated by the different, seemingly impenetrable boundaries constructed by the text. However, boundaries are violated and disruptions do occur. The narrative centred on the rabbit locates one version of the story at the level of the story's primary, or diegetic, world: a world in which a rabbit borrows books from a library while the secondary (hypodiegetic) narrative focuses on the world of grey wolves. These two different levels project 'possible worlds' (McHale, 1987) whereby readers 'abandon' *their* real world and adopt (temporarily) the ontological perspectives of the literary work. The rabbit enacts this very process as the story progresses and perhaps his fate is a warning to real readers that allowing themselves to be wholly drawn into a text leaves them vulnerable to the ideology of that text.

In constructing the primary world the text draws upon a discourse of 'libraries and books' represented largely pictorially by the borrowing card and due date slip, illustrations of a large 'Shhh' sign, as well as a well-stocked bookcase. The text relies on readers' intertextual knowledge of libraries to draw inferences and fill in the gaps to construct the world of 'library' from these minimal visual references. The playful language of the primary narrative supports the ontology of this world with its 'burrowing library' and 'rip-roaring tails' and so on. Mackey (2008, p. 108) comments that it is a discourse that relies on 'the nostalgia of the old-fashioned library' and certainly the illustrative text features a library in which patrons are expected to maintain a respectful silence (indicated by the large 'Shhh' sign) and borrowing procedures appear to remain somewhat antiquated by today's online library systems. However, rather than being appreciated as nostalgia, the book has a playful and parodic appeal, particularly to the implied adult readers of the text (remembering the dual audience of picturebooks referred to in the Introduction). The secondary narrative constructs a world of grey wolves in which the register is that of a documentary, recording such details as where they live ('Anywhere from the Arctic Circle to ... the outskirts of towns and villages') and their physical attributes ('sharp claws ... bushy tails'). However, the humorous visual text undercuts the register of the written text. For instance, the reference to the Arctic Circle is accompanied by an illustration of two snarling wolves beside a snowman that has antlers rather than ears, in keeping with the specifics of its location.

In discussing the violations and disruptions that occur in this text, Mackey (2008) proceeds on the premise that it is the wolves that break out of their own world to invade the rabbit's ontological space, while Pantaleo (2010) suggests that the different diegetic levels converge. Certainly, on one occasion a wolf peers round the edges of its own text and enters the ontological space of the rabbit's world. However, this is a momentary violation made possible by its disguise as an old woman. The major breach of ontological boundaries is perpetrated by the rabbit. As the rabbit reads the library book entitled 'Wolves' the frames of that book increase in size until the rabbit is absorbed into its ontological space. This gradual transgression of the secondary narrative by the rabbit is advanced through the playfulness of the illustrative text. As the story of the rabbit progresses, the pictorial text juxtaposes an illustration of the rabbit reading his book (the primary narrative) with a double-page spread of the page from 'Wolves' (the secondary narrative). As the rabbit becomes immersed in the book on wolves, the frames of that book expand until they have taken up most of the double opening of the primary text, *Wolves*, and the rabbit is absorbed into its ontological space. This is signalled by the disappearance of the red frame of the secondary text which allows the rabbit to (however, unconsciously) breach the boundary (represented by the red frame) between the wolves' world and that of the primary world of the text: the 'real' textual world (such as it is) of the rabbit. There follows four openings without frames and with considerable white space in which the rabbit, its head resolutely buried in the book, walks past the wolf's paws, up its tail and along the ridge of its back to arrive on the end of its snout. The fifth opening of this sequence shows the moment of realisation of the danger in which he has placed himself, signalled by both the rabbit's startled expression and the reappearance of part of the red frame. The latter (the reappearance of the red frame) acknowledges that the action is taking place within the hypodiegetic world of the library book about wolves rather than that of the primary world of the rabbit.

Because the rabbit has entered the world of the wolves, the ontological status of the wolf in relation to the rabbit changes from construct to 'real' and thus enables it, at that level, to pose a real threat to the rabbit. Pantaleo (2010, pp. 19–20) sees these metaleptic transgressions as a:

> result of the different narrative levels constructed by the visual and verbal text. Although the words and images occupy the same space on a page, readers move from one ontological level to another as they go back and forth between the image and text worlds of the picturebook.

This violation of the ontological barriers between the primary and secondary narrative worlds draws attention to the fact that these worlds are constructions which, in turn, foreground narratives, not as reflections of reality, but as constructions. As indicated earlier, Hutcheon (1988) explains that realism is a particular way of ordering and understanding the world around us. If the 'order' of the fictional world can be destabilised through, for instance, the violation of boundaries such as has occurred in *Wolves*, then the 'truth' of such worlds becomes provisional.

In addition to raising questions concerning the status of the fictional world(s) and their characters, *Wolves* also stages what McHale (1987, p. 70) describes as a *postmodernist ontological confrontation* between the text as formal object and the world it projects. In other words, as the text establishes a particular ontological world in the narrative it also playfully draws attention to the text as an artefact, which disrupts the reading process as well as the text's 'air of reality'. The text as an object is highlighted in a number of different ways. Reference has already been made to the replication of the endpapers and the provision of a lift-out library card and a due date slip. Added to this is the accumulation of letters on the doormat on the back endpapers of 'Wolves', particularly the overdue notice from the library complete with its own envelope from which it can be removed and read. Appropriation of the jacket of *Wolves* provides endorsements from a number of newspapers including *The Hareold* which claims that *Wolves* is 'a rip-roaring tail'. Also, the name of the author of 'Wolves', Emily Grrrabbit, plays on both the name of the real-world author of *Wolves*, Emily Gravett, and the subject matter of the text, a rabbit. These word-plays and other visual playfulness disrupt any seriousness of the narrative and draw attention to the text's status as fiction. The fictional nature of the text is further enhanced by the use of direct address. The first instance is a visual 'demand' image as the rabbit realises he is about to be eaten. It looks out at the audience in a typically 'startled rabbit' appeal thereby implicating readers in its fate. The second occurs when the author openly addresses readers (see below) about the alternative ending. By foregrounding its status as material object in these ways, the fictional worlds represented in the text are momentarily eclipsed by the real-world object (McHale, 1987). The former, that being read by external readers, is a real-world object, while the latter is a signifier for which there is no (real-world) signified.

Postmodern texts, such as *Wolves*, lay bare their (self)-referentiality through the self-conscious use of intertextual references, which carry traces of other ontological worlds into the primary text. In *Wolves*, a playful intertext occurs with a pictorial allusion to the wolf in Little Red Riding Hood when it is disguised as the girl's grandmother. This reference relies on readers' prior encounters with fairy-tale wolves as sinister figures and serves in this text as a sign of danger for the rabbit. The sequence in which the pages of the library book expand until the red border disappears also alludes to a 'rumpus' such as occurs in the picturebook *Where the Wild Things Are* (Sendak, 1963) in which Max and the Wild Things embark on a rumpus free from adult constraint. The 'rumpus' represented in *Wolves* is that of the rabbit in its gradual, if unintentional, invasion of the ontological space of the wolves' world. Another intertextual layer is created by the extensive use of iconography on the library card, the letters on the mat, as well as the advertising flyers (Hall, 2008; Mackey, 2008). These simulated real-world artefacts contribute further layers of complexity to the ontology of the text.

As suggested in Chapter 2, endings occupy one of the most salient positions in the structure of a conventional text. According to McHale (1987, p. 109), readers expect either clarity (closed ending) or opacity (open ending), but *Wolves* creates a sense of 'non-ending' (McHale) by providing an alternative ending. At this point the implied author adds another layer to the already complex ontology of the text by intruding into the ontological space of the text with the following disclaimer:

> The author would like to point out that no rabbits were eaten during the making of this book. It is a work of fiction. And so, for more sensitive readers, here is an alternative ending.

This alternative ending claims that the wolf was actually a vegetarian so the rabbit and wolf became best friends and shared a jam sandwich, thus projecting yet another 'possible world', but one that could only exist in fantasy. Consequently, this world does not hold up to any scrutiny as grey wolves are not vegetarian and would be unlikely to eat a jam sandwich as an alternative to a rabbit. The illustration accompanying the alternative ending is a collage of torn pieces taken from the original narrative (presumably torn in the fracas when the wolf devoured the rabbit) and hastily glued together. The level of modality of the illustration is at the lower end of the scale, which diminishes its credibility. The change in representational style of the alternative ending clearly signals this ending is playful and parodies the conventional belief of some adults that children's literature requires a happy ending.

There is a final ironic note played in *Wolves*. In the final pages new 'evidence' is brought to readers' attention in the form of accumulated, uncollected or unanswered letters addressed to the rabbit, most notably a library overdue notice for the library book 'Wolves'. Readers are required to examine the alternative ending in light of the implicit conclusion and the evidence of the endpapers, determine the degree of its 'validity' and proceed to draw their own conclusions. Regardless of conclusions drawn, the non-ending destabilises the ontology of the projected worlds which creates uncertainty about the rabbit's fate, along with possible amusement for the readers, despite Hall's (2008) view that it is a bleak tale. The real irony here is that no rabbits *were* killed in the writing of this story because the text is not telling a true story about real animals, but is a literary construction. Despite the violation of ontological boundaries, the playfulness of the text, the intertextual references and the ironic (non)-ending combine to construct a text which, while playful and entertaining, raises serious questions concerning the ability of fiction to represent reality with any degree of authenticity. In the next text, *Wait! No Paint!*, the ontological disruptions that occur are caused by the 'Illustrator'.

The unconcealed presence of the implied author or the intrusive narrator is a common feature of stories for children, even in realist fiction where attempts are traditionally made to eradicate intrusiveness and enhance objectivity. Postmodern picturebooks take this further by deliberately drawing attention to the presence of the narrator. In the picturebook *Wait! No Paint!* (Whatley, 2001) there is an intrusive illustrator whose actions lead to the layers within the text being made explicit. While *Wait! No Paint!*, a parody of *The Three Little Pigs*, does not employ a fairy-tale register, it does begin in a similar manner to the pretext with the pigs building their homes of straw, sticks and bricks. By the fourth opening, however, a disruption to the narrative occurs when, just as the wolf approaches, the first pig hears a splash followed by 'a Voice' which says 'I spilt my juice.' The visual text shows a glass in the foreground tipping over and spilling an orange liquid over the first little pig's house causing it to collapse. While the identity of the Voice is not immediately revealed, this interruption to the narrative also signals the first metaleptic violation of the ontological boundary between the world of the narrative and the 'real' world of the implied illustrator. Following this incident, the first pig runs ahead of the wolf to the second pig's house. The pigs slam the door on the wolf, bending its nose. Again the intrusive Voice comments: 'Wait. I've got to redo the nose.' As a brush, pencil and eraser appear from *off-stage* and begin work on the wolf's nose, the two little pigs race to the safety of the house of bricks.

It is the third little pig who works out to whom the Voice belongs: 'It's the ILLUSTRATOR,' he explains. At this point the (implied) Illustrator joins the conversation to admit that 'he' is, indeed, the illustrator painting the story in which they are located. This self-reflexivity adds another ontological layer to the text, inserting this implied Illustrator between the characters of the story and the real author/illustrator. He further informs them that he has run out of red paint, which is why they are all white rather than the usual pink. The announcement has a (melo)dramatic effect on one of the pigs: 'The first pig felt so faint he had to sit down.' McHale (1987) describes the narrative strategy whereby the author penetrates the fictional world, introduces him/herself to the characters, and explains their roles to them as *short-circuit* which, while logically impossible, *appears* to happen regularly in postmodernist fiction. Intruding into the picture plane of the next illustration is a thoroughly squeezed, but nevertheless empty, red paint tube and a paint brush, the relative size of which suggests they are external to the interior narrative space.

The intrusion of the Illustrator into the narrative creates a degree of ambiguity surrounding the ontological levels within the narrative.

McHale (1987) notes that by visibly representing himself (sic) in the narrative, an author (in this case, illustrator) represents himself as a fictional construct just as the other characters are also constructs. Thus the ontological status of the Illustrator is also fictional, a character within the text as demonstrated by the use of the capital 'I' for Illustrator, which indicates his name rather than his function. This Illustrator operates at a higher ontological level than the pigs and wolf as he appears able to control aspects of the narrative such as the colour of the pigs as well as repair the wolf's nose. However, he does not seem able to alter major aspects of the narrative. Instead he uses his insider knowledge to warn the pigs that the wolf is coming: 'But be careful [...] The wolf's coming.' Thus, the Illustrator uses his position of omniscience to play the role of conspirator. The *real* artist, according to McHale (1987), always occupies an ontological level superior to that of his projected, fictional self and is therefore doubly superior to the fictional world. Thus, Bruce Whatley, the author/illustrator of the actual text, operates on the level of reality; the Illustrator operates at a metadiegetic level, while the pigs and wolf operate at the primary, or diegetic, level of the narrative. The illustrative text, as McCallum (2008) notes in another context, reinforces these ontological levels by representing the primary world of the narrative through low modality and cartoon-style illustrations of the pigs and the wolf, while the art paraphernalia representing the Illustrator is rendered in a much higher, quite realistic, modality.

Another aspect of the ontological debate being enacted in this narrative is the extent to which characters are aware of their fictional status. Unlike the townsfolk in *Bad Day at Riverbend* (discussed in Chapter 2), who are totally unaware of their status as fictional folk, the three pigs and gradually the wolf become aware of their fictionality through their conversations with the Illustrator. They call upon him to take action ('Do something quick!'), dispute his colour choices ('You made us *green*?') and eventually emphatically demand to be removed from the story ('WE DON'T WANT TO BE IN THIS STORY ANYMORE!'). Only characters aware of their own fictionality could participate in these discussions. This hierarchy of ontological levels also draws attention to the status of the text as artefact: the processes of fiction are exposed and the devices of art are (literally) laid bare. The pigs and the wolf seem prepared to work with the Illustrator to get the narrative finished until conditions become untenable: the Illustrator has placed them into the story of 'The Three Bears' creating yet another ontological shift within the text. Neither the pigs nor the wolf look happy with this solution. The final illustration shows the pigs taking action against the illustrator by forming a picket line and waving banners demanding a new painter. This metaleptic action on the part of the characters of the text playfully foregrounds yet another ontological boundary: one between readers and characters. The illusory reality of the fictional world is disrupted and what becomes real is the author/illustrator's role in creating that world.

Chinese-box structures

A popular strategy employed by postmodern picturebooks for raising awareness of the ontological status of various worlds, both fictional and 'real', is having a character enter, by various means, the projected world of a book. This strategy contrasts the 'real' world of the protagonist with that of the fictional world(s) within the book. It also self-consciously exposes the writing process as well as the fictional text as artefact. McCallum (2008, p. 181) suggests such strategies 'problematize the relationships between fiction and reality, and the world of stories and that of readers'. This situation is played out in *Who's Afraid of the Big Bad Book?* (Child, 2003) when a young boy, Herb, goes to sleep and falls into a book of fairy tales. Through the utilisation of a Chinese-box structure, typographical experimentation and self-conscious intertextuality violation of the ontological boundaries between worlds is made possible. The picturebook is modelled on what McHale terms a Chinese-box or layering structure of narrative, which consists of several stories-within-a-story, thereby instantly creating a number of different fictional levels or 'possible worlds' within the text. This slippage between narrative worlds is anticipated on the front cover on which Herb is depicted reading an almost identical book to the book being read by external readers and so acts as a *mise-en-abyme* for the text itself. Such self-consciousness is designed from the very beginning to draw readers' attention to both the text's own awareness of its constructedness and the narrative processes through which 'possible worlds' are created.

Within the Chinese-box structure the central ontological world is located at the primary diegetic level, in this case the world of Herb's bedroom. When Herb wakes with a start he is surprised to discover that he is in Goldilocks' story;[1] this forms the first hypodiegetic level Herb encounters. Goldilocks is quick to show her displeasure at the intrusion: 'WHAT ARE YOU DOING HERE? HOW DARE YOU BE ON THIS PAGE? I AM THE STAR AND I SAY YOU ARE NOT ALLOWED IN THIS STORY!' The register is that of an attention-seeker[2] of the late twentieth century rather than that of a mid-nineteenth-century child. This anachronism, along with the feisty Goldilocks and three particularly polite bears, destabilises the ontology of the book's projected world into which Herb has 'fallen'. He quickly makes good his escape. While running on a path through the woods Herb enters what could be called a 'zone' (McHale) in which a number of possible worlds share a common space. These possible worlds are presented through intertextual references to various fairy tales in progress, including Hansel and Gretel, Rapunzel and Puss-in-Boots. This zone constitutes a second hypodiegetic level. When Herb calls out to Hansel and Gretel at the Witch's cottage to 'Be careful' they tell him to 'Get lost', which is rather ironic given that they are the ones who are literally lost. These self-conscious intertextual references to other ontologies further undermine the ontological stability of the main narrative.

A third hypodiegetic level is created when Herb eventually arrives at an enormous door through which he enters an opulent ballroom where he stumbles upon the Cinderella story. The doors (pages) fold out to form a four-page spread showing the ballroom. The arrangement of the characters is fairly linear, which has the effect of making the characters appear static. This creates a freeze-frame effect: the Prince is missing and the Cinderella narrative cannot continue without him. It is possible, because of the physical construction of the book itself, to stand it up and fold out the four-page spread to form a diorama, which further emphasises the doubly constructed nature of the text as both narrative and artefact. It is a spectacle to be observed rather than a 'real' world with which to engage. Further slippage between the 'real' world of Herb's bedroom and the imaginary world of the ballroom of the Cinderella story is achieved through the anachronistic appearance of a telephone and Herb's pencil case on the palace floor. These elements of the primary world have violated the ontological boundaries between the primary and hypodiegetic levels. This ontological uncertainty is reinforced by a number of dramatis personae (or additional characters) who wander into the text from history, other fictions and/or popular culture. These 'transmigratory figures' (McHale, 1987, after Eco) from other ontological worlds are not mentioned in the written text but are evident in the visual text. They include Agnetha and Benny from the band ABBA, a John Lennonesque figure in a Sergeant Pepper's-style costume as well as a recurrent character (*personnage de retour*), the Little Wolf, from another Lauren Child picturebook, *Beware of the Storybook Wolves*, who bides his time, waiting to dance with the Prince. These intruders come from a range of ontological realities, and bring traces of those ontologies with them which disturb the established ontology of this particular hypodiegetic level, the Cinderella story, as well as highlight the constructedness of such fictional worlds.

Of all the intruders in the ballroom, Herb is of the most interest to the discussion. He is represented through the visual text as small and on the margins of the story. Readers most often view him from a high vantage point – making Herb look small and insignificant. When Herb enters the ballroom from the Cinderella story, the text sets up an opposition between the cardboard 'cut-out' characters at the ball and Herb as the only 'real' person present. That the characters in the Cinderella story are constructs is underlined by the fact that Herb has been able to draw glasses and moustaches on a number of them. He has also cut out Prince Charming and completely removed him from the ball. This action has considerably upset the progression of the Cinderella story and the King and Queen are furious but powerless to restore their son to the narrative. The Prince, in particular, lacks agency as he has no ability to object to being cut and pasted according to Herb's uses for him. Herb, unlike the other characters, exercises a degree of agency as he is able to alter the appearance of various characters and, when he is pursued, cuts a hole in the floor of the ballroom and makes good his escape. Herb's ontological status as a 'real' person is highlighted by the fact that he is the only character present in the Cinderella story to cast a shadow, which seems to indicate a presence that is 'real' as opposed to the other characters who are, consequently, make believe. The irony is that Herb too is a construct, merely a sign on the page.

Herb's sojourn in the fairy-tale world represents a carnivalesque disruption at play. Typical of the carnivalesque, order is restored not only by Herb's return to the relative safety of his bedroom but also by the actions of Herb, and his friend Ezzie, who re-establish order to the narrative by erasing drawn moustaches, telephones and so on, and place the upside-down page right way up. The Prince, previously cut out and relocated on a card for Herb's mother in an entirely different role, is finally resurrected and pasted back into the original story (although the text mentions in an aside that he will never quite dance the same again). However, Herb and Ezzie cannot resist a moment of transgression when Herb draws a lock on the Three Bears' cottage and Ezzie draws a brown wig on Goldilocks. Readers are left with the image of Goldilocks, now with brown hair which alters her appearance and sense of self, trying desperately to get access to the Bears' cottage but is prevented by the lock Herb has attached to the door.

Another text to feature Herb is *Beware of the Storybook Wolves*, as noted above. This text relies on a reversal of the character-falls-into-a-book strategy of *Who's Afraid of the Big Bad Book?* Rather than Herb falling into the world of fairy tales as occurred in the previous text, in this story some of the characters from a collection of fairy tales Herb's mother reads to him each night enter Herb's bedroom as he lies in bed. He first becomes aware of this transgression when he hears a rumbling sound accompanied by a 'not-very-nice' smell. As he switches on his bedside light two wolves (the second wolf seems to act as apprentice) from the 'Little Red Riding Hood' story appear in his room. This act of switching on the light signals a break in the narrative frame and enables the wolves to enter from the storybook world (hypodiegetic level) to the world of Herb's bedroom, the 'real' world (primary diegetic level). The wolves are determined to eat Herb and he is forced to rely on subterfuge ('I wouldn't eat me yet [...] little boys are for pudding') to keep them at bay. This action takes place in Herb's bedroom over several openings. However, on the sixth opening the verso page is split into two parts with the far, one-third of the page devoted to Herb and his current dilemma with the wolves. The other two-thirds of the page shows a page from Herb's book of fairy tales in which the princess had fallen asleep at her own birthday party. This juxtapostioning of the 'real' story and the fairy story makes obvious their differing ontological realities. The right-hand page of this opening is completely taken up with an illustration from the fairy tale which shows a table full of birthday party treats, including jelly. The next double opening shows Herb's hands intruding into the fairy-tale world in order to borrow the jelly with which to fob off the hungry wolves. This violation of the borders of the fairy tale indicates that boundaries between the worlds are not fixed but provisional.

The wicked fairy also disregards the borders between the fictional and 'real' worlds of this text. Herb's plan to distract the wolves is thrown into disarray by the wicked fairy who has left the book to inform the wolves that Herb has tricked them, and everybody knows: 'little boys are starters, jelly is pudding'. In desperation, Herb takes hold of the book and shakes it until the Fairy Godmother, accompanied by a sparkle of sequins, tumbles out onto the floor. Herb displays a double opening of the book that shows Cinderella at the sink (this is almost an exact replica of an illustration two openings further into the book readers are viewing) while the other side is pink wash but otherwise empty – indicating the space where the Fairy Godmother was until Herb shook her from the book. The Fairy Godmother accidentally waves her wand and supplies Little Wolf with the dress intended for Cinderella to wear to the ball. Little Wolf is so pleased with his appearance that: 'he jumped into the fairy-tale book and went to the ball himself' and danced with the Prince. This provides a wonderfully 'queer' moment in which the conventional discourses of gender are challenged. More pertinent to the current discussion, however, is this ability of the characters, both 'real' and fairy tale, to move between the 'real' world of Herb's bedroom and the pages of the storybook (as well as the pages of another book altogether, as described above). It creates uncertainty about the ontological status of both worlds and their characters and raises questions about the ways in which fiction and reality are constructed, represented and understood.

By violating the boundaries between fictional worlds through a variety of metafictive strategies, the postmodern picturebooks examined in this chapter destabilise the ontological veracity of these fictional worlds which, in turn, undermines the integrity of their represented realities. This uncertainty draws attention to the constructed status of fictional worlds and reminds readers of Hutcheon's contention that rather than containing essential truths, fiction is merely one way of ordering and understanding the world around us.

If uncertainty has been brought to bear on the ontological status of the fictional and 'real' worlds of these and other texts, what then is the status of historical events 'recorded' through conventions similar to those of narrative? The problematisation of historical knowledge is the subject matter of a genre of postmodern literature Hutcheon (1988) has labelled *historiographic metafiction*, which is examined in the next chapter.

4
Interrogating Representations of the Past

> Because we cannot directly encounter the past [...] we employ a narrative fulfilling a two-fold function, as both a surrogate for the past and as a medium of exchange in our active engagement with it. History is thus a class of literature. (Munslow, 1997, p. 6)

According to Hutcheon (1988, p. 9), postmodernism attempts to transgress 'previously accepted limits: those of particular arts, of genres, of art itself' by consistently blurring the distinctions between conventional hierarchies such as those of 'high' and 'low' culture. This results in a fluidity between borders of, for instance, literary genres. Hoberek (2007) suggests that this genre shifting of postmodern fiction is quite self-conscious. One particular genre which has emerged as a result of this self-conscious blurring of boundaries is historiographic metafiction. In its examinations of history, postmodernism has created a paradox in which interest in historical context has been reactivated while simultaneously problematising the entire notion of historical knowledge. Hayden White (1976) has been a key voice in working to expose the 'conceptual apparatus' which previously gave sense and order to the principles of historiography. White (1978, p. 69) argues that 'every representation of the past has specifiable ideological implications'. This point aligns with the view expressed by Michel de Certeau (1975) that no research of the past is free of socio-economic, political and cultural conditions. Following these views on the difficulties of achieving a mediated-free knowledge of the past, Hutcheon (1988) points to a shift from 'validation to signification'. Rather than attempting to validate historical representations, a postmodern approach recognises that historical narratives function as signifying systems, thus any meanings drawn from such systems will always be constructed and imposed. This provides a pluralist view of historiography which allows for differing constructions of past realities – what Jenkins (1991, p. 78) refers to as a 'multiplicity of histories'. These constructions are based on the documents remaining from that past such as archival evidence, witnesses' statements and other primary sources which are already 'textualised' and therefore mediated.

Historiographic metafiction questions the view that history has a claim to the truth. According to Hutcheon (1988), it does this by interrogating that claim to truth in historiography: insisting that both history and fiction are discourses and therefore human constructs or signifying systems. Munslow (1997, p. 6) takes this further, as indicated in the epigraph to this chapter, by labelling history as a class of literature. It is through historiographic metafiction that history is shown to be a signifying system constructed from the textual remains of the past. This textualisation of the past makes problematic any claims to 'the truth' of, or about, historical events and personages. As discussed briefly in the Introduction, historiographic metafiction is a form of postmodern fiction which, according to Nicol (2009), uses metafictional techniques to draw attention to the fact that history does not naturally equate with 'the past' but is constructed, based on the texts of that past. McCallum (1999, p. 69) points out that history is often presented as a progressive or developmental narrative which utilises 'linear, chronological, causal and teleological relationships between events and people' in its representation of the historical past. Historiographic metafiction works to unmask these seemingly 'natural' features of history by disrupting such frames. This disruption is achieved through the use of many of the metafictive strategies discussed above but aimed specifically at problematising the representations of historiography. This problematisation may be either implicit or explicit.

The postmodern interrogation of conventional representations of history, namely historiographic metafiction, is achieved, according to Hutcheon (1988), through the utilisation of a range of textual strategies that include: mixing historical and fictive elements; disruptions to the 'objective', third-person narration of historiography;

transgressions of conventions of historiography; challenges to the conventions of narrative; destabilisation of notions of continuity; questioning the status of historiography's 'facts'; and the exploitation of intertextuality and anachronism. These metafictive strategies reveal the interpretative nature of historical writing, allow critical distance which prevents nostalgia, create uncertainty concerning the evidence provided by historiography, and draw attention to history as a form of textuality, and thus implicated in ideology. While these strategies and their effects on reading positions may seem sophisticated they are, nevertheless, utilised across a selection of postmodern picturebooks which endeavour to raise questions about the status of historical knowledge and how this knowledge is conveyed through narrative structures.

A common strategy of historiographic metafiction is parody which, through critical distance, questions the authority of any act of writing and therefore, according to Hutcheon (1988, p. 145), foregrounds its 'paradoxical use and abuse of the conventions of novelistic and historiographic reference'. Intertextuality, on the other hand, functions to both close the gap between the past and present and rewrite that past in a new context (McCallum, 1999). Other strategies include mixing the historical and the fictive in order to destabilise the historic referent; disruption to the so-called objective third-person narration with alternative or multiple points of view which reveal the interpretative and selective nature of historiography; and the interrogation of extraliterary discourses of historiography such as diary entries, interviews, public records, artefacts and so on, by questioning the authenticity and/or authority of such texts. These strategies of historiographic metafiction self-consciously remind readers that, while events did occur in the real empirical past, these events are named and constituted as historical facts through processes of selection and narrative positioning (Hutcheon, 1988), and thus need to be subjected to scrutiny, or at least be regarded as provisional.

The notion of a particular form of postmodernism in literature for children, raised in the Introduction, is particularly pertinent to the interrogation of the discourse of history within postmodern picturebooks. The format and length of the picturebook (normally 32 pages) do not generally allow for interrogation of extraliterary genres and discourses such as artefacts, interviews, public records, diary entries and so on to the same extent that Young Adult (YA) historiographic postmodern novels such as *Strange Objects* (Crew, 1991) are able to do. Additionally, the primary audience of picturebooks is generally young children[1] who are still developing a sense of the world around them, including a sense of the history of this world. Therefore, the following picturebooks are arguably modified historiographic metafiction designed to accommodate both the format and implied audience of the picturebook. On the other hand, while the implied audience may be children, the texts convey a sophistication that will possibly appeal to a wide range of readers. This critique takes a number of different forms. Many of the texts tell of an historical event from a different perspective from the 'authorised' version (*The Rabbits*, Marsden and Tan, 1998; and *A Coyote Columbus Story*, King and Monkman, 1992), some of the 'documentary' evidence on which a historical report relies may be shown to be suspect (*Memorial*, Crew and Tan, 1999), while another text overtly draws parallels between historical discourse and that of the fantastic (*The Tin-Pot Foreign General and the Old Iron Woman*, Briggs, 1984; and *The Discovery of Dragons*, Base, 1996). In addition, I examine another picturebook, *The True Story of the 3 Little Pigs* (Scieszka and Smith, 1989), which interrogates an 'historical' event from the annals of children's literature which I have chosen to call *fictional* historiographic metafiction. These strategies demonstrate that historical events are mediated through language and other textual processes which work to position readers to receive the historical account in particular ways.

Uncertain memories

As its title indicates, *Memorial* by Gary Crew and illustrated by Shaun Tan is a story about a specific memorial of war (a tree) but it is also about people's memories (and stories) of various wars. It works as historiographic metafiction largely on an implicit level. The written text contains two main narrative strands. The first strand is a series of fragmented memories offered by three generations of a family to a young boy of the family. The second strand consists of the boy's comments on the remembered histories. The memories of the boy's parents, grandparents and great-grandparents centre on a Moreton Bay fig tree[2] planted as a living memorial to the soldiers from the town who died in World War I. The tree is also used as a focal point in the town's celebrations at the end of World War II and the Vietnam War. McCallum (1999, p. 167) suggests: 'concepts of personal identity are formed, in part, through an awareness and understanding of the past and of a sense of relation in the present to personal and social histories'. *Memorial*'s anecdotal 'record' of history, archived through family stories, is designed to give a sense of the past in relation to the present through a storytelling format (older generations recalling their memories of significant events in their lives) that would be familiar to many readers.

The written text relies on 'I' statements of the witnesses providing a supposedly accurate account of the events. However, a number of conflicting memories highlight the instability and unreliability of memory. For instance, when Old Pa says 'your grandma' the boy corrects him with 'My great-grandma'; and later Pa says: 'The council's been saying that since they put the traffic lights in,' but Old Pa claims it was: 'Since they spread the bitumen.' These differing perspectives destabilise the truth claims of these stories. The boy's editorial asides such as: 'He [Old Pa] remembers the tiny details but forgets [...] the big picture' and 'I'm remembering that old people forget' also place the truth of these claims under review. The uncertainty this creates is reinforced by the visual text which is a pastiche of photographs and 'historical' artefacts such as medals, tiles, rusted ironwork and hessian. While such artefacts implicitly evoke the 'archaeological' processes of historical records of the past (McCallum, 1999), and perhaps represent attempts to authenticate it, other pictorial elements undermine these attempts. For instance, while photographs are usually regarded as having high modality or 'truthfulness', the photographs on display in this text are faded photographs that reflect the faded memory of some of the storytellers, and thus endow them, in the minds of readers perhaps, with a similar level of uncertainty. The photographs are in black and white so lack the colour of 'real' life. The past of the photographs will always be rendered, pictorially, in black and white and thus can only ever be known as such. The past will always present an incomplete picture of history and must therefore be seen as provisional.

Absences within the narratives of history are also implicitly evoked. For instance, when the boy asks his father about the Vietnam War his Dad replies: 'There's some things you don't want to remember, son ...'. Readers are led by the three points of the ellipsis to turn to the next page which contains a close-up illustration of a large black hole in the old tree. This black hole can be read as a metaphor for the psychological traumas endured, and then repressed, by the veterans. The absence or empty space also serves as a reminder that when the very people who participated in these wars (the soldiers, nurses and other paramilitary) have not made available their versions of the events (or not been given the opportunity to do so), historical accuracy is compromised. Such editorial and pictorial commentaries undermine the authenticity of the accounts, and readers are positioned to treat them as provisional narratives rather than as 'true' facts. This historiographic postmodern picturebook raises questions about our ability to know the past from our position in the present. By implicitly disrupting distinctions between memory, history and narrative, the text undermines history's ability to provide a true and accurate account of events when the methods of historical record are seen to be provisional, partial and unreliable. Another popular strategy of destabilising the reliability of historiography is through the use of alternative perspectives.

Conflicting [hi]stories

The picturebook *The Rabbits* by John Marsden and illustrated by Shaun Tan operates on a number of narrative levels. On one level, the narrative tells the story of small, hybrid marsupial animals which are displaced from their natural habitats by the arrival of rabbits, an introduced species to a place which represents Australia. As is the wont of introduced species, the rabbits multiply beyond expectation and now live in plague proportions across the land that has been decimated by their activities. On another level, the text can be read as an allegorical representation of the British settlement of Australia in which the marsupials represent the Indigenous peoples of Australia, and the rabbits are representative of the British colonists. This use of allegory points to a strategy which Bradford (2007, p. 199) labels as: 'a key form of counter-discourse [...] by which colonist versions of history and dominant modes of representation are contested and resisted'. The presentation of an alternative view to the 'authorised' history of the settlement of Australia initially works to position the text as historiographic metafiction.

History is generally written from the point of view of the dominant social and cultural groups of any particular society. Consequently, the authorised versions of history are inclined to replicate and validate the ideologies of the dominant culture. Until the latter part of the twentieth century the 'past' of Indigenous Australians was represented as 'myth' or 'legend' rather than as history (McCallum, 1999). This representation allowed Aboriginal history and culture to be marginalised in order to bestow legitimacy on the colonisation of the country (Hodge and Mishra, 1990). This legitimacy was further strengthened by the adoption of a *terra nullius*[3] approach to sovereignty over the land. *The Rabbits* seeks to address the gaps, absences and silences of the 'authorised' versions of these events by providing an alternative perspective on the British settlement of Australia and to destabilise previously entrenched discourses in the process.

The verbal text is constructed to resemble an oral tale – an appropriate form, according to Mallan (1999b), that reflects the culture of Indigenous peoples who have a strong oral tradition for storying and educating their children. The written text consists of a series of sparse statements which creates a mood of despondency. The narration includes documentation in the form of how and when statements: 'They came by water' and 'The rabbits came many grandparents ago', as well as warnings: 'They won't understand the right ways. They only know their own country.' The text utilises a first-person plural voice that indicates that the narrator is speaking on behalf of the represented Indigenous peoples. Bradford (2007) warns that such worthy intentions do not, however, guarantee that texts produced by non-Indigenous writers and illustrators will be free of stereotyped and colonial views. While Kathleen Pleasants (2006) claims that the opening statement: 'The rabbits came many grandparents ago' positions the narrators as Indigenous inhabitants recounting their own history, the reference to linear time contests this – since an Aboriginal view of time and the past, associated as it is with the Dreaming, is far more complex. By contrast, the illustrations, in typical postmodern fashion, use an excess of detail to represent aspects of the story. The visual text is full of the pomp and power of the rabbits in which the might of the colonising power is symbolised by metanarratives of Progress, Civilisation and Science, and reinforced by the motto MIGHT=RIGHT repeated regularly throughout the visual text. There is a succession of towering ships, architectural splendour and mechanised, agricultural innovations. The reading positions provided by the text do not construct these as positive images. Rather, through exaggerated, surrealistic imagery they show the colonists as insensitive power-mongers who ride roughshod over both the Aboriginal peoples and the environment using not only the sheer force of their numbers ('there were too many rabbits') but also the 'superiority' of their knowledge, machines and weaponry: all signifiers of their power.

Transitions of colour occur throughout the text, symbolising the devastation being wreaked by the colonisers on both the Aboriginal peoples and the environment. The colour palette ranges from the bold ochres, blues, and reds of the' Australian desert landscapes which competes with the gold, red, black and blue of the uniforms and braids of the colonists, through to the softer pastel shades of the billabongs[4] which are gradually replaced by the greys, browns and sepias of the pages that deal with conflict and destruction. The final pages are mostly black and reflect despair and a lack of hope for the future. Through these contrasts the text positions readers to see the ceremonial and official costumes of the colonists as signifying destructive power and force and therefore to respond more positively to the tranquillity of the billabong scenes on the endpapers. The illustration of the arrival of the settlers by sea, heralded by the writ-ten text: 'They came by water,' is a case in point. The relative size of the ship, bathed in a golden light combined with its billowing sails, speaks of an almost-anointed power. The prow of the ship, along with the sweep of colonists up the beach, form non-transactional vectors pushing forward into the vast land. The stylised Union Jack flag consists of a series of arrows radiating out from a central point which signals the colonists' intentions to spread their influence in all directions over the entire land. The motif of the flag is repeated throughout the text. The forward thrust of the figures of the land-ing party as they march up the sand, along with the supercilious expressions on their faces, position readers to see this as an act of aggression. Two small hybrid marsupials, crouching behind a sand dune and clutching simple spears, observe their arrival and provide a stark contrast to the seeming splendour. Tan[5] explains he based this image on a nineteenth-century painting by E. Phillip Fox on Cook's landing at Botany Bay. Thus, the motivation for this particu-lar illustration in *The Rabbits* was a twentieth-century interpretation of a nineteenth-century representation of an event that occurred in the late eighteenth century. While McHale (1987) discusses the use of deliberate anachronism of attitudes and ideologies as an interrogation of history, Tan's use of the painting has been imitative rather than satiric. Tan has (unintentionally) committed the very act that historiographic metafiction seeks to interrogate.

The methods (observation, measurement, collection and recording) of the colonists as they extend their areas of influence and domination are also strategies of historians who use similar tools to authenticate their historiographies. The visual text on the opening which begins with a word of caution: 'But our old people warned us. Be careful. They won't understand the right ways. They only know their country,' shows a number of the colonists measuring, testing and observing in their attempts to categorise, quantify and constrain elements of this new land. There is a proliferation of test tubes, instruments of measurement and observation, as well as a scattering of random numbers, letters and eyes all pointing to an obsessive need on the part of the colonists to regulate, assess and observe the environment for their particular purposes. These activities are in stark contrast to how the book imagines Aboriginal peoples interpret the environment and live in harmony with the natural landscape. The ridiculing of the colonists' activities within the visual text not only interrogates the discourses (metanarratives) of Progress and Science but also undermines the practices of history itself. To this point *The Rabbits* represents a historiographic metafiction which interrogates the discourses of history by offering an alternative perspective to the authorised version of history. The text, in its endeavours to revision the authorised history of Australian settlement, plays a dangerous game according to Bradford (2001). A closer examination of aspects of *The Rabbits* identifies examples of 'ideological drift' (Pennell, 1996) whereby the overt, or explicit, ideology of the text (interrogation of the authorised history of the British settlement of Australia) may (inadvertently) be subverted by its covert, or implicit, ideology (in which the Aboriginal peoples are represented as victims, and the landscape is represented through a Eurocentric lens). Because the colonial past remains 'powerfully present in many attitudes and ideologies that appear natural' (Bradford, 1996, p. 92) it is not until these attitudes and ideologies are subjected to scrutiny that their covert meanings become more apparent.

The written text documents a sequence of the Aboriginal peoples' changing reactions to the invaders which range from curiosity

('At first we didn't know what to think'), caution ('our old people warned us'), resistance ('Sometimes we had fights'), despair ('The land is bare and brown [...] Where are the great billabongs?') and, finally, hopelessness ('Who will save us from the rabbits?'). In this sequence the Aboriginal peoples are depicted as primitives and victims who are largely incapable of agency, adjustment or adaption to these new circumstances (Bradford, 2001). Bradford suggests that two scenes in the picturebook particularly bear this out. The first scene is the depiction of the stealth of the Aboriginal children[6] which seems to suggest acquiescence or complicity, as the thumbprint on the documents – which allow the children to be taken – *seems* to indicate that the Aboriginal peoples were complicit with the removal of their children, whereas they would have been pressured to sign accordingly. The second scene is the final illustration of the text, that shows a single rabbit and lone hybrid marsupial who, together, look into a small waterhole accompanied by the written text: 'Who will save us from the rabbits?' These instances may characterise the ambiguous or indeterminate conclusions of a postmodern text; nevertheless they also undermine any attempts to represent the Aboriginal population as other than victim. Furthermore, the Indigenous peoples, represented by the marsupial animals, remain for the most part confined to the margins of the illustrative text, almost invisible. While allegory may be a suitable vehicle through which to contest various embedded colonist ideologies, to collapse 'animal' with 'Aborigine', without problematising this construction, is to risk invoking colonial discourses and older ideologies which are no longer acceptable (Bradford, 2001). Rather than interrogate older versions of history, these particular representations, however unintentionally, reinforce many of them.

While Pleasants (2006, p. 190) claims that: 'One of the key tools employed by Marsden is to give voice to the indigenous species [sic]', Bradford (2001) questions Marsden's ability, as a white Australian, to speak on behalf of the Indigenous peoples and their experiences of the invasion. In a similar vein, Tan,[7] by his own admission, draws upon the work of various illustrators and a number of prominent Australian landscape artists, including Arthur Streeton, Fred Williams and Brett Whitely, to represent the Australian landscape, such as that which accompanies the opening which begins: 'At first we didn't know what to think.' His inspiration is drawn, however, from white Australian artists trained primarily in a Eurocentric art tradition and therefore not able to represent the Australian landscape in ways appropriate to the Aboriginal peoples of Australia. Rather than exploit the intertextual possibilities as a means of disruption and dislocation as historiographic metafiction does, Tan has, probably unconsciously, subsumed a number of ideological implications of their works into his own. Once again, the text undermines the import of historiographic metafiction by reinscribing some of the attitudes and representations of older ideologies. In challenging the legitimacy of the authorised account of Australian history and attempting to provide a counter-discourse, *The Rabbits*, through the particular narrative strategies utilised, has at times undermined and marginalised the very people whose story it attempts to promote.

In a similar manner to *The Rabbits*, the picturebook *A Coyote Columbus Story* (King and Monkman, 1992) provides an alternative view of an historical event which its title implies. McHale (1987) contends that alternative histories either supplement or displace the officially accepted version of an event. This picturebook displaces the accepted account of the discovery of the so-called New World, offering in its stead a First Nations' perspective of the arrival of Christopher Columbus in the Americas. Not surprisingly this version differs quite significantly from authorised historical accounts. Unlike *The Rabbits*, however, this text is told by author Thomas King and illustrator William Kent Monkman, both of whom have First Nations ancestry. This enables the text, according to Bradford (2007), to locate historical events within Indigenous systems of narrative and history rather than those of the colonisers. The events are told in the manner of an oral tale which is entirely appropriate given it is focalised through Coyote, a trickster in the guise of a female creator figure. A trickster is an ideal conduit through which to tell the tale as she changes the rules to suit her own purposes. For instance, she sings and dances to conjure players for baseball. First, she conjures the beavers and other animals and then human beings. Coyote, however, plays to win and, when things do not go her way, she changes the rules to suit her purposes. This mocks the ways in which history is told to suit the purposes of the victors. The text exploits the parallels between traditional storytelling and historiography. In this case the practices of traditional storytelling parallel the mythmaking of history surrounding Columbus and his impact on the Americas. For instance, history claims Columbus was the first European to discover the New World, but this is now disputed owing to evidence that the Vikings, among others, may have arrived centuries beforehand. Rather than a tale of largely passive acceptance of the invasion, Coyote as female Creator appears to be very much mistress of her own destiny, although she ends up being too clever by half and inadvertently contributes to the exploitation of her own peoples. Coyote is cheeky, brash, competitive and careless of her powers of creation. A sign of trouble is when she becomes bored. This is foreshadowed by the narrator's comment: 'That silly one sings a song and she dances a dance and she thinks really hard. But she [...] doesn't watch what she is making up out of her head.' She conjures up Christopher Columbus.

One of the most common strategies used by historiographic metafiction is parody. By parodying aspects of an authorised historical account, historiographic metafiction questions the authority of the act of (historical) writing and therefore, argues Hutcheon (1988, p. 145), foregrounds its 'paradoxical use and abuse of the conventions of novelistic and historiographic reference'. This picturebook parodies the manners, mode of dress and obsession with 'treasure' exhibited by the Spanish sailors. Coyote complains, 'These people I made have no manners.' The Spaniards display a level of arrogance matched only by the foolish vanity of Coyote. Columbus and his men demonstrate disrespect for the local people ('I'll bet these are Indians'), disregard for the environment ('These things aren't worth poop') and ignorance of the value systems of the First Nations people. In fact the text exposes the so-called explorers for what they are – invaders. In a similar vein, the inappropriateness of the mode of dress of the explorers is parodied, especially through the illustrative text (see Figure 4.1). The text comments: 'some people in funny-looking clothes carrying flags and boxes of junk' arrived. What would be acceptable, nay, required, dress according to the prevailing cultural norms operating at the Spanish Court of the time seems totally incongruous in the woodland setting of the Americas in which the action of the picturebook takes place. The text ridicules the dress of the explorers who are portrayed as clown-like figures with ruffs around their necks, or cross-dressers who wear stilettos and fishnet stockings. Columbus is depicted in boots, leggings and what appears to be a little frilly skirt, accompanied by ruff collar, cape and epaulettes. One character sports both an automatic weapon and an Elvis quiff. This Elvis look-alike is wearing high heels

Figure 4.1 Illustration from *A Coyote Columbus Story* by Thomas King and William Kent Monkman (1992)

and a cross and chain (which appears to be more a fashion statement than a religious symbol). Another sailor looks like a shady salesman complete with suitcases and cloth cap. These are telling visual comments on how dress (and what may be the height of elegance and rank at the Spanish Court) can be viewed as ridiculous by another society. These regalia point to the incongruity of their clothes in this particular setting and contrast with Coyote's informality in singlet top, shorts and sneakers and, similarly, with the local people and some of the animals. Mendoza (2007) argues that by dressing the First Nations people in casual, contemporary clothes this signals to readers that this is the norm and the Spaniards are portrayed as outlandish, even bizarre, by contrast. These representations contradict Western historical accounts which construct these men as heroic figures who were intrepid explorers. Columbus Day, for instance, is still celebrated every October in North America (although there is some resistance to this). The text, on the other hand, depicts them as buffoons, and, later, as opportunistic mercenaries.

In a similar vein, Columbus disregards the riches of the First Nations people: the land, streams, an abundance of animals and crops. In contrast to the work ethics of the beavers, moose and turtles that build dams, relax in the pond and generally value the environment Columbus is blind to the real worth of the country. The text relates that he is intent on finding gold, India, fame and chocolate cake. This bizarre proclamation, along with Columbus' iteration throughout the text that he is 'sailing the ocean blue' (the rhyme children through the centuries have used to remember dates), points to the absurdity of the situation. Unable to find any 'treasure', Columbus says to his men in an aside: 'I'll bet this is India [...] I'll bet we can sell these Indians.' The subterfuge of it being India points to the way in which history (and in this case geography) has been manipulated to suit the purposes of those writing it. Having established, to his satisfaction, anyway, that he is in India, Columbus indicates his intention of taking some 'Indians' back to Spain to sell. The people of the land say 'This is a bad idea full of bad manners' but Coyote is struck by the absurdity of the idea and laughs and laughs. Bradford points out that Coyote is not indifferent to the fate of her people; rather she misreads Columbus' intentions which show herself as a bad judge of character and a foolish optimist.

However, while Coyote is still laughing, Columbus takes some of the people prisoner, and, as they are rowed to his ships, he stands on the shore rubbing his hands together in eager anticipation of the sale. When the auction of the First Nations people takes place, the written text lists potential bidders, with some irony, as rich people such as baseball players, dentists and baby-sitters. Within the visual text a mitre points to evidence of the presence of representatives of the Church. This suggests that the Church (another powerful institution whose historical records require scrutiny) is complicit in these dealings. In the foreground of the illustration is Columbus in a sports coupé with fluffy dice hanging from the rear-view mirror and four bags of money along the back seat. Ironically, it is a black auctioneer who sells off the people. Columbus tells his friends, 'another couple of trips like this, and I'll be able to buy a big bag of liqorice jelly beans and a used Mercedes'. The jelly beans reference trivialises the import of the auction and its human cargo and speaks to a comment by White (1978, p. 69) that: 'every representation of the past has specifiable ideological implications'. Columbus' trips were seen by European historians as significant for opening up the New World for trade and colonisation, yet this text provides a very different representation: it portrays Columbus as a mercenary only interested in how much money he will make.

Meanwhile the animals and remaining people berate Coyote for what she has allowed to happen. They say: 'you better look out or this world is going to get bent'. Coyote admits she made a little mistake but she will put it all back: 'you'll see, everything will be balanced again'. She holds up her hands, placating them, then she sings her song and dances her dance. When she looks around there is another bunch of funny-looking people there – it is the French explorer Jacques Cartier and his crew. All the people say 'oh, oh, [...] Coyote has done it again' and either disguise themselves as animals or catch the first train to Penticton.[8] This points to a proactive stance against colonisation rather than the dominant account of powerlessness or complicity. Mendoza (2007), for instance, points to the people being kidnapped as indignant rather than stoic. Cartier is looking for India but Coyote says he should forget India. However, there is no room for nostalgia in this text: Coyote reverts to her fall-back position: 'Maybe you want to play ball?' As Columbus is replaced by Cartier this heralds an impending procession of explorers who will come in search of 'treasure' in the Americas over the next couple of centuries. As alluded to earlier, McCallum says history is often presented as a progressive or developmental narrative, and yet these explorers, and the settlers who followed them, wreaked havoc on the lands they discovered and changed forever the ways in which life was lived. The picturebook uses parody and irony through references to contemporary popular culture to interrogate any notions of 'progress' and 'development'. The First Nations people travel by jeep and pick-up trucks, they go skydiving and on cruises, attend casinos and sponsor wrestling matches. Much of the humour in the picturebook is a result of what McHale (1987) would call 'creative anachronism', whereby the material culture of the twentieth century has been imposed on the fifteenth. The animals wear nail polish and fashionable sunglasses, watch TV ads and enjoy cooling drinks around the pond, all of which trivialise their lives compared with their idyllic surrounds pre-Columbus. The use of anachronism produces tension between the past and present and creates an impossible temporal hybridity which, nevertheless, provides a light-heartedness that belies (or softens) the serious (implicit) messages of the text.

Despite the cheeky, playful register of both the visual and verbal texts of *A Coyote Columbus Story*, the book serves a serious purpose. Mendoza (2007, p. 198) reminds us that 'Laughing at outrageous situations is, after all, part of the Indigenous tradition of survival.' Through the utilisation of a range of metafictive strategies such as parody and creative anachronism it points to the similarities between the practices of historiography and fiction, and challenges Euro-Western accounts of history by presenting an alternative, Indigenous view of Columbus' trips to the Americas. The veracity of historical records is also problematised through references to the fantastic in the following picturebooks: *The Tin-Pot Foreign General and the Old Iron Woman* (1984) by Raymond Briggs, and *The Discovery of Dragons* (1996) by Graeme Base.

Fantastic [hi]stories

The roman à clef picturebook *The Tin-Pot Foreign General and the Old Iron Woman* is another multi-layered text. The primary level appears to be a story about the two eponymous characters who squabble over a 'sad little island at the bottom of the world'. The text parodies the heroic war figure and both protagonists, the Tin-Pot Foreign General and the Old Iron Woman. The illustrative text with its overt sexualising of the body – guns blazing from the breasts of the Iron Woman and an overabundance of phallic symbols – constructs them as 'warring human-machine hybrids who exhibit excessive displays of warrior-like behaviours' (Mallan, 2002b, p. 20) which are consequently subverted by their childish posturing over the sovereignty of the 'sad little island'. The protagonists are depicted as children in the playground fighting over toys: 'It's MINE! [...] I bagsied it FIRST! DID! DID! DID!' Their behaviour is childish in the extreme. They deploy toy ships to the island and engage in self-aggrandisement that 'construe[s] a world of playful fantasy, including sexual fantasy' (Martin, 2006). The combination of eroticism and aggression signals that both sides of the conflict indulge in a fantasy of lust and power in their attempts to invade or defend the island.

On another level, the narrative refers to the events of the Falklands War[9] of 1982 in which General Galtieri of Argentina ordered his troops to occupy the Falkland Islands, a remnant of Great Britain's colonial past but, geographically, Argentina's neighbour. This story uses the Falklands/Malvinas War as its historical subject to provide a satirical account of war and imperialism through its blending of history and fantasy. Although war was never declared, hostilities broke out and some 900 military personnel, along with three civilians, lost their lives. Great Britain, under the leadership of then Prime Minister Margaret Thatcher, eventually regained control of the Islands. In the text both sides take the high moral ground and invoke nationalistic symbols such as flags and medals, yet both are shown to have less than noble motives. Through the presentation of an alternative point of view, mixing historical and fictive elements, and highlighting absences within the accounts of a particular event, the text undermines a number of aspects of historiography and the particular ways in which history is recorded and represented.

Historiographic metafictions, in presenting an alternative view of an historical event, often juxtapose the official version of that event with another (McHale, 1987). Through a change in illustrative style and medium, *The Tin-Pot Foreign General and the Old Iron Woman* moves from the extravagant fantasy of the first section of the text (colourful caricatures and cartoonish drawings), to the stark reality of the impact of the conflict upon the soldiers of both sides (sombre pencil and charcoal drawings of the soldiers injured or dying). Martin (2006, unpaginated) argues that the effect of these sombre drawings is to highlight the universal application of these particular circumstances to all conflicts while downplaying the horror of the injuries sustained:

The illustrations clearly represent real men, not toys, but involve minimal attribution, and no circumstantiation. This has the effect of generalising the soldiers' fate as applicable to any man [sic], and avoiding a sensationalised representation of the physical ghastliness of their deaths.

This move from fantasy to reality in the illustrative text is accompanied by a similar shift in the written text from satirical, bedtime story – 'Once upon a time' – to hard news reporting – 'Some men were shot. Some men were drowned.' The sudden switch in both visual and verbal registers draws attention to the existence of an alternative perspective on the war, that of the soldiers.

Another strategy of historiographic metafiction is the mixing of historical and fictive elements. Rather than being a 'sad little island' occupied by a few shepherds, as the text suggests, the Falklands is made up of two large islands and some 776 small islands. During the war three civilians were killed; however, they were women, not shepherds.[10] Within the narrative the 'sad, little island' serves as a symbol of the Falklands and its previous insignificance in world affairs. However, as historical fact, its representation as one little island is misleading. The shepherds, too, are presented as one-dimensional figures through the uniformity of their dress, clothes and food. Their lifestyle is depicted as simple, almost monk-like, but far from idyllic. This use of 'ironic nostalgia' (Hutcheon, 1995) suggests that they do not 'count' as being important. This sentiment is also expressed through the treatment of the returning, injured soldiers who are excluded from the victory parade: 'in case they spoiled the rejoicing'. The illustrations highlight this absence by the choice of charcoal and pencil in which the illustrative text of this section is rendered. These media are impermanent and, like the photographs in *Memorial*, will fade, as will the public's memories of the soldiers who lost lives or limbs in the war.

The absence of women (apart from the masculinised Old Iron Woman) and children from the text highlights how history silences individuals and groups of people through its selection processes. Hutcheon (1988) argues that if storytellers can silence, exclude and absent past events and people, so too can historians through their selection and rejection of documentary evidence. By contrast, the Old Iron Woman's visage on the television screen, watched by the injured, is brightly coloured and preserved through the medium of television for all to see and recall through video replay. The rhetoric of victory is invoked through the words 'there was a Grand Parade to celebrate the Great Victory'. Such constructions of history often serve the interests of particular groups while excluding others.

Postmodernism poses questions about whose history survives, as the stories of the seemingly insignificant 'players' of history often become lost to official memory. The blatantly emotive language and wildly exaggerated illustrations in the text undermine the possibility of objectivity of historical records and promote a pluralist view of history (Hutcheon, 1988) where different but equally meaningful constructions of past realities co-exist. While first and foremost the picturebook highlights the senseless loss of life in the Falklands/Malvinas War, it also problematises the discourse of history and its authorised accounts, as does the next picturebook to be examined.

The Discovery of Dragons (Base, 1996)[11] parodies the historical periods of exploration and discovery as well as the scientific endeavour that often accompanied such expeditions. It takes the form of a collection of letters written by three adventurers whose expeditions are documented by Professor Rowland B. Greasebeam (an anagram of Graeme Base), B.Sc (Serp), F.R.Aud. (Melb), Editor, Melbourne. The introduction reassures readers that the work has been 'exhaustively researched' and is 'scientifically accurate'. Greasebeam goes on to claim that: 'I clearly establish that dragons [...] are indeed part of the natural world.' This reference to dragons immediately raises questions about the scholarship of the work as do the letters after Greasebeam's name: 'F.R.Aud.'. The book has a General Introduction in which Greasebeam makes reference to his previous, largely overlooked, work, *Dragons, Draaks and Beasties*, introduces the three adventurers/explorers and makes some disparaging comments about a rival colleague, 'Professor' Marty Fibblewitz. While this is fictitious and playful, it reminds readers of the interpretative nature of historical writing: that representations of past events may also be compromised by the rivalries and particular agendas of the authors/editors of the so-called documentary evidence and the selection process inevitably involved. The General Introduction is followed by three chapters, each with its own introduction by Greasebeam, but largely devoted to the letters of an explorer/adventurer. These include bumbling opportunist and Viking, Bjorn of Bromme, writing to his cousin Olaf the Grim around the 850s AD; devoted but disobedient daughter Soong Mei Ying writing, in the Middle Ages, to her ailing silk merchant father, Soong Chen Yi; cartographer and amphibiologist Dr E.F. Liebermann, writing from Darkest Africa and later Tasmania to his fiancée, Prunella Hapsburgenfries, in mid-nineteenth-century Munich.

The materials on which Greasebeam relies for the documentation of the existence of dragons are extraliterary artefacts, primarily letters, which are accompanied by drawings and paintings of the dragons discovered. These letters are written variously in scratchy writing on hide (Bjorn), calligraphic script (Soong Mei Ying) and typed word (Liebermann). Each letter is accompanied by a large colour plate of the dragon detailed in the letter it accompanies, while along the bottom of each opening runs a frieze which depicts, often humorously, the scenes detailed in the letter above. For instance, when one of Bjorn's travelling companions, Dagbar, is killed by a dragon the frieze announces his death with the heading: Dagbar*Defunctus*Est. Each colour plate has an inset map showing the location of the particular dragon as well as a sketch comparing the size of the newly discovered dragon to an animal already known to the recipient. In the inset alongside Plate 2, for instance, the dragon is shown to be a similar size to a horse. This supposedly adds further documentary evidence to the information yet, because of the nature of the subject (dragons), playfully interrogates the practice of utilising documentary evidence to verify the 'truth' of past events.

This book problematises the discourses of history and science but undermines its own interrogations. In the introductory remarks to Chapter 3, Greasebeam reveals that his ex-colleague and arch rival, 'Professor' Fibblewitz, claims that Greasebeam wrote the letters himself. This only confirms what readers have probably already suspected. Of course, as a work of fiction documenting the discovery of dragons which are mythical creatures, readers are already positioned to take the documentary evidence provided as provisional, at the very least. However, the text uses a number of the strategies of historiographic metafiction to further, playfully, undermine the veracity of its own claims. The use of anachronisms in historiographic metafiction is both playful and parodic; it undermines the authenticity of any historical evidence presented and highlights the difficulty of the knowability of the past from a position in the present. In other words, even when historical documents are reliably accurate readers find it difficult not to be (subconsciously) influenced in their interpretation of these documents by the prevailing conditions in which they (readers) exist. *The Discovery of Dragons* is littered with self-conscious use of anachronisms. These range from out-of-context references to the inclusion of broader concepts. The former are evident in popular cultural references to, among others, beach volleyball, used-rickshaw dealers, karaoke and medical licences. Of the latter, two examples stand out. Bjorn of Bromme's letters incorporate the use of informal language ('bit of a flop', 'pop down to Portugal', 'Anyway, must fly') which are inappropriate for the time period in which they were supposedly written. Secondly, it would have been almost impossible for a young girl to travel alone throughout Asia in the Middle Ages. Soong Mei's self-deprecatory style also gives rise to a number of ironic references to traditional gender roles. She regularly refers to her timidity and her skills at needlepoint yet spends several years in pursuit of dragons, during which she establishes the Soong Institute of Dragon Research, and sets out to write an encyclopaedia on dragons. These anachronisms not only provide moments of playfulness throughout the text, but also remind readers that any understandings of the represented events of the past at which they might arrive are (unconsciously) mediated by their positions in the present. The playfulness allows readers to develop a degree of critical distance which prevents a nostalgic view of the past and underlines the provisionality of any representations of that past.

Historiographic metafiction often self-consciously draws attention to the parallels between the processes of historiography and those of narrative, and this text is no exception. Greasebeam highlights these parallels by pointing to his use of 'mock parchment' and goes on to say: 'people want Colour! and Big Headings! and Snappy Dialogue sprinkled with Amusing Anecdotes!' He follows this up with a direct address to his arch rival Fibblewitz: 'that's the way to present a theory to the public – reel 'em in with a bit of Mystery and Romance. Never fails.' This reinforces the fact that the events of the past have been mediated through language which is not neutral and can be manipulated to present events in particular ways. The characters' names, too, particularly in the letters from Liebermann, bear resemblance to names utilised in nineteenth-century novels, such as those by Charles Dickens. Examples include Fibblewitz and Kurt von Spanklebot, which give readers an insight into some aspect of their character or situation, or satirise the character by having a ridiculous name. Prunella's surname, Hapsburgenfries, appears to reference the Habsburg dynasty but challenges any links to this ruling family by making the end of the name sound like a fast-food order for (ham)burger and fries. The characters cannot be taken seriously, nor can the historical events being documented – all is provisional and unstable. Finally, the 'Afterword' states that Prunella and Kurt lived happily in a picturesque cottage deep in the Black Forest: language which evokes fairy-tale discourse and, perhaps, serves as a wry comment on the 'historical' events of the text. Further destabilisation comes with the less than happily-ever-after ending when Kurt dies in a skiing accident in Switzerland. While this text is very loosely based on periods of history (Vikings, Middle Ages, Age of Discovery and so on), the next text is based upon an 'historical' event which owes any 'real' existence to the annals of fairy and folk tales. And yet, to me, this seems entirely appropriate within the framework of postmodern children's texts.

An alternative [hi]story?

The True Story of the 3 Little Pigs (1989), by Jon Scieszka and Lane Smith, rather than employing historiographic metafictive strategies to problematise the representation of events from the empirical past, interrogates a fictional event that has nevertheless been recorded in children's literature as 'fact'. While the other texts discussed in this chapter largely rely on fantasy and allegory to tell their tales, they are centred on actual historical events such as various wars, the colonisation of Australia and the Age of Discovery. However, *The True Story of the 3 Little Pigs* is entirely based on a folk tale. It has been included in this discussion on historiographic metafiction because it could be argued that fairy and folk tales represent an 'historical truth' of sorts for small children. When that historical truth is interrogated, it introduces the very young to the notion that some 'histories' may not be stable and knowable to the extent previously projected. This raises awareness that all representations of past events should be treated as provisional.

This picturebook, as can be predicted from the title, is a retelling of the popular folk tale of the 'Three Little Pigs'. I examined a carnivalesque retelling (*The Three Pigs*, Wiesner, 2001) of the original tale in Chapter 1. However, this account has more in common with the other texts discussed in this chapter as it is an attempt to present an 'historical' event from an alternative point of view. White (1976) suggests that historiographic metafiction makes overt the conceptual *apparatus* of historiography which orders and makes sense of historical knowledge. In this text, the wolf, traditionally cast as Big and Bad, calls upon this 'apparatus' to mount his own case to raise doubts about the case previously outlined against him. He becomes an historian – presenting evidence, gathering additional data which offer a competing sequence of events, using eyewitness accounts to substantiate his particular version of 'history' and, not without some irony, drawing parallels between fiction and history. Thus, the wolf becomes complicit in the methods of history in the very act of refuting history itself. Throughout the story, however, as the wolf attempts to discredit the pigs' tale, he constantly undermines the veracity of his own account.

The front-cover illustration of the picturebook appears as the front page of a newspaper, the *Daily Wolf*. The headline exclaims: 'The True Story of the 3 Little Pigs!', with the exclamation mark creating an emphatic tone. The article is attributed to 'A. Wolf. As told to Jon Scieszka', all of which suggests a testimonial from the main protagonist in an attempt to clear his name. This newspaper is clearly aimed at wolf readers, which immediately alerts readers of the picturebook that this could be a one-sided report. Readers are therefore positioned to treat the testimonial with caution. In addition, in the lower right corner of the cover, the newspaper is being clutched by a pig's trotter, which suggests that already the story is being closely examined by unsympathetic eyes. The page is crumpled by the way it is being held, which has made the lines of print go awry, signifying, pictorially, that the story has a particular slant.

The opening paragraph of the book sets up readers to doubt the original 'real story'. The wolf points out that nobody has heard his side of the story, thereby alerting readers to the existence of another point of view. He introduces himself formally as Alexander T. Wolf but adds: 'You can call me Al.' By introducing this casual register Al attempts to encourage readers to identify with him, to bring them onside. This may prove difficult as readers already are positioned by their intertextual knowledge of how wolves traditionally behave in fairy and folk tale. Furthermore, McCallum (1999) cautions that a chronicler may deliberately present a false image of themselves and events. In this text, the image begins with the way in which the wolf is dressed. Al is very nattily attired in dark trousers, pinstriped jacket, white shirt, and a small, red polka-dot bow-tie which is sober rather than flamboyant. At this point he is looking out of the book, directly at the readers of the picturebook. Such 'demand' acts, according to Kress and van Leeuwen (2006), both acknowledge the readers and demand that they enter into some kind of imaginary relationship with the character – in this case, Al. He is in the act of adjusting his glasses, which suggests a certain vulnerability, although the glasses worn also create a degree of authority and an air of seriousness. However, one side of the glasses is lowered so that he can make direct eye contact with readers, which suggests that the glasses are an affectation. Furthermore, he is not wearing shoes, which, in a similar manner to the chef in *The Great Escape from City Zoo* (see Chapter 5), suggests that the wolf does not fully understand the norms of the society into which he is attempting to ingratiate himself. This suggests to readers the possibility that the wolf's tale is as unreliable and unknowable as the original, just as the 'facts' of history are never totally knowable from our position in the present.

Al is relying on the story that he was baking a cake for his dear old granny's birthday, thereby projecting himself as a kind and thoughtful grandson rather than as a determined predator. He claims he simply went to borrow a cup of sugar from his neighbour, a pig. However, because he had a cold he sneezed so violently that the little pig's house of straw fell down and killed the pig inside. So, he insists, the whole story was about a sneeze and a cup of sugar. To further validate his version of events he presents this 'evidence' on the verso page of the second opening in the form of a mathematical formula on a blackboard: 'Sneeze + Sugar'. In support of this discourse of logic, on the recto of this double page is his opening statement: 'This Is The Real Story', which is spelled out using a collage of elements from the story including a pig's tail, snouts, bricks and straw, and at the very bottom of the page is a pair of ears, pricked, as if listening carefully.

While events did occur in the empirical past, as Hutcheon (1988) notes above, these events are subsequently constituted as historical facts by a process of selection. So, too, the wolf reselects and repositions in order to make favourable his account. In telling his story, Al cleverly appropriates aspects of the original story and fits the 'facts' to suit his version of events. This use of partial truths is powerful in convincing readers to at least consider an alternative to the 'established truth' of the traditional story. For instance, the original story relates that the wolf 'huffed and puffed', which sounds like a deliberate action, whereas Al claims he 'huffed and snuffed', which suggests an unintentional or involuntary result of his cold. So, too, when Al knocks on the door of the second pig's house and calls out, the second pig replies, according to Al: 'Go away wolf. You can't come in. I'm shaving the hairs of my chinny chin chin.' This reply constitutes an explanation on the pig's part rather than the emphatic rejection of the original: 'Not by the hairs of my chinny chin chin'. The illustration accompanying this exchange shows the interior of the second pig's house. While readers only see a glimpse of the wolf through the window, the second pig is clearly seen shaving the hairs of his chin. The illustration appears to confirm this particular aspect of the wolf's story. When the second house blows down and the pig inside is discovered dead, Al makes eating the second pig seem natural or logical: 'you know food will spoil' and 'think of it as a second helping'. He attempts to enlist readers' empathy by pointing out that he can't help it if some parts of a wolf's diet (pigs and bunnies) are cute. He further justifies his actions by drawing parallels with humans and their habit of eating meat: 'If cheeseburgers were cute, folks would probably think you were Big and Bad, too.' Rather than deny eating the pigs (a stretch too far perhaps?), Al naturalises it by equating it with humans eating meat products. This is a clever attempt to align readers with his point of view.

Finally, when Al is, in his opinion, rudely rebuffed at the third pig's house he explains: 'Now I'm usually a pretty calm fellow. But when somebody talks about my granny like that, I go a little crazy.' Consequently, he admits, that when the 'cops' drove up he was trying to break down the door. The visual text shows the wolf breathing fire and generally looking threatening. He is, however, also shown to still have the cup in which he was hoping to borrow some sugar which could, perhaps, lend some credibility to his story. Across the foreground border of the opening, police are depicted arriving with truncheons drawn, and accompanied by reporters, one of whom is clutching a microphone and notepad. They are mostly visible as shadows and silhouettes but are undeniably all pigs, which, aside from the play on the slang term for police being 'pigs', raises concerns about the chances of Al getting a fair hearing (both in court and in the newspaper) as the supposed victims are also pigs. The following illustration is of the *Daily Pig* newspaper with huge headlines proclaiming: 'Big Bad Wolf!' The price of this newspaper is listed, ironically, as two cents – a play on the saying 'have your two cents' worth', which refers to the offering of a tentative or unfounded opinion. This seems to imply that the newspaper is not an authoritative medium. The 'photograph' used in the *Daily Pig* story is the same as the illustration of the wolf on the previous page of the picturebook. Yet, two very different pictures are painted of the wolf from the one image, which highlights potential problems with relying on photographic representation with regards to historical records. Under the illustration of the *Daily Wolf* newspaper is the comment: 'The rest, as they say, is history', which is a wry comment on the processes of historiography and the way in which the authorised historical account and, in this case, the processes of the justice system often favour the dominant group in society (in this instance, pigs). It questions how the wolf can get a fair hearing if the power lies with the very group whose history he is denying.

White (1976) argues that history is mediated through narrative. *The True Story of the 3 Little Pigs* self-reflexively draws attention to the conventions of narrative in the same way as historiographic metafiction draws attention to the narrative and linguistic strategies of historiography. The wolf overtly, if unintentionally, acknowledges that his story is embedded within the conventions of narrative. This is immediately evident as the wolf begins in that time-honoured tradition of familiar folk and fairy tales, although his version is slightly different: 'Way back in Once Upon a Time'. This temporal reference to a mythical time creates a degree of scepticism for readers from the very beginning and immediately undermines the authenticity of his tale. Other examples of intertextual references to storytelling are evident through Al's references to his granny, particularly the photograph on the wall of the third opening in which granny looks remarkably like the wolf in the Little Red Riding Hood story after it has eaten the grandmother. The conventional, authoritative third-person narration of historical tracts is replaced by the first-person commentary by Al – the main protagonist and 'historical personage' with the most to gain from this retelling. He attempts to interpellate readers through friendliness and direct address to listen to '*my* side of the story'. To this end Al also employs a range of linguistic modifiers in relation to the pigs. In contrast to original modifiers such as 'cute', 'little' and 'small', which paint the pigs as vulnerable and innocent, Al uses 'lazy, 'rude' and 'porker' to counter the conventional images usually utilised.

The text employs shifts in register rather than keep to the more formal register of the fairy-tale genre. Al adopts a friendly, informal register: 'And you know what?' This accords with McCallum's (1999) argument that shifts in register foreground the function of language in constructing and concealing its object. He also uses a form of linguistic subterfuge when he tells readers 'you are not going to believe it, but', which acknowledges the implausibility of the event yet, at the same time, expects readers to believe it. Furthermore, Al uses a number of popular sayings to advance the story. This allows Al to utilise the natural gaps which occur in narratives to further his own ends. By saying 'The rest, as they say, is history,' Al glosses over the details of the ensuing legal proceedings against him where opposing versions of events would, no doubt, be presented. Al also relies on a number of popular sayings by way of glib explanation of what happened next. In reference to the *Daily Pig* newspaper report he claims that a story about a sick guy wanting to borrow a cup of sugar wasn't very exciting: 'So they jazzed up the story [...] and made me the Big Bad Wolf.' Later he resignedly tells readers: 'That's it. The real story. I was framed.' Al constructs a fairly plausible tale and recruits readers to at least consider his version of events but at the same time makes more problematic the signifier 'real'. This reference to gaps is also evident in the illustrative text where the regular use of windows and doorways contributes to a sense of visual framing and frame-breaking. Al is often positioned on the margins of the illustrative text, the result being that he does not appear as the aggressor. However, it also suggests that he is not in full control of the narrative despite it being *his* version of events, as the windows and doors present barriers, as well as represent gaps, in the narrative.

Despite insisting throughout that his version is the *real* story, the wolf constantly undermines the truth value of his account. He undoes any trust readers may have placed in his version of events. On the one hand, Al tells a reasonably valid story – he went to borrow a cup of sugar to make a cake for his granny's birthday. This presents Al as the good guy and invites readers' empathy and, perhaps, trust. However, the cake mixture he is baking for his granny has a pair of bunny ears in it, and, as noted above, the photo of his granny on the wall bears a remarkable likeness to the wolf posing as Little Red Riding Hood's grandmother (all signifiers of the wolf's 'true' nature), and the cheeseburger has evidence of tails and paws poking out from within. At one point he exclaims: 'Wolf's honour!' when attempting to get readers to believe his account. Readers, no doubt, are well aware of the irony of this pledge, positioned as they are by intertextual knowledge of wolves and their behaviour in fairy tales. But it is the final image of Al that creates the greatest uncertainty in readers' minds. The wolf, in prison clothes, leans through the bars of a prison and says: 'But maybe you could loan me a cup of sugar.' There is a double irony in this sly remark, creating, as it does, a sense of unease or threat and undermining any chance of having his version of events accepted. In the initial illustrations of the picturebook when the wolf begins his story (that is, in current story time) readers get glimpses of Al's sleeves, which are black and white stripes. However, it is only with hindsight that readers realise this is prison garb, which also undermines any trust in the story developed so far. The wolf's long grey beard in the final illustration suggests that a considerable time has passed, which also suggests that he received a considerable sentence for his crimes. These factors, when considered by readers in light of previous evidence for and against, seem to work against the case presented by the wolf.

The playfulness of postmodern picturebooks is evident in the texts examined in this chapter despite the serious subject matter of most of them. That postmodern texts take delight in the parody of particular genres is already apparent from the discussion thus far. However, the picturebooks *The Discovery of Dragons* and *The True Story of the 3 Little Pigs* are doubly parodic in that they parody not only the conventions of historiography but also the genre of historiographic metafiction. The final text, *The True Story of the 3 Little Pigs,* further blurs the already slippery boundaries between the genres of historical fiction and historiographic metafiction. Through the use of specific metafictive strategies that include parody, intertextuality, disruption to the 'objective' third-person narration, and the mixing of historical and fictive elements, all of the above texts interrogate, with varying degrees of success, the reliability of historical methods and the veracity of 'historical' texts to recognise that history, like narrative, is a discourse and therefore a human construct or signifying system through which it derives its claim to 'the truth'. Readers are thereby positioned to treat historical 'facts' as provisional and contested rather than truthful and certain. Chapter 5 examines hegemonic discourses of liberal humanist societies which privilege unity over diversity.

5
Problematising Unity through Ex-centricity and Difference

> Cultural homogenization too, reveals its fissures, but the heterogeneity that is asserted in the face of that totalizing (yet pluralizing) culture does not take the form of many fixed individual subjects [...] but instead is conceived of as a flux of contextualized identities: contextualized by gender, class, race, ethnicity, sexual preference, education, social role, and so on. (Hutcheon, 1988, p. 59)

The previous chapter discussed how authorised versions of history exclude or privilege one group over another. This chapter considers how individuals are marginalised by hegemonic discourses of society which privilege unity and, in turn, advance homogeneity and consensus over heterogeneity and diversity. Adherence to a discourse which favours homogeneity over heterogeneity can lead to the marginalisation of those alienated from dominant discourses by virtue of their race, gender, sexual preferences, class, ethnicity, education, social and other positionings. Hutcheon (1988) sees postmodern practices, such as parody, as a way to give space to these previously silent or marginalised individuals or groups to challenge the 'normalising' discourses of liberal humanist societies. Christopher Butler (2002, p. 46) argues that these normalising discourses actually bring into being what many postmodernists call *the other*. This concept of otherness, according to Hutcheon (1988, p. 65), has associations of: 'binarity, hierarchy, and supplementarity that postmodern theory and practice reject in favour of a more plural and deprivileging concept of difference and the ex-centric'. As a result, postmodern fiction not only gives recognition to those on the margins and celebrates their difference, but simultaneously questions discourses which isolate the 'other'.

Postmodernism is committed to difference and interrogates any notion of unity or homogeneous identity. Underpinning this attention to difference is a postmodernist tendency to promote the politics and ideology of the marginalised rather than those of the centre, redressing the concern expressed by bell hooks (1990) that master narratives silenced many marginalised voices. Sarah Joseph (1998, p. 41) endorses this view: 'we should listen to the voices which were submerged by the grand narratives'. Postmodernism does not call for those on the margins to be moved to the centre, however, as that would be merely replacing one hierarchy with another. Hutcheon, in light of this, refers to those on the margins as 'ex-centrics', playing on both the eccentric/other label as well as the position they occupy outside of the centre. This commitment to the marginalised has seen the emergence of fiction, including a number of picturebooks, which foregrounds a diversity of characters and situations not previously seen in mainstream publishing circles for both children and adults. In any examination of the representations of otherness and difference in postmodern picturebooks, however, it is necessary to return to the notion that children's literature exhibits a particular type of postmodernism. While Angela Carter, for instance, offers, at times, radical alternatives such as the grotesque circus freaks in her adult novel *Nights at the Circus* (1984), postmodern picturebooks generally offer a range of characters who are less extreme (often they are anthropomorphised subjects), who suffer social exclusion, live on the margins of society, are alienated by difference, or work to be accepted by the dominant society.

Minor marginalised characters appear in a number of the picturebooks discussed already. For example, the railway porter in *Black and White* exemplifies Hutcheon's contention that those existing on the margins of society paradoxically operate from both the inside and the outside. The porter, othered by class, wears a uniform ('inside'), that generally signifies authority and power, yet when the train is late the porter has no knowledge ('outside') of its whereabouts and, consequently, is largely ignored by the passengers. He has no access to official information, no authority to act, and thus remains 'invisible'. Another example is the Little Red Hen (*The Stinky Cheese Man and Other Fairly Stupid Tales*), whose marginalisation can be seen as a result of her gender. She is female, small but feisty, yet projected as possibly mad or irrational. This irrationality is implied through the red font of her speech, the strident tone of her voice, as well as her incessant questions. In this way she fits with Hutcheon's observation that ex-centrics are often relegated to: 'the realms of the irrational, the mad or the very least, the alien' (1988, p. 68). However, while these first examples are of characters on the margins of their stories and peripheral to the main texts, a more complex form of marginalisation or otherness occurs in a number of picturebooks by two Australian author/illustrators, Tohby Riddle and Shaun Tan. The chapter examines three picturebooks by Riddle: *The Great Escape from City Zoo, Nobody Owns the Moon* and *The Singing Hat*, followed by *The Lost Thing* by Tan.

'Ex-centrics'

Liberal humanist discourses tend to privilege unity and therefore often attempt to erase difference. The animals in the picturebook *The Great Escape from City Zoo* (1997) represent those whose difference has led to their being incarcerated within the confines of a zoo where they are treated as exotic others, and subjected to the regulation of the prevailing norms of the zoo, which include surveillance by the keepers as well as the gaze of visitors. Bauman (1998, p. 106) argues that: 'Spatial separation leading to enforced confinement has been [...] almost a visceral, instinctual fashion of responding to all difference, and particularly such difference that could not be, or was not wished to be, accommodated within the web of habitual social intercourse.' Thus, when four distinct animals – anteater, turtle, flamingo and elephant – escape from the city zoo they are relentlessly pursued by the zookeepers in order to return them to the confines of the zoo. After being on the run for a while, eventually all but the flamingo are recaptured. The paradox within the story relies on two contradictory discourses. On the one hand, it is the regulatory impulses of the liberal humanist society that holds the animals captive, pursues and ultimately recaptures them. On the other hand, the animals escaped from the zoo where they have been kept as virtual prisoners in the hope of experiencing a liberal humanist life of supposed freedom and self-determination. These are, however, illusionary metanarratives of the Enlightenment and are therefore unattainable. Thus, the animals' escapade is doomed from the beginning.

The visual text is rendered in monochromatic tones, evoking a bygone period – the era of the silver screen. The individual illustrations are framed as stills[1] from a black and white movie with the written text appearing as captions to the pictures. Within the illustrations are allusions to a number of iconic (Western) cultural references such as the original King Kong movie, the intertextual use of artwork (René Magritte, Edward Hopper, et al.), the Beatles' Abbey Road album cover, the film version of *The Grapes of Wrath*, as well as influence of the American photographer Ansel Adams and Renaissance painter Paolo Uccello.[2] Stephens (2008, p. 98) sees these 'cited components' as serving more than just a pictorial pastiche – instead a pastiche of language and story elements. Certainly, the written text, with its use of clichés and linguistic playfulness, calls upon many classic narrative traditions such as escape ('over the wall'), adventure ('heading west, out of town') and danger ('hot on their trail') among others. The overall effect is one of wry humour although intermingled with a sense of the vulnerability of the four escapees. Despite the playfulness of the text and its seemingly straightforward narrative structure of escape, adventure/freedom, followed by return home, or in this case capture, the underlying examination of alienation and difference offers a bleak scenario (McMillan, 2000).

In their attempts to blend in, in order to avoid recapture, the previously marginalised animals experience some of the cultural activities available to those at the centre of society. They visit the movies where they witness the original 1933 *King Kong* movie – ironically the story of another 'exotic other' that is pursued, tormented and exploited by the existing society. Rather than blend in, their obviously defiant (animal-shaped) silhouettes in the cinema betray them as different, at least to readers, if not to the other (human) cinema audience. Hutcheon claims that the ex-centric or 'off-centre' is ineluctably identified with the centre it desires but is denied. This point is played out in the text when the animals acquire clothes and get jobs (as construction and railway workers, and miners) in attempts to conform to the socialising norms of the society in which they find themselves. These attempts represent their desire to fit in by conforming and moving towards the centre. The animals also betray their 'ex-centricity' by misunderstanding or misreading cultural signs when they visit an art gallery. Ironically, the animals, who were positioned as exotic others in the zoo and subjected to the gaze of the paying public, are now in a position of being the ones required to gaze, yet they do not know what is expected of them. This uncertainty is depicted by the contrasting stances between the humans and the animals which convey their differential knowledge of the ways of looking: a woman has her hands behind her back, the man in the foreground has his hand on his chin, while the man in the background has his hands in his pockets. These poses all signify contemplation of the artworks. Meanwhile the animals reflect confusion. Their hands are limply by their sides, they are staring straight ahead, not, as expected, at the artworks. Their behaviour marks them as outsiders or ex-centrics, a status which is further denoted by their clothing. For instance, the anteater, who is wearing the clothes of a chef (which is entirely appropriate when working in a kitchen), does not seem to understand that to wear a chef's hat and apron to an art gallery is inappropriate according to the social norms of the existing society. By failing to read such cultural signs he signals his outsidedness.

Rather than achieve acceptance, the animals are exposed as outsiders and recaptured when, one by one, they falter in their masquerade as 'normal'. Stephens (2008) points out that, ironically, it is the very characteristic which sets each animal apart which eventually leads to its downfall; however, in a society that privileges unity, this is to be expected. For instance, the tortoise falls on its back and is prevented from getting up again by its shell: this very characteristic, which sets it apart from the other animals, also makes it vulnerable. The only time the animals achieve a measure of legitimacy is in the cabin in the mountains where the written text claims: 'Things were finally working out.' But this is only because they are isolated from the very society in which they had hoped to participate and relatively safe from the threat of exposure. Their failures to read the cultural signs are not significant in their isolation. Once again they are relegated to the margins although they fail to fully recognise that their isolation is a particular form of marginalisation and continue to strive towards the centre of acceptance. The only one to avoid recapture is the flamingo[3] around whose fate there is some (typically postmodern) indeterminacy. It seems to have eluded capture by taking on the signs of the culture in which it has sought freedom. Readers can detect an isomorphic resemblance between various flamingo-shaped objects such as a hotel sign, a Loch Ness Monster (itself another abject 'other') and a garden statue among others. The flamingo is forced to sublate its difference to take on the cultural signifiers of the dominant society and thus becomes complicit with the regulatory regime rather than having its difference recognised or acknowledged. Despite its seeming freedom, the flamingo has had to conform to the prevailing cultural norms in order to remain 'free'. Thus, all four animals remain alienated from the prevailing social norms of the society in which they have found themselves. There is no celebration of their difference; they remain as 'ex-centrics' confined to the margins. The second Riddle picturebook examined, *Nobody Owns the Moon*, follows the mixed fortunes of a fox named Clive Prendergast and a donkey named Humphrey.

A first reading of *Nobody Owns the Moon* (2008) presents a whimsical tale of friendship and belonging. However, closer inspection reveals layers of meaning which problematise issues surrounding marginalisation, indifference, ambiguity, contradiction and the provisional nature of postmodern existence. The cityscape on the front cover establishes the postmodern setting in which the events take place. The two friends have learned to live in this city, admittedly with varying degrees of success: both characters reflect the attributes that writers commonly assign to these animals in children's fiction – the quick and clever fox and the docile, dim-witted donkey. Clive oozes confidence whereas Humphrey presents a more dejected figure. The text claims, in documentary style, that the fox is the only wild creature that can successfully make a life for itself in the city. And this certainly seems true of Clive. Readers are treated to a view of him reclining in an armchair surrounded by the creature comforts of home: feet on a footstool, a coffee mug close at hand, a collection of books waiting to be read and a painting on the wall. Clive has accumulated the infrastructure necessary for living within the mainstream of this society. The commentary makes the observation that other animals have limited success compared with the fox, a point reinforced by the visual text which shows a crocodile in a lumberjack's cap and coat, moving along low to the ground and looking very much like a misfit among the people on the streets of this city. However, the crocodile is better off than the dancing bear

Clive has witnessed: a creature bereft of any of the trappings of city life and forced to dance inanely while subjected to the gaze of various (human) onlookers. This bear embodies the abject other. Clive's friend Humphrey, by contrast, is able to walk upright and has had a variety of jobs and thus appears better able to blend into the urban landscape.

Humphrey's life, however, is not without its difficulties. He finds it hard to keep a job and doesn't always have a fixed address and, unlike Clive, he does not have a surname, which suggests he is a nobody. As if to reinforce this down-on-his-luck position, the visual text at one point shows Humphrey sitting somewhat dejectedly in a doorway and, later, loitering at the base of a statue in a park. Because of his inability to adapt completely to an urban life, Humphrey lives a provisional existence on the fringes of the society. While Clive has his comfy armchair and mug of coffee, Humphrey sits on a step and carries a thermos and a book in his tote bag, which appears to contain all his worldly goods. Two objects in Humphrey's tote bag prove significant. The book, Walt Whitman's *Leaves of Grass* (1855), celebrates the diversity of nineteenth-century America, including a wide range of people from all walks of life. Upon publication this work was met with both disapproval and critical acclaim. While this extra-textual knowledge has no direct bearing on the story, it could extend the kind of mixed reception Whitman experienced to the provisional nature/reception of postmodern art and to Humphrey's changing fortunes. However, the narrative focuses not on the Whitman text, but shifts readers' attention to the intriguing blue envelope in the bag. It turns out to be an invitation to the opening night at the theatre of the production of *Nobody Owns the Moon*. Clive suggests they can go, and they do.

Regular theatre-goers could find the sight of a fox and a donkey in the dress circle of an elegant theatre and partaking of hors d'œuvres and, later, coffee and cake somewhat surprising or amazing. But fiction allows for the incongruous and the unexpected. This sequence of scenes at the theatre confirms the postmodern contention that boundaries between high and popular culture have been dismantled, including those that separate who can legitimately participate in, or attend, such cultural activities. In a previous age neither Humphrey, nor Clive for that matter, would have gained admittance to a theatre such as the one pictured in *Nobody Owns the Moon*. When readers encounter Humphrey sitting in a doorway (referred to earlier) he is surrounded by posters advertising vaudeville shows. Unlike the 'high' culture of the theatre, vaudeville is regarded as an example of popular or mass culture. As if to emphasise this, one of the posters shouts: 'Bring all the family.' This is the milieu to which the likes of Humphrey conventionally belong. As cultural boundaries are no longer so rigidly defined, Humphrey, who lives on the margins of society, is able to move to the centre, however briefly, when the opportunity presents itself in the guise of (free or acquired) tickets to the theatre. This dismantling of boundaries reflects the postmodern world of the city and enables the friends to enjoy the high cultural activity of the theatre. Whether this signals a tentative step towards mainstream society's acceptance of their difference or is simply a result of indifference on the part of the other patrons evident in the visual text is uncertain.

Paradoxically, the night at the theatre also exposes the contradictory nature of postmodernism. We can understand this theatre experience as offering 'multiple provisional alternatives' to a traditional fixed unitary idea of the theatre-going experience (Hutcheon, 1988). The night breaks down boundaries between high/popular culture but also perversely demonstrates the appeal of high culture traditionally reserved for those at the centre of society and perhaps desired by those on the margins. Unlike the zoo animals when they visited the art gallery in *Great Escape from City Zoo*, Clive and Humphrey are better able to read the cultural signs pertaining to attendance at the theatre. This is not only evident in the visual text where, despite being (admittedly, anthropomorphised) animals among people, they appear to go unnoticed by the human patrons. Their ability to blend in is also reinforced in the written text: 'In all the right places, they laughed and sighed.' This aspiration to fit in contradicts the postmodern impulse to accept, even celebrate, difference. This is the paradox of postmodern children's fiction: while on the one hand it celebrates difference and interrogates unity it also (perhaps inadvertently) reinforces the appeal of the centre, the desire to be accepted into the mainstream.

While the written text of *Nobody Owns the Moon* presents a fairly linear tale, the illustrative text speaks of a postmodern world where notions of time and space are more indeterminate, reflecting the impermanence of existence. The text's disruption of conventional sequences and spatio-temporalities is typical of postmodern fiction. Mixed media, including pencil, pen and watercolours, as well as coloured paper and photo collage, are all utilised within the illustrative text of the picturebook to achieve various effects. These detached visual effects point to the provisional state of existence which, it is now acknowledged, does not conform to order and uniformity as implied by realist texts but rather is partial and incomplete. Representations of the past are depicted in black and white in contrast to the main storyline which is rendered in colour and appears to be in the present, although, in typical postmodern uncertainty, this cannot be confirmed. These strategies work to undermine the temporal organisation of the written text. Use of iconography (signs, posters and so on) comment on, advance and/or disrupt the sequence of the narrative. For instance, visual references to matryoshka dolls in the body of the text as well as in the endpapers signal the repetition of daily life. A similar repetition occurs with the mention, and nature, of Clive's job in a factory in which he 'puts the same two parts together – over and over'. These, in turn, stall any sense of ordered progress.

The city appears to be populated by people resembling cardboard cut-outs placed on the background in a fragmentary and provisional manner of the postmodern urban environment. There is also repetition of particular figures in the visual text. A woman in an orange coat (and sometimes a hat) makes several appearances: in the queue for the theatre, at the waiter's right shoulder as he serves hors d'œuvres and behind Clive on the street. Other recurrent figures are featured in another of Riddle's picturebooks, *The Singing Hat*, and include a man who looks remarkably like the main protagonist, Colin Jenkins, especially in profile. There is also a man with a long white beard who bears a resemblance to the ornithologist in *The Singing Hat*. Another figure, most often in silhouette, speaks of Orson Welles or newspaper magnate Randolph Hearst. This urban space is not represented as a homogeneous community; rather people appear inserted, random and self-absorbed. In this busy, lonely postmodern space there is no sense of connectedness between, what McHale would call, 'transmigratory figures', which appear as separate figures reflecting the isolating effects of an urban existence. While Clive appears to maintain a stable position within the mainstream of society, Humphrey's life appears to be subjected to random events such as the blue envelope rather than by any ordained plan.

At the close of the story, Clive and Humphrey optimistically pro-claim: 'This is our town.' Yet any sense of joint ownership is imme-diately tempered when they 'go their separate ways'. This separation reinforces their 'difference' from each other: Clive manages to live a reasonably comfortable life within the mainstream society whereas Humphrey ekes out a living on the margins. Both characters, how-ever, exhibit physical differences from the human characters and thus remain separated from the general populace. There is no happy ending for either of the friends. Another Tohby Riddle picturebook, *The Singing Hat* (2000), follows the story of another character margin-alised by his so-called 'ex-centric' behaviour.

While I do not necessarily consider *The Singing Hat* is a postmodern text *per se*, its treatment of unity and conformity is a useful means of comparison with the other Riddle books discussed in this chapter. The story tells of a man, Colin Jenkins, who falls asleep under a tree and while he is asleep a bird builds a nest on his head. Rather than disturb the nesting bird, Colin leaves it where it is and attempts to carry on as normal. However, this act of 'virtuous disobedience' (after Judith Butler) is met with various reactions. As a result of his actions, 'Colin Jenkins made some new friends ... and lost some old ones.' Unlike the exotic animals in *The Great Escape from City Zoo*, Colin is, to this point, part of the mainstream of society. He is a businessman who wears a suit and tie, carries a briefcase and holds down a steady job, all signifiers of a person in tune with the norms of the prevailing society in which he lives. However, because of the disruptions caused by the bird and its nest (which can be read as a metaphor for almost any sign of 'deviant' behaviour or nonconformity), Colin is rejected by a number of his friends, loses his job and, as a consequence, is turned out of his home. Despite the bird being identified as an extremely rare species, Colin's efforts at conservation are ignored and he becomes alienated from the centre of mainstream society.

Colin and his young daughter are forced to move from the cen-tre to the margins of society, thereby becoming one of Hutcheon's 'ex-centrics' in both senses of the word. Their change in circum-stances is marked in the visual text by a change in Colin's clothing from suit and tie to baggy corduroy trousers, cardigan and open-neck shirt. His lowest point occurs when another bird drops a large white splat upon his shoulder and, at low ebb, he considers returning the bird's nest to the tree under which he had fallen asleep so that he can return to his old life at the centre of things. However, he refuses to succumb to societal expectations and allows the bird and its nest to stay. His actions accord with Hutcheon's contention that the different, the other, can become 'vehicles for aesthetic and even political consciousness raising [...] perhaps the first necessary step to any radical change' (1988, p. 73). The illustrative text uses the monochromatic tones familiar to readers of Riddle's work for the background. However, photo collages foreground particular elements such as the crown of the tree, the cityscape at night and an office plant, while the action of the narrative is played out in cartoon-style pen and ink drawings. Colin is changed by the experience and 'never took another job like the one he had', which suggests that he has become somewhat disillusioned with the society in which he lived. While he returns to functioning within society he does not embrace its adherence to conformity and unity, but rather has seen, and enacted, other (different) ways of being. The eponymous 'lost thing' in Shaun Tan's picturebook, too, enacts another way of being.

A place for difference

The Lost Thing (2000) depicts a futuristic Melbourne (Australia)[4] as a dystopic city in which people, as well as lost things and different things, are left behind in the meaningless pursuit of the information industries of a post-industrial society. The story is focalised through a young boy, Shaun, not the author but the character who signs himself Shaun on the postcard to Pete on the back cover. This confusion between naming and identity is also typically postmodern. Shaun relates the time he came across a 'thing' which was obviously lost ('it had [...] a sad, lost sort of look'). Shaun tries to find where it belongs. After a number of false starts, including caring for it at his home, he eventually arrives at a place 'in a dark little gap off some anonymous little street' that appears to be called Ut*qIA, to which he consigns the lost thing. Throughout this journey the text installs and interrogates a number of binary opposites, including lost/found, dystopia/utopia, same/different, homogeneity/heterogeneity, and contrasts the boy's life of sameness with the lost thing's life of difference. *The Lost Thing* is told through minimal written text accompanied by a sequence of crowded canvases in which physics and engineering equations, arrows, posters and ticket stubs, and other iconography, as well as intertextual references to a number of well-known Australian artworks, compete for readers' attention. Debra Dudek (2005) identifies three texts among this postmodern excess of signs: pages from Shaun's Dad's old physics and engineering textbooks, that are overlaid by the visual painted text, and the narrator's story written on scraps of lined paper from an old exercise book. Dudek (p. 58) notes: 'the composition of each page challenges the reader to move beyond the linear narrative and into the layered margins'. This act of reading reflects the impulse of the text and requires both readers and characters to also look beyond the normative society to life on the margins.

The decaying society in which the lost thing has surfaced is a bureaucratic labyrinth from which there seems to be little chance of escape. The cityscape is one of cubes, straight lines and imposing structures inherited from the modernist period which celebrated so-called metanarratives of 'progress' and the veracity of 'science' (embodied in the background visuals of physics and engineering texts). However, the idle cogs and wheels, rusted pipes and dislocated machinery of the visual text reflect the obsolescence of the machinery and suggest a shift from industrial to post-industrial.[5] The tension between these references to post-industrialism in opposition to the modernist cityscape and the regulation and conformity of the depicted society represents an example of a postmodern chronotope as there appears to be conflicting periods of time co-existing in the one place. This spatio-temporal relation further contributes to the dystopian setting and creates a sense of discontinuity which signals not only the loss of the utopian dream of progress (Mallan, 2005), but also the placelessness of the lost thing.

Stephens (2008) argues that the text's capacity to proliferate meanings, together with the manifest otherness of the thing itself, enables it to be read both as a story which deals with immigrant displacement in a postcolonial, multicultural state, and as an attack on consumerism and a future interpretation of a destroyed environment. While the picturebook interrogates all of these social, political and environmental phenomena (and more), it seems restrictive, despite the multiple agenda outlined here by Stephens, to limit the condition of the lost thing to immigrant displacement.[6] *The Lost Thing* deals with an 'ex-centric' or alienated other for whom there is no possibility of acceptance or familiarity in the dystopian society depicted. In this city people are treated as problems to be solved and put in their place by bureaucratic centres such as the Federal Dept of Odds and Ends (whose motto 'Sweepus underum carpetae' mocks any pretence to it offering any serious government service). The wheels and cogs of the visual text are metonymic of the bureaucratic nightmare through which people must fight to establish their place or identity. This is evident in the faces of the people in the city queues who appear like automata, staring mindlessly and numbly ahead rather than attempting to engage with those around them. This image suggests that the citizens have no desire or will to resist, but are resigned to submit to the norms of the society with its regulation and conformity: the image of conformity is vividly conveyed in Tan's appropriation of John Brack's 1955 painting, *Collins St., 5pm* (see Figure 5.1). While the original work is already a satirical depiction of the conformism of everyday life (Stephens, 2008), Tan's reworked illustration with the lost thing in the background creates a striking contrast to the lines of faceless, sightless robotic figures wending their way along the street. The visible faces of the people in the foreground are uniformly grim. By contrast, the lost thing is the embodiment of difference and therefore poses particular problems for a society that values uniformity, repetition and sameness. It does not fit into the available norms of the society in which it has been 'found'. It is not seen as a subject but a 'thing' to be catalogued, archived and forgotten: its namelessness (thingness) thereby reveals its status as nonentity.

The only spontaneity expressed in the visual text is in the sequences of what appear to be wisps of cloud which at times appear to be engaged in dance, a baby morphing into abstract shapes, or Elginesque figures. One even appears to resemble the duck that is a constant in Leunig's cartoons.[7] This spontaneity stands in contrast to the monotony of the endpapers which display Shaun's bottle-top collection. The bottle tops are uniform white on which are superimposed symbols from physics and engineering texts – except for one on which is the word 'entropy', signalling the current state of this society, while a second is green with a swirl of cloud. This second bottle top seems to represent the antithesis of the uniformity and rigidity of the bureaucratic society in which the lost thing is trapped, and perhaps symbolises, as Dudek suggests, the 'utopian impulse' that pervades *The Lost Thing*. Dudek bases this utopian assertion on the three figures (Shaun, Pete and the hybrid custodian) who,

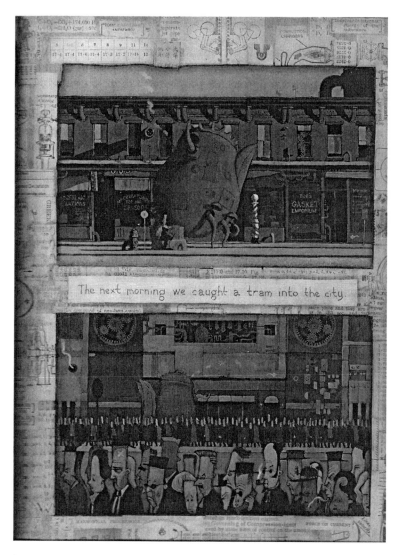

Figure 5.1 Illustration from *The Lost Thing* by Shaun Tan (2000)

through small individual acts of resistance, contribute to the lost thing's arrival in Ut*qIA (which can be read as a corrupted version of Utopia). Shaun helps the lost thing even if his actions are a bit misguided. He reverts to binaries in his assumption that if something is 'lost' it can be 'found'. However, his friend Pete says some things are 'just plain lost' and that 'Maybe it doesn't belong to anyone.' Dudek (2005, p. 64) says this observation: 'opens the possibility for another way of being for both the boy and the reader'. That is, it raises awareness within the boy and readers of other ways of being, to possibilities outside of 'lost and found', and 'belonging and home'. Through the timely intervention of a hybrid custodian, itself marginalised by both its difference as a cyborg and its occupation as a cleaner, who points the way to Ut*qlA by way of a sign consisting of a wavy arrow, Shaun is able to find a place for the lost thing. The search is not without its problems however as the wavy arrow is difficult to locate through the excess of other signs within the text.

Eventually they arrive at their destination which is housed 'in a dark little gap off some anonymous little street': in other words, tucked out of the way on the margins or limits of the bureaucratic society. The text, too, exceeds its own limits, not only by requiring readers to turn the book in order to examine this image, but also by having the layers of written text and background pages of science and physics equations removed, so that Ut*qlA stands alone framed in black, a place set apart. The arches of this Ut*qlA are soft and rounded in contrast to the harsh, straight lines of the modernist cityscape. It is occupied by a great many hybrid characters, including a birdcage with wings, a barometer/protractor and an accordion/typewriter. These playful hybrids bring to mind Haraway's (1985) cyborgs which, by being assembled not born, are freed from the 'biology as destiny' fate that allows the possibility of producing new social identities and connections. Ut*qlA thus represents a decentralised community in which alienated otherness gives way to difference, and exhibits the contention that difference operates within each of the challenging cultures as well as against the dominant. This is a space of nonconformity and acceptance which celebrates difference rather than condemns or corrals it, as Dudek (2005, p. 58) puts it: 'It is a world of fluidity and delight and difference and play.'

The best option for the lost thing seems to be to live in Ut*qlA because this regulatory, bureaucratic society has made people (including Shaun) into sameness, automata who cannot envisage a society in which difference is acknowledged or embraced let alone celebrated. By contrast, the cyborgs that exist in Ut*qlA are outside society's recognised norms but exhibit the principle that postmodernism encourages the 'other' to become, namely, the 'different'.

The centralised and centralising authority has not been challenged by the narrator, Shaun and the thing, merely circumvented. To live on the margins may be seen as a pyrrhic victory, but, unlike the animals in *The Great Escape from City Zoo* that remain subjected to surveillance and spatial confinement, the lost thing has been led to a place which could be read as a place of belonging and acceptance. Whether this space represents a utopian space as Dudek contends, or whether it merely operates as a safe space, away from the regulatory bureaucracy which has no place for those who are 'different', is, perhaps, a moot point. It remains, however, in a back street, tucked out of sight from the mainstream society. Bhabha (1994), following an idea after Heidegger, argues that the border is not only the limit or the end of a particular thing, but the place where the presencing of something else begins. The boy's comment: 'I didn't know what to think but the lost thing made an approving sort of noise,' suggests that the thing recognises a place in which it will be accepted and where, perhaps, the presencing of something else is possible.

In addressing the ways in which a postmodernist approach interrogates liberal humanist notions of unity and conformity, this chapter has shown that the four picturebooks examined foreground characters who are marked by various forms of 'difference' and who, as a result, are marginalised and/or excluded from mainstream society because of this ex-centricity or difference. While the eponymous 'lost thing' eventually finds a separate place where its difference is accepted, perhaps celebrated, it is forced into seclusion. Humphrey, in *Nobody Owns the Moon*, remains on the margins of society despite his visit to the theatre, and three of the four animals of *The Great Escape from City Zoo* remain incarcerated from the mainstream society in which they yearn to find a place. The fate of the fourth animal, the flamingo, remains unclear. The man in *The Singing Hat*, Colin Jenkins, chooses not to return to the 'centre' of society after his experiences of ostracism and rejection. As a result of postmodernist interrogations of notions of difference, Fuery and Mansfield (2000) suggest that ethnic, national, class and gender groups, as well as those defined by sexual orientation, have seized the opportunity to express and theorise their differences from others, especially from central, conventional, 'normal' value systems. These impulses evident in picturebooks have contributed to a growing trend whereby various fields are achieving autonomy from the label *postmodernism* by creating their own discourses; the growing *politics of identity* is one such field. Chapter 6 addresses the shift in the direction of postmodernism outlined in the Introduction, by analysing the contrasting ways in which a number of postmodernesque picturebooks engage with issues of postmodernity such as globalisation, and its associated components – mass media and consumerism.

6
Towards the Postmodernesque Picturebook

> I have felt uncomfortable for some time that post-modernism is losing its power to worry, provoke and to question, especially to question its own nature and origin. (Smethurst, 2000, p. 11)

> What is undeniable is that globalization, in one form or another, is impacting on the lives of every-one on the planet [...] It is changing consciousness, too, as everyone everywhere becomes more globally aware and oriented. In this sense globalization might justifiably be claimed to be the defining fea-ture of human society at the start of the twenty-first century. (Beynon and Dunkerley, 2000, p. 3)

As documented in the Introduction to this book, in recent years a shift has become evident in children's literature from postmodern to what I term *postmodernesque literature*. That such a shift has occurred is not surprising. According to Barth (1967) all literary trends follow a cycle of a resistance–acceptance–decline and eventually reach a point of exhaustion when the particular strategies and themes of the movement become clichéd. Concurrent with this decline, a literary trend will often take new directions, undergo modification and morph into a related, but recognisably different, development. Certainly adult postmodern fiction has experienced a number of shifts and changes in emphasis in the latter part of the twentieth century. One such shift, despite the reservation expressed by Smethurst in the first epigraph, is a turn from a focus on the ideologies and practices of liberal humanism to engage with the discourses of postmodernity (see Hassan, 2001; Connor, 2004; McLaughlin, 2004; Hoberek, 2007). A number of commentators (Lewis, 2001; McLaughlin, 2004; Kirby, 2010) refer to the resultant fiction produced as post-postmodernist texts. In a similar vein, Hutcheon (2002) argues that postmodern fiction, that she defines as fiction which *both* disrupts the conventions of narrative *and* interrogates aspects of liberal humanist society, is now a thing of the past. I argue that, just as adult postmodern fiction is undergoing change, a similar process is occurring within the postmodern picturebook.

Throughout the final years of the twentieth century, and into the twenty-first century, the postmodern picturebook has continued to evolve and change. While some picturebooks reflect a decline into cliché (as briefly discussed in the Introduction), others have evolved to the point where a separate designation is justified. In marked contrast to the concerns of the postmodern picturebooks, examined in earlier chapters of this book, such as *The Stinky Cheese Man and Other Fairly Stupid Tales, Black and White, The Three Pigs* and *A Walk in the Park,* which (in line with Hutcheon's definition) interrogate liberal humanism, a group of picturebooks has emerged which critique aspects of postmodernity. In order to differentiate between these newer texts and those that Hassan (2001) might designate as 'classic postmodern' texts, I use the term *postmodernesque picturebooks.* Where postmodern fiction questions naturalised notions of eternal truths, reality and a knowable past as well as the concept of a stable individual (all aspects of a liberal humanist world), postmodernesque picturebooks turn their attention to the critique of the postmodern world: a globalised, mediated, hyperreal world in which, seemingly, the only way to make any sense of it is through the rampant consumption of goods, services and signs, and in which individuals construct multiple identities and learn to navigate through multiple realities. In this respect, to paraphrase Woods (1999), these books (postmodernesque picturebooks) are not so much postmodern picturebooks as picturebooks *about* postmodernity.

In its analysis of the postmodernesque characteristics of the fictional worlds depicted in a number of recently published picturebooks, this chapter examines three, interrelated, areas of interest. The first section deals with the effects of globalisation, the second section examines the reach of mass media and the third critiques patterns of consumer consumption. The picturebook *Il Libro piu corto del mondo* (*The Shortest Book in the World*, Cox, 2002) reflects on the effects of technology and communications innovations on global relationships, while *The Empty City* (Megaritty and Oxlade, 2007) and *In the City* (Harvey, 2007) take up issues relating to the globalisation and glocalisation of cities. The next section looks at the diverse ways in which the mass media, through available technologies and communications, impacts upon everyday lives and how this impact is played out in the picturebooks *The Short and Incredibly Happy Life of Riley* (Thompson and Lissiat, 2005) and *The Race of the Century* (Downard, 2008). The final section centres on the rampant consumption of goods and experiences (*Riley* and *In the City*) and the construction of identity through consumption (*Riley* and *The Race of the Century*). In their accounts of globalisation, mass media and consumerism these picturebook narratives use detachment (*Il Libro*), playfulness (*The Empty City* and *In the City*), celebration (*The Race of the Century*) and censure (*Riley*) to represent their responses. These postmodernesque texts draw attention to the effects of globalisation, the influences of the mass media and the results of rampant consumption on a number of fictional worlds. They do this by drawing on their postmodern precursors, employing familiar characteristics of style and format that have been discussed throughout this book.

Globalisation/glocalisation

As indicated in the second epigraph above, globalisation just might be the defining feature of society at the beginning of the twenty-first century; however, different trajectories for the onset of globalisation range from several hundred years to the final decades of the twentieth century. Despite the history of globalisation, Roland Robertson and Kathleen White (2007) claim that widespread academic usage of the term has been adopted only over the past 20 years, marked by the fall of the Berlin Wall[1] (Bauman, 1998). The most recent phase is marked by the accelerated rate of globalisation. Globalisation, like the term postmodernism, resists definition and it may be more accurate to write of *globalisations* to reflect its diversity, not only of its processes, but also of understandings and theories surrounding it. The earliest discussions on the effects of globalisation focused primarily on the economic sphere through which most ordinary people formed an understanding of what globalisation meant (Tomlinson, 2007). Approaches to the term are now more multi-dimensional. Bullen and Mallan (2011, p. 58) argue that: 'Globalization is predicated on new forms of political, economic, and cultural interconnectivity and interdependency.' Within these political, economic and cultural domains are other areas of concern such as human rights, environmentalism and the fate of the nation-state. Bauman (1998, p. 60) argues that the term globalisation has evolved to a point where it is now understood 'to primarily refer to global *effects* [...] notoriously unintended and unanticipated [...] it is about *what is happening to us all*'. It is these *effects* which are the subject of both theoretical debate and how they play out in postmodernesque picturebooks under examination in this chapter.

Opinions differ amongst writers as to whether globalisation is a feature of modernity or postmodernity. While a number of commentators including Robertson, Giddens and Meyer see globalisation as 'the universalisation of the institutions of modernity' (Robinson, 2007, p. 138), Mike Albrow (1997) sees the transition from modernism to postmodernism as the defining feature of globalisation. However, Barker (1999) acknowledges that the first waves of globalisation were part of the spread of Western modernity. Increasingly, however, global flows rather than neat, linear determinations are more a series of 'overlapping, overdetermined, complex and "chaotic" conditions' (p. 41) – all indicative of postmodernity. Further, Ien Ang (1996) argues that the global spread of consumer capitalism (a product of modernity) encourages consumption and gives rise to the constant identity transformations and heterogeneity of postmodernity, a point which the previous chapter discussed. Perhaps globalisation is best understood as a phenomenon which began with modernity and continues to develop and change with postmodernity. The postmodernesque picturebooks discussed in this chapter reflect this development and resultant changes.

As early as 1992, Robertson contended that the major directional tendencies of globalisation were connectivity and an increasing global consciousness: 'Globalization as a concept refers to both the compression of the world and the intensification of consciousness of the world as a whole' (p. 8). This degree of connectivity and increasing global consciousness is made possible by constantly updated information and communication technologies which allow for increasingly rapid and frequent global access. In fact, Howard Tumber and Frank Webster (2007) suggest that it would be impossible to conceive of the scale and scope of contemporary globalisation without the availability of such technologies. Robertson and White (2007) suggest that the latter (consciousness) indicates a shared sense of the world rather than a consensus and that this aspect is often neglected in favour of the former (connectivity). The level of connectivity created concerns in early discussions on globalisation regarding the possible domination of local cultures by the West, particularly the dominance by American transglobal corporations (TGCs), expressed through terms such as McDonaldization or McWorld.[2] It is now increasingly recognised that globalisation is no longer unidirectional but rather a process of uneven development that fragments as it co-ordinates (Barker, 1999). Barker draws upon Gilles Deleuze and Félix Guattari's (1987) model of the rhizome to explain the connectivity paths and his notion of 'fragments as it co-ordinates'. The dynamic interplay between the global and the local as a process by which the global becomes integrated into the cultural particularities of local life (Caldwell and Lozada, 2007) has been labelled 'glocalization' by Robertson (1992). Bauman (1998) argues that Robertson's term 'glocalization' exposes the unbreakable unity between 'globalising' and 'localising' – not, as some argue, a term indicating an anti-globalisation stance. Rather than an impulse to homogeneity as many feared, glocalisation is seen as contributing to a heterogeneous global world. Further, Garcia Canclini (2001) argues that globalisation is not characterised by homogeneity, as Barber (1995) asserts, but by fragmentation and recomposition into hybrid cultural forms. In relation to picturebooks, Stephens (2008, p. 89), for instance, writes of 'glocal postmodernism [and ...] whether the dialogue between internationalism and local concerns has produced a glocal version of postmodernism, what may be termed a postmodern hybridization'. I would argue that, rather than either of the awkward neologisms used here, such picturebooks could be accommodated under the *postmodernesque* designation. What makes globalisation the dominant concern at this point in the twenty-first century, according to Caldwell and Lozada (2007), is that the degree of rapidity, influence and reach of transglobal flows is changing the very fabric of everyday life in profound ways: a feature which is examined in the following discussion of postmodernesque picturebooks.

Globalisation, according to Waters (1995) and others, is marked by the increased speed and volume of goods, messages and symbols which have largely been freed of spatial and temporal constraints by technological and communicational innovations. The advent of computer technology and satellite television, for instance, has had significant impact on the conceptualisation of time in the postmodern era (Heise, 1997). These innovations have also impacted on conceptualisations of space and consequently time–space dynamics. The information technology of the Internet has contributed to the creation of a space in which information circulates virtually without any temporal delay. Twenty-four-hour news visually juxtaposes quite different times and spaces, blurs any sense of distinction, and creates a culture of instantaneity and simultaneity. These technologies have given rise to the notion of 'technological time', which, according to Paul Virilio (1991), constructs a permanent present. Heise (1997) claims this is particularly evident in computer games where players become immersed in an extended present, detached from any sense of past or future, yet they are transported by the game to a multiplicity of ontological spaces. Not surprisingly, given the age of their primary audience, not many picturebooks focus on the effects of globalisation. However, as Bullen and Mallan note, theories of cultural globalisation offer a means of revealing how various globalising processes are expressed in children's narrative culture. By utilising a number of metafictive strategies, particularly irony and excess, as well as typographical experimentation, three postmodernesque picturebooks, *Il Libro piu corto del mondo*, *The Empty City* and *In the City*, address aspects of society emanating from the rise in global trends as discussed above.

Spirals of interconnectivity

Il Libro piu corto del mondo (Cox, 2002) draws attention to the constructed nature of both the book as an artefact and illustration as an artifice, particularly through typographical experimentation. The first is immediately evident from the physical construction of the book made of thick card with a spiral binding. The spiral disrupts the conventional notion (and function) of front and back covers and the linear approach of reading from beginning to end. The format therefore denies any sense of closure and uses typographical experimentation to provide multiple reading itineraries (there is no fixed starting point) and spatio-temporalities (there is no logical sequence or anchoring of images). In appealing to its target audience of very young children each page consists of a seemingly simple illustration rendered in primary colours. The repetition of the only written text, consisting of the one word *intanto*, meaning 'meanwhile', is the sole written evidence of a narratorial presence, and provides a tenuous narrative link between the images. These pictures, some 116 in all, consist of a wide diversity of images that range from a woman milking a cow by hand to a hospital operating theatre, a submarine, a factory working at night and another working by day. Other images reflect a range of activities associated with weapons, sport, leisure and weather events.

The motif of a clock is regularly, if randomly, repeated throughout the text. While the vast majority of images do not seem to be connected, some appear to be linked. For instance, there is an image of a figure atop a ladder picking a bunch of bananas while another image is of a peeled banana being proffered by an unseen person. In yet another sequence a man runs down a set of stairs, and in a later image what appears to be the same man runs up the same set of stairs while being filmed. Another image is of a lion tamer while a later image shows a circus tent. These images represent the connectivity of the globalised world, although in typical postmodern fashion there is no certainty that any of the links forged will remain constant or that they are indeed connected.

The title of the text: *Il Libro piu corto del mondo* (*The Shortest Book in the World*) with some 58 pages (remembering that the average picturebook is approximately 32 pages in length) cannot refer to the actual length of the text. Instead it refers to what Genette (1980) calls *durée*, or duration (the time covered by the story of the text or narrative time), which in this case is but a single second or instant, which again reinforces the notion that we live in an extended present detached from any sense of past or future (Allan, 2006). Thus, the clocks that randomly appear throughout the texts do not record the passage of time in the conventional sense, but rather show lives being lived, simultaneously, in different time zones throughout the world. This simultaneity, across time and space, reflects the postmodern contention that events are moments in time not necessarily linked to the past or future. Rather than being used as a narrative device, as is most often the case with spatio-temporal disjunctions in postmodern picturebooks, it is this self-reflexive attention to its own rending of the postmodern notion of time–space here that marks the postmodernesque. Beynon and Dunkerley (2000, p. 31) argue that the instantaneity of television allows viewers to be both 'here' and 'there'. This 'global immediacy' reflects the time–space compression of globalising forces and is derived in part from the capacity of media technologies and institutions to dislocate conventional notions of time and space (Tomlinson, 1991). This dislocation of time and space, a postmodern chronotope, will continue to be experienced through a range of technologies that includes advances in Virtual Reality technology. A global consciousness, rather than an inner consciousness characteristic of postmodern fiction, is also raised in *Il Libro*. Where once postmodernism was regarded as a phenomenon of the Western world, with the advent of, in particular, television and the Internet,[3] inhabitants of Third World countries are able to tap into, even if they cannot participate in, the events, lifestyles and consumer culture of the West (Boli and Petrova, 2007, p. 106). This is evident in *Il Libro* where perhaps the defining image in this respect is a figure in a coolie hat sitting on some stairs with what appears to be a laptop on the knee. This juxtaposition of traditional Eastern cultural accoutrement with Western technology seems to confirm the notion that postmodernism/globalisation is no longer confined to the West. Through the availability of global technology such as the Internet, globalisation spreads its influence throughout the world by increasing connectivity and raising global awareness. Thus, despite *Il Libro*'s appeal to the very young through its seemingly simple drawings, use of primary colours and thick card with spiral design, the picturebook is a sophisticated text that, through its inventive design, cleverly engages with issues of time and space, globalisation, interconnectivity and global consciousness. Another feature of postmodernity examined in two postmodernesque picturebooks – *The Empty City* and *In the City* – is the emergence of the globalised city.

A tale of two cities

The Empty City (Megarrity and Oxlade, 2007) documents a visit by a boy and his mother to the centre of a large city. Readers soon discover that the purpose of the shopping expedition is the crockery department in what appears to be a large department store. From the first opening the boy is shown as ambivalent about being dragged along on this trip with his mother. Overcome by boredom, the boy commits an unnamed/unseen transgression for which he is relegated to waiting outside the store while his mother delights in the 'proliferation of choice' on offer. As he becomes restless the boy begins to 'make mischief' in a similar manner to Max from *Where the Wild Things Are* (Sendak, 1963). The title page depicts the cityscape as a conglomeration of towering buildings, traffic, people, movement and signs all seen from the perspective of the young boy whose view is from a much lower point than that of the adults on the streets. This low-viewing position contributes to a sense of disorientation and possibly intimidation for the boy. This orientation is given a pictorial prolepsis and analepsis through the cover and endpapers with the bottom two-thirds black and top one-third scenes of people's shoes. The boy appears in the bottom right-hand corner, a position Kress and van Leeuwen term 'the unknown'. With hindsight it becomes clear that he is being dragged along by his mother who, perhaps in eager anticipation of the consumer goods waiting to be bought, has already left the scene. This positioning prompts readers to turn the page and thus promotes the narrative forward in the left to right direction of the Western style of reading.

The people represented in the visual texts are an eclectic mix of ethnicity, age, gender and possibly class, reflecting the 'migrating tribes' of globalisation. Their diversity is represented through a pastiche of colours, fabrics, textures and patterns which reflect Canclini's (2001) contention that globalisation does not lead to homogeneity as many fear, but rather fragmentation and recomposition. The connectivity of globalisation is also emphasised through the visual text, which includes a telephone booth, headphones, television sets for sale in shop windows, the movies and the, now inevitable, big screen which dominates public spaces and brings shoppers news and entertainment 24/7 (whether they want it or not). Yet many of the people have their eyes closed as if oblivious to those around them, seemingly intent on their own concerns. This orientation points to one of the ironies of the postmodern world that, despite being fully connected by way of the Internet and various forms of social media, people often fail to make face-to-face connections with those around them. The rectangular high-rise buildings in the foreground of the title page are rendered in black, so appear somewhat foreboding and remain unidentifiable, which reinforces the notion of the faceless corporations of the global world as described by Kellner and Pierce (2007). This city, despite its brightly coloured palette, does not appear to be a child-friendly space, nor is it a 'local' space. It is left up to the small boy to attempt to carve out some recognisably 'local' or familiar space for himself in this frenetic cityscape.

Once the boy has been banished from the department store he becomes increasingly bored waiting for his Mum. He causes chaos when he attempts to go up the down escalator. The chaos is only inferred *after* the event by the pile up of shoes at the bottom of the 'UP' escalator and his admonishment to himself 'Ooh. Better wait here for Mum.' Suddenly there is a shift in the text as he becomes aware that there are no people around. In a similar manner to Max, in Sendak's book, the boy seems to have created an escape through his imagination, although this is by no means certain. The city is now empty of people, traffic and other adult distractions, providing instead a city of child-friendly pursuits. He looks out of the text and turns his direct gaze upon the readers and asks: 'What would you do ... in an empty city?', thereby implicating readers in the 'rumpus' which follows. In the ensuing sequence of pages the boy navigates his way through a bewildering but exciting array of temptations such as fast food, music, cookies and chocolate, much in the way he might negotiate his way through a gamescape, ticking boxes and moving to the next level. In this, the boy characterises Jonathan Crissman's (2009, unpaginated) 'younger generation' who, unlike older generations (represented here by the boy's mother), 'has developed the ability to juggle a variety of different and, sometimes, opposing realities, futures, and possibilities' of postmodernity. The temptations or rewards on offer are all designed to appeal to a small child and all look very generic in their packaging and appeal, suggesting the McDonaldization of consumer products for children. The ultimate destination in this gamescape is Mr Crazy's, a toy shop which, the boy gleefully informs readers: 'is totally filled with ... STUFF!' There is a point in the toy shop when the boy is tempted to take something; the toys on display are the 'seductive goods' referred to in another context. Yet again he looks towards the reader and, by way of explanation, says: 'And who would you show it to anyway?' Perhaps this second-person address and question indicate that consumer goods only have merit when they can be displayed and coveted. He resists the temptation and moves on.

The toys that the shop stocks, however, are old-fashioned toys dating from previous eras, including train sets, rag dolls, castles, alphabet blocks, globes and a replica of the 'Blue Flame' racing car. They represent a nostalgic return to an idealised past through which the boy attempts to escape the inadequate present of the global city. David Lowenthal (1985) argues that nostalgia, while previously confined in time and space, now engulfs the whole past. And certainly these toys cover a diverse range of time periods. The past may be readily accessible through electronic and mechanical reproduction of images of the past, yet the boy cannot know the past of the toy shop from memory. He can only assemble a past that is projected by the artefacts in the toy shop. So, it is a constructed nostalgia which, in the end, cannot compete with the present which is all the boy has known. Ultimately the boy rejects the nostalgic escape offered by the toy shop and returns to the present. His return is heralded by the 'Welcome back!' he shouts to the people as they return to the visual text.

A subsequent opening is divided into four panels, each representing a different play on the words 'look' and 'out': Lookout – Look out – Look – Out; these connote a viewing space, a warning, an enticement and an exit. The final panel 'Out' shows a small lean-to on a rooftop which has an open door through which readers can see the boy's shoe and part of his lower leg disappearing inside. A sign above the door says Exit. This signals the boy's exit from the gamescape and anticipates his return to his mother. The return is reinforced by the following opening which has a display of plates similar to those in the department store and on some of which is written the message 'Now back to where you were first lost'. The ensuing opening reverts to gamespeak as he examines the escalator and says: 'Then back to where they start again [...] Up. Down. Around. Start again?' He goes down the Down escalator and reaches for his mother's outstretched hand. While the boy's mother, unlike Max's mother, is visible through the illustrative text, she is on the periphery of both the narrative itself and the visual text. In a similar manner to Max's mother, the boy's mother appears to remain unaware of his absence and appears to reward him for his transgression when, at his insistence, she returns to the toy shop with him and buys him a toy.

As alluded to earlier, the text is a revisioning of *Where the Wild Things Are*. Both are carnivalesque texts and in the tradition of carnivalesque literature the boy has had his moment on the carnival square which is marked by a temporary liberation from the established order, including the suspension of norms and prohibitions (Bakhtin, 1968, p. 75). This temporary suspension allows the boy to wander freely through the city without adult supervision or constraint, just as Max was able to be king of the wild things. Appropriately, *The Empty City*, written some 45 years after *Where the Wild Things Are*, has replaced the domestic space of Max's bedroom with the cityscape of a global metropolis. And rather than escape to a wild land as Max did, the boy in this text escapes into what appears to be a gamescape. This move heralds a shift from the carnivalesque to the postmodernesque. He is, whether he likes it or not, a child of the globalised world and must learn to navigate his way through the, at times, bewildering array of spaces, signs and goods on offer. Unlike Max, the boy is unnamed and this anonymity adds to the lack of identity of the global subject. In a reversal of the title-page opening the final opening shows the boy dragging his mother along the street towards the toy shop. He has a smile on his face and is pointing ahead in eager anticipation of the shopping spree to come. He has succumbed to the pleasures of the global city and its consumerist ethos. Similarly, the three siblings featured in the following picturebook, *In the City*, appear to revel in all that the globalised city has to offer.

In the City: Our Scrapbook of Souvenirs (Harvey, 2007) relates the details of three siblings, Frankie, Penny and Henry, who, along with their parents, travel from their home in the country to the city where their Uncle Kev lives. The only written text, in a conventional sense, is a series of journal entries (or perhaps blogs) written by the siblings reporting the events of each day. Their entries incorporate copies of other 'texts' such as newspaper bulletins, a questionnaire, photographs and a certificate. The blogs are placed on the far side of the verso pages so that readers who are used to the Western style of left-to-right reading will encounter them first. These playful accounts of the siblings' trip to an urbanised space could be viewed as mimetic representations of various forms of social media (Myspace, Facebook, Twitter) which create space for the (self-indulgent) musings of the postmodern subject. The majority of the commentary, however, is carried through the densely packed illustrations that include iconography, much of which constitutes playful, linguistic games. For instance, vehicles on the bridge in the first opening carry slogans such as *Tree-z-a crowd* and *'snappie' rubber bands*. In typical post-modern excess, the pages are also full of other texts: mainly signs comprising directions (Exit), place names (Lester Square), businesses (Golden Dragon) and so on.

As is characteristic of the postmodernesque picturebook, *In the City* interrogates notions of 'space' and 'place' in a globalised city. The represented city is depicted as a glocalised space as it contains many of the elements of a globalised city, while at the same time it includes a montage of characteristics of numerous cities in Australia which are identifiably Australian. For instance, there is an amusement park named Luna Park in the picturebook – Sydney and Melbourne both have amusement parks named 'Luna Park'. Another example is the suburb of Carlington which could be a combination of Carlton (Melbourne) and Darlington (Sydney). A play on the name Ma's Den may also be a reference to the suburb of Marsden in Brisbane. The bridge the family travel across on their arrival could be a conglomeration of Sydney Harbour Bridge, Westgate Bridge (Melbourne) or the Storey Bridge (Brisbane). The map on the endpapers includes Black Mountain (Canberra), complete with its landmark tall communications tower. There are no definable characteristics which enable readers to identify the city by a specific name or location as it is composed of hybrid suburbs and fragments of a number of cities. Despite some Australian qualities, the fragmentation and hybridity create a global, postmodern space which gives rise to a sense of place-lessness where one 'place' is less easily differentiated from another; Smethurst (2000, p. 33) suggests that: 'Cities and towns appear more uniform because the same signs, shops, building styles etc. can be found almost everywhere.' Nearby suburbs are marked on the map featured on the endpages as 'another suburb', 'another suburb' (and yet) 'another suburb', reinforcing Smethurst's (2000) notion of the 'undifferentiated suburbia' of the global city.

Globalisation, with its transglobal corporations,[4] has given rise to a proliferation of non-places or 'pseudo' places within cities such as airports, hotels and holiday villages, petrol stations and restaurant chains. These non-places, according to Smethurst (2000, p. 33), 'emulate place-bound familiarity but undermine essential characteristics of place'. In other words, while airports, hotels and restaurant chains strive to present a comforting sense of familiarity they lack any of the individualism that makes a 'space' a place. Similarly, the map on the endpapers of *In the City* abounds in 'pseudo' places which lack defining characteristics, but conform to a global standard. This conformity is playfully interrogated by labels such as 'Gov't Building', 'Big City' sign, 'Town Hall', 'China Town'. The only buildings to be labelled with any sense of 'place' are an office tower named as 'Uncle Kev's Office' and another which, with some irony, claims to be the '8th highest semi-resident'l tower in the world as we know it'. The marked points for generic China Town or Town Hall could be China Town or Town Hall for any major city in the world, much in the same way that a McDonald's or a Sheraton Hotel looks much the same everywhere in the world.

A postmodern sense of 'place' is never a finished construction, according to Smethurst (2000), but reaches backwards and forwards in time. The cityscape, as illustrated on a number of openings, represents the complexity of a global city with its high-rise, futuristic (forwards looking) buildings juxtaposed against buildings that reflect a cross-cultural influence with minarets, a Moorish-style building, a New York brownstone with its fire escape on the outside, alongside European-style domes (backwards looking). This complex hybridity, typical of postmodernity, looks back to the past as well as forward to the future and is playfully rendered through the juxtaposition on opening ten of both a medieval village complete with church and castle, and a number of futuristic buildings, such as a glass and steel helix. The atrium, too, is a typically postmodern space whose only use value, Woods (1999) suggests, is as spectacle. Other views of the cityscape include high-rise buildings in the shape of a pencil case, a double-door fridge and a milk carton, all of which reflect Nigel Watson's (2005, p. 42) contention that: 'postmodern buildings and cityscapes are characterized by a sensitivity to context and self-conscious playfulness in which different styles and references to different historical periods are mixed together in an ironic and eclectic way'. These buildings interrogate notions of homogeneity levelled at globalisation, by presenting a heterogeneity through ludic recomposition and resignification of architectural styles. Within this globalised cityspace the glocal emerges, bringing with it a sense of the local (for many Australian readers), but even this identification of the local is corrupted through language play.

The futuristic and fantastic architecture of the city contrasts sharply with the buildings in the suburb of Carlington which are both 'old and cool', according to Henry's blog. The architectural style used on the opening when the children visit Carlington reflects an identifiably traditional Australian domestic style with its tin roofs and overhanging verandas. While globalisation is, by its very definition, a worldwide phenomenon, there is a paradox at work. The development of a universal culture, which potentially could destroy any sense of national culture, may be seen by some as inevitable. However, the growth in activities at a local level to ensure the survival of local cultures is growing (Featherstone, 2007). The influence of globalising forces is somewhat tempered by a glocalising impulse whereby the global becomes integrated into the cultural particularities of local life. This is demonstrated with typical postmodern irony in this city where the city generally exhibits characteristics of a global city. However, specific local attractions – a 'Quaint Old Pub' and a statue of a 'Big Local', marked on the map on the endpapers – are named with a gentle sardonic humour. Other expressions of local flavour come in the form of an amusing play on words that alludes to well-known Australian children's writers and illustrators, which includes a block of apartments named Spud Villas, a park called Ruth Park and billboards outside a bookshop asking 'Is Marg Wild?' and 'Is Shaun Tan?' These 'in-house' puns refer to Australian authors and illustrators Anne Spudvilas, Ruth Park, Margret Wild and Shaun Tan.

The text also plays with the social, cultural and economic divides that exist between occupations which operate in either global or local arenas; a typically postmodern phenomenon. Opposite the shopping centre visited by the children (discussed below in the section on consumer culture), is a high-rise office building containing, among other offices, an information desk, a lecture theatre, a room full of computers (at one of which sits a skeleton) along with a number of offices in which workers are engaged (or not) in transactions in which they are disengaged from the output of their labour, thereby creating a sense of postmodern alienation. On the other hand, down at the wharves a bakery produces its daily bread, a shopkeeper places a sandwich board on the footpath, and fishermen ready their boats for a day at sea. Gentrification of the docklands, a particularly global pursuit, has not yet happened in this city. The watercolour washes of the early morning gloom evoke a sense of 'collective nostalgia' (Robertson, 1992, after Davis, 1974) for times past. Buildings appear to be aglow as they are lit from within by, in many cases, a single light. There is a sense of industry and purpose to the activities underway which forms a strong contrast with that of the workers in the city offices who are remote from the products of their labour.

At the same time that these activities are occurring, a number of questionable activities are taking place nearby. A fire has broken out in an old shed, while next door is the 'Dept. Of Suspicious Activities' outside of which is a parked van proclaiming to belong to 'ROBBERS R US' (a play on the global Toys R US brand and its many franchises). Douglas Goodman (2007, p. 37) says of globalisation that the poor will be invited to admire the seductive goods of the consumer society 'through a window of a locked door'. Knowing this, it is hardly surprising that some have taken it upon themselves to break down those doors and help themselves to the 'seductive goods' on show. While these activities provide some of the playfulness of the text and contribute to the multiplicity of reading paths available in the text they also point to the underbelly that exists in any large city. These localised activities represent the enactment of various *petits récits* within the urban landscape and contrast strongly with the frenetic activity of the city centre.

'Mediatization' of daily life

If globalisation is the defining feature of a postmodern society in the twenty-first century, then perhaps the defining feature of globalisation is the far-reaching influence of the mass media on all aspects of our lives. In fact, Tomlinson (2007, p. 81) argues that the media is an *'ensemble* of technologies and institutions which have become the dominant cultural form in our time, the mode and context of an increasing proportion of human experience [which has led to] the "mediatization" of daily life'. A number of postmodernesque picturebooks engage with aspects of the daily influence of mass media, demonstrating its pervasive and often intrusive presence. This influence takes two separate forms. On the one hand, it represents a range of technologies (particularly television and the Internet) that has facilitated the exponential growth of global trends in communications, technologies and cultural practices in recent years, which has contributed to the compression of the dynamics of time and space. This aspect of mass media has been discussed in relation to globalisation in the preceding section (*Il Libro*). On the other hand, the mass media, through its pervasive presence in everyday life, also provides multiple images, representations and simulations of life and culture. It is this aspect of mass media and its representation in postmodern-esque picturebooks which will now be addressed.

The centrality of the medium of television in everyday life is evident in a number of Lauren Child's picturebooks which feature the television set as a central element to the story. *Clarice Bean, That's Me* (1999) is focalised through the eponymous Clarice, who takes readers on a guided tour of her family, each member of whom seems to seek time to be alone. However, the final illustration is a double opening of Clarice and her whole family, along with a couple of 'extras' or transmigratory figures, gathered around the television set watching their favourite programme – *Martians in the Kitchen*. Even Clarice's angst-ridden teenage brother, Kurt, has emerged from his room to watch it. This is a particularly ironic scene of what passes as family life in the postmodern era. In previous generations many families would come together around the dining or kitchen table (or wireless), whereas this family's dining table, observed in the first opening, is covered in the general detritus of family life, which renders it redundant as a focal point for family gatherings. Instead, this role is now fulfilled by the television set, which is the focal point of the room and labelled 'Our TV' (labelled, presumably, by Clarice, who has labelled everything else in the room from her perspective). All the furniture in the room, including a couch, an armchair and a footstool, is arranged facing the television. Thus, the line of sight forms a transactional vector between the set and each of the viewers, and indicates the television's central role in the family's life; a centrality not featured in the postmodern picturebooks examined in earlier chapters where the focus is on interrogating aspects of liberal humanism (see *A Walk in the Park, Ooh-la-la (Max in Love)* and *Granpa*). Similarly, in the picturebook *My Uncle is a Hunkle Says Clarice Bean* (examined in Chapter 2), Clarice and her Uncle Ted watch westerns on television while dressed in cowgirl/boy clothes and eating egg and beans, appearing to be totally immersed in the action on the screen. When Grandad goes missing he is eventually found at a neighbour's house watching horse-racing on television. Clarice explains her grandfather's motivations as, 'Mrs Stampney's got a bigger television set.' Finally, when Clarice and her siblings are playing together under Uncle Ted's supervision, Clarice declares: 'we are like one of those families on your television who always say things like please and thank you and sorry'; such self-reflexivity also parodies the media's role in constructing 'the real' for many viewers. The text's emphasis on the dominant part television plays in the life of Clarice and her family resonates with the paradox of this medium that Butler (2002) makes in another context: on the one hand, television's presentation appears to be 'transparent' (in a similar manner to photography), on the other hand, so much of it is contradictory, commodified and motivated by economic interests it engenders a degree of postmodern scepticism.

Postmodern society is subjected to a saturation of sensory effects and images, in magazines and advertisements, and through television, radio and the Internet. While Derrien (2005, p. 173) writes of 'a flood of simultaneous messages' emanating from the media, Featherstone (2007) nominates the MTV television channel as the epitome of globalised television as its 24-hour format represents a 'timeless present'. In a similar manner, each page of *Il Libro* is framed in such a way as to directly call to mind images of a television or computer screen. The illustrations are constructed by utilising pixel-style dots which reinforce the suggestion of a communications screen, while the spiral design allows readers to flip through the images in a manner similar to that of viewers using a remote control to channel surf, or computer users surfing the 'net' – juxtaposing disparate times and spaces (Allan, 2006). As mentioned previously, the flexible spiral of the text allows a non-linear approach to the reading process, which enables readers to encounter differing sequences of images each time they engage with the text and choose to begin at a different point. Repetition in the text, with minor variations, is utilised when a soccer game is played 'live' in one scene, yet watched on the big screen by two children in another. In a third illustration the game is on television being viewed by two different children. This repetition raises questions of whether the game is being played and watched simultaneously or played at different times because of delayed telecast. Then again, perhaps this question of time delay is no longer relevant to television viewers. Just as the 'post-tourists' (discussed below) are content to experience the simulacra of theme parks instead of the 'real' thing so, too, sophisticated television viewers of the postmodern era are adept at channel surfing through differing times, genres and formats.

Television, too, has led to the creation of 'media spectacles', initially through coverage of various wars[5] and, more recently, political events such as the 2000 US Presidential Election and the 9/11 attacks in New York and Washington. However, other occasions, not only sporting events, natural disasters or war zones, but more localised occasions, have been sensationalised through excessive media coverage and hype. The concrete referent is no longer required to attribute meaning to its spectacle form which results in blurring the boundaries of each. *The Race of the Century* (Downard, 2008), with parodic playfulness, examines how the media, particularly television, has contributed to the 'production and construction' of otherwise ordinary events into major media affairs that then become defining features of the postmodern world and, therefore, subjected to playful scrutiny in postmodernesque picturebooks.

This text is a retelling of the Aesop fable of 'The Hare and the Tortoise'. While the moral of the story (slow and steady, rather than fast and flashy, wins the race) remains intact, this particular version is told through the hype and glamour of the media. Tom Tortoise, tired of constantly being taunted by Flash Harry Hare, challenges Harry to a race. With Harry's more-than-willing cooperation, the media turns the event into a spectacle. While Flash Harry prepares for the race by disco dancing à *la* Travolta,[6] Tom Tortoise takes to exercising with dumbbells made of pumpkins. Flash Harry lives up to his name in terms of his self-presentation and promotion, producing autographed posters to hand to his fans. By direct inversion Tom attempts to keep a low profile and trains at the somewhat dubiously named 'Jim's Gym: home of champiums'. Inevitably, news of the race spreads and it becomes a major media event: 'The Race of the Century was on every beak, muzzle and snout, as well as in every newspaper and magazine. It was even on TV!' The exclamation mark signals the kudos which comes with an appearance on television. It can also be read in terms of Baudrillard's (1983) ironic claim that it is not real unless it happens on TV. The event is broadcast 'live' around the world on CNN's Donkey's Wide World of Sport programme with anchorman, Don Key (who is literally a donkey with a perfect smile, toupee and false beard) – a parody of the globalised television programme *Wide World of Sport* and its commentators. The accompanying illustration features a double-page spread with a television set in the bottom left of the verso page out of which emanates a series of 'waves' which form transactional vectors connecting to a series of bubbles with an animal in each of the bubbles watching a television set featuring the race. The animals include a giraffe, penguins, reindeer and meerkats, playfully indicating the global reach of the programme.

The illustrative text is composed of what Downard refers to as 'photo illustration',[7] which consists largely of photographs that have been digitally manipulated, thereby rendering their authenticity provisional. The effect is a pastiche of styles, genres and periods, including visual references to reporters and photographers of the 1940s and 1950s with their pork-pie hats and large, external camera flashes. The television sets also date from an earlier era with manual dials and outmoded aerials – there are no plasma screens here. The start of the race is reminiscent of big American pageants and tickertape parades complete with brass bands, marching girls (cows), pennants, balloons and sponsorship (a pig playing a French horn is wearing a hat trimmed with gold braid and bearing the words *Critterville Croon* embroidered on it). The illustrations are littered with a variety of exclamations and exhortations: 'Gasp!!, Gosh! And Hoo-rays' reminiscent of the 1950s-style Superhero comics that reflects the rise of the nostalgia industry in which symbolic objects from the past are utilised to trigger a 'collective nostalgia' (Robertson, 1992, after Davis, 1974). It also represents a version of popular culture which has been manipulated by various groups who appropriate use of particular signs to further specific interests (Featherstone, 1995). Robertson (1992) argues that such acts of appropriation constitute a constructed nostalgia which is doubly globalised: by being 'collective' on a global scale and at the same time directed at (resisting) globality itself. Given the 1950s inflection of the illustrative text, the animal in the bottom corner of the verso page with what appears to be a modern, portable video camera recording the start of the race is an anachronism. In the small screen of the video camera, readers can see almost the exact scene on the double-page spread in front of them. This *mise-en-abyme* effect is a playful reference to the propensity for many people to remain glued to their video cameras recording an event rather than experiencing it as it happens. Typical of the postmodern viewer, they appear transfixed by the representation of the event, the simulation, rather than the real experience.

The race is surrounded by all the marketing and media hype associated with such events and there is no shortage of playful puns, both visual and verbal. Globally recognised brand names such as Sony ('Pony') and Toys R US ('Carrots R Us') are mocked, chooks eat plates of corn ('popcorn') while watching the race on television, and the rabbits are watching a Telebunnikins TV set. By contrast, Tom Tortoise remains persistent and dull throughout the challenge but his efforts are thwarted by the media coverage. While Flash Harry cultivates the attention of the media, Tom seems to despise it, signalled by his repeated 'hurrups'. Ironically, when Tom wins the race he too courts the media and appears to enjoy the attentions of the press. He uses it to pose with what appears to be a newspaper advertising placard proclaiming: 'Flash Harry Hare Has Bad Hare Day.' Tom has been seduced by the power of the media. In the postmodern world global citizens are not only seduced by the reach of the media but also by the goods on offer. The following texts, *In the City*, *The Short and Incredibly Happy Life of Riley* and *The Race of the Century*, display a range of, at times, conflicting attitudes towards aspects of the rampant consumption on open display in the globalised world.

A consuming culture

Jameson (1991) points to postmodernism as an expression of late capitalism in which knowledge and services, in the Western world in particular, are more important than the manufacturing and production of goods. Bauman (1998) suggests that where modernist society was a society of producers, the postmodern world is a society of consumers. This shift has led to changes in the production, consumption and circulation of cultural goods and practices in the West and other parts of the world. Featherstone (1995) recognises two such shifts and notes that postmodern consumption is no longer considered an outcome of production but is central to social reproduction. Consequently, consumer culture not only points to the increasing production and salience of cultural goods as commodities, but also to how the majority of cultural activities and signifying practices become mediated through the consumption of signs and images (of goods) – as well as the consumption of experiences and pleasure (leisure practices). The most common site of such consumption is the city – a postmodern space saturated with signs and images in which people come together in fluid, 'postmodern tribes' consuming goods and experiences (Featherstone, 2007). The picturebook *In the*

City is a good example of a postmodern site in which consumption of goods, services and signs proliferates. The unnamed city offers a cacophony of sights, sounds, people and experiences as well as spectacles, interactivities and consumer products.

The shift from production to consumption has seen shopping become a legitimate leisure activity: a shift that began in modernity but has accelerated since the end of the twentieth century through globalisation processes. A visit to 'the biggest store in town' (*In the City*) emphasises the consumption of goods and shopping as a leisure activity of postmodernity. The profile drawings, almost cartoon in style, reveal multiple levels of separate departments within the one store. Shoppers appear to be engaged in a frenzy of consumption as these huge shopping malls are designed to keep people moving, diverted and entertained in order to avoid time spent devoid of commercial value. Each department is full of shoppers inspecting goods, trying on clothes, playing with toys and buying. Not only is each of these departments devoted to a particular group of products (toys, camping and wilderness equipment, hats, books) but also within each of these departments there is a playful proliferation of choice that is typical of postmodernity. For instance, in the hat department shoppers can buy, not only ladies hats, but also canoe hats, chest hats as well as 'hats for cats'. This proliferation of choice is replicated in the book department with cook books, crook books, chook books, took books, science friction and diction fiction on offer. While there is an element of linguistic playfulness to this range of hats and books, it also subtly alludes to what Watson (2005) refers to as the generation of false needs by the advertising industry and Bauman's (1998) argument that providers must seduce consumers in order to outdo their competitors. Signs, too, proliferate: 'Ask about our free offer!!', 'BARGAINS', 'Launch in city today', 'Complaints', 'Lifts' and so on which adds to the confusion and creates an overload of instructions. It is not so much that the text highlights consumption *per se* but rather it is the playful parody of the proliferation of signs and choices which marks it as postmodernesque.

Great cities, as cosmopolitan places, embody notions of globalisation in the way inhabitants and visitors experience them. Bauman (1998, p. 25) argues that: 'the water well has been abolished', meaning that the traditional focal point of local communities has been lost and been replaced by artificially constructed city squares such as the square featured in *In the City*. At the centre of this square, replacing Bauman's water well, is, ironically, a pool in the shape of a grand piano on which the stairs, painted black and white, represent the keys. Nothing is as it appears and the pool only has decorative value rather than any functional use. The square is full of shoppers and spectators surrounded by businesses, particularly restaurants, which supports the notion that in the postmodern era, just like shopping, eating has become a leisure activity. Further activities in the square include buskers and various other forms of entertainment as well as strollers and spectators. A key feature of the consumer culture, according to Featherstone (1995), is the fragmentation and overproduction of culture. Cultures from around the world are represented on the streets of globalised cities, and judging from the playful references to the array of cuisines, languages and consumer experiences available in the square, this city typifies Featherstone's point. The city square is a patchwork of 'denationalized ethnic and folk motifs' (Goodman, 2007, p. 342) masquerading as shop signs, '*Ristorante*', advertisements and place names such as 'Broccoli est Bene et Verdi'. The translation of the latter (Broccoli is good and green) indicates the playfulness at work. The text parodies the postmodern appropriation of cultural difference as a resource through which to tempt consumers. The presence of a town crier and a date plaque (1321) on one building demonstrate that the antiquities of the city are appropriations from European city cultures rather than being typically Australian. (The latter is an impossible date as Australia was not settled by Europeans until 1788.) Goodman (2007) claims that cultural difference becomes a resource of the postmodernist, consumerist culture which randomly draws upon diverse cultures for its ever-changing, new-and-improved content – such a consumer culture is represented in this text.

The consumer society is no longer restricted to the consumption of goods but extends to the consumption of sensations and experiences. The children's blogs document trips to the zoo, the beach and a hot-air balloon ride, all of which position the participants as spectators who revel in the experiences and sensations on offer. Featherstone (2007) argues that museums and galleries, once restricted sites of high art and institutions of learning, have discarded their exclusive label to cater for wider audiences where the emphasis is on: 'the spectacular, the popular, the pleasurable and the immediately accessible'

(p. 94). This blurring of boundaries between high and popular art, as well as surrendering to the world of simulation and hyperreality (all features of postmodernity), is celebrated in the text *In the City*. The children visit the city museum in which the foyer is given over to a display on 'Where did I come from?' which features a giant ovum being bombarded by balloons tied with coloured string to represent sperm. Other exhibits playfully feature a 'Prince of Whales', and 'Arctic Python' with the warning 'Do not thaw'; these are included along with the familiar museum objects such as dinosaurs, Indigenous artefacts, snakes and early model cars. The most prominent display is the 'Giantest Scientist', an extremely large model of a man (presumably a scientist) in which visitors enter through his mouth, continue on through his intestines, and exit from his anus, by way of his alimentary canal, down a slide into a wading pool. This model is supposedly an instrument of learning but presents as a carnivalesque figure of the grotesque in which the 'lower, bodily functions' (Bakhtin, 1968) are celebrated and a parodic inversion of the museum's former standing as an elite institution of learning. *In the City* celebrates the popular appeal of such simulations through an excess of activity, colour and playfulness but in true postmodernist style avoids making any direct value judgements other than the use of a mildly ironic tone.

   A further effect of globalisation is that culture is used as an attraction for capital development and tourism (Goodman, 2007). Spencer (2005) asserts that among the culture industries, it is the heritage industry which has experienced the most sustained boom. Thus, a different simulation is encountered when the siblings visit what Penny claims is the oldest part of town but which appears to be a replicated historical village in the style of, for example, Sovereign Hill near Ballarat in Victoria, Australia,[8] which demonstrates Spencer's (2005) claim that every aspect of the past has been mediated, packaged, presented and represented. According to Penny's blog, activities include: 'a kid's gallery with dress-ups and DVDs of the olden days and you can be an orphan and I saw a chimney sweep and convicts!' The slippage in language here is interesting as Penny seems to recognise the 'unreality' (or hyperreality) of the village where, on one hand, 'you can [pretend to] be an orphan' but then she claims to have seen a (real) chimney sweep and convicts. Here she fails to make any distinction between the 'real' people and those merely playing a role – the boundaries have been blurred for Penny. Such appropriation of the past epitomises the postmodern process, where a past is nostalgically recreated as a form of substitute reality (Watson, 2005). As this text illustrates, consumers pay their money and in return are entertained by consuming second-hand experiences which once formed the basis of everyday life. This is the power of the simulacrum where the hyperreal replaces the real.

In her blog Penny also displays a black and white postcard and comments: 'This postcard was from when everything was black and white.' This comment resonates with the point raised in Chapter 4 of the difficulties of representing the past from a position in the present. While Penny and her brothers may experience a simulated version of the 'olden days', it can only offer them various reconstructions of past realities. The black and white postcard reinforces the postmodern message that simulations and representations of the past will always (re)produce an incomplete picture of history and must therefore be seen as provisional. This understanding could be extended to the provisionality of all simulations, not just of history. It is also possible to see Penny's statement as referring to nostalgia or misremembering of the days when life was seemingly clear-cut and unambiguous, not mediated through a flood of images, simulations and hyperrealism. Featherstone (2007) argues that resorts, theme parks and museums provide spectacles and simulations for today's 'post-tourists' who seek the: 'surface sensations and spectacular imagery, liminoid experiences and intensities without the nostalgia for the real' (p. 59). His point accords with Berger's (2003, p. 15) assertion that: 'Representations of the real have become stand-ins for actual, lived experience.' The post-modernesque element of this is the inference that these post-tourists know that what they are witnessing has little relation to the real, but they are happy to accept that, as thrill and pleasure are paramount compared with authenticity and the real. This preference can be seen in an example from the Outback Spectacular on the Gold Coast in Australia. Visitors are aware that, despite the advertising hype on the website,[9] this is not the 'real' thing. However, as Berger (2003) points out, what is 'real' then becomes judged against the simulated productions which usurp reality in such a way that reality pales in comparison to the 'blockbuster' experience.

Another text that comments on the consumer society and its propensity for consumption for consumption's sake is the picturebook

The Short and Incredibly Happy Life of Riley (Thompson and Lissiat, 2005). The picturebook is fairly conventional in its linear narrative and sense of closure; however, it also incorporates the playful and parodic appropriations of a number of famous paintings (*Mona Lisa* and *The Scream*), a pastiche of illustrative techniques, as well as a number of different framing styles. Added to these stylistic features is the text's comment on consumerism as a feature of postmodernity, all of which contribute to the postmodernesque status of this picturebook. This text compares the simple life of Riley, a pink rat who is extremely happy with his simple lot ('He was always happy, even when he was asleep'), with that of a generic group 'people', epitomised by the character of Norman, who seeks all things bigger, better, faster: 'People, of course, want more than that.' The consumption of food in the Western world has little to do, any longer, with the notion of hunger and/or health but rather excess (as implied by the text). While Riley is content with 'some fruit and maybe a couple of slugs on Tuesday or Friday', people want 'double-fudge-chocolate-caviar-sausage-gourmet-jumbo [...] burger'. This declaration is accompanied by an illustration of an adult and child representing the grotesque bodies of the carnivalesque in which hair and bulging flesh predominate. The small child is gorging on a jumbo-sized burger, dripping with cheese, from which protrudes what looks to be a cat's paw. This particular text depicts postmodernity's consumption as greed, whereas the market scene in *In the City* celebrates not only abundance, but also variety and sensation. Goods, too, are consumed and superseded as suggested by the illustrative text in *Riley* of an old car made up of a multitude of wheels and cogs, with a mix of old and new technologies including a gramophone alongside an iPod which seems to playfully evoke the notion of 'collective nostalgia' discussed previously. Featherstone (1995) argues that consumption is no longer a simple appropriation of utilities, or use values, but a consumption of signs and images. A rat as the figurehead on the front of the bonnet of a car is a parody of the more refined emblems used by prestigious companies such as Rolls-Royce (Flying Lady) and Jaguar (sleek jaguar) to signify power and status. The text seems to suggest that as luxury goods gain greater prestigious signification they become more readily desired in order to provide social gratifications. Thus, this text illustrates Goodman's point that use values and consumer practices are socially constructed and integrate individuals into global consumer society.

The culture-ideology of rampant consumerism of postmodernity is characterised by a belief that the meaning of life is to be found in the things we possess (Goodman, 2007). This point is mocked in the picturebook *Riley*: '[People] want microwave-video-dvd-sms-internet-big-car-cost-more-than-yours [...] electronic-gigabyte-fastest- [...] machines'. The running-on of the words suggests the haste and excessive desires that characterise the urgency to consume. It would seem that to consume is to be fully alive. The irony is that, with goods rapidly becoming obsolete or passé, one must continue to consume in order to stay abreast of trends to achieve any sort of cultural cachet or existence. The obsessive consumption, epitomised by Norman, in this picturebook, has broadened in recent years to become the art of living whereby the home, car and body are all regarded as extensions of one's persona (Featherstone, 2007) and must, therefore, be stylised, updated and constantly replaced. Such obsessions have seen the emergence of new cultural intermediaries (after Bourdieu) such as chefs, interior designers and beauty therapists who replace the doyens of high art as the new taste masters. Featherstone argues that these trends result in general stylistic promiscuity and playful mixing of codes typical of postmodernity. These trends are evident in the visual text of *The Short and Incredibly Happy Life of Riley*.

Desire impacts on identity and postmodern subjectivity and, because individuals lack a coherent identity, they seek products to reinforce and affirm whatever subject position they occupy at any given moment (Berger, 2003), or they use products to construct a more desirable one. While Riley looks in the mirror and simply sees 'Riley', people, including Norman, 'want to be taller-shorter- [...] -smooth-skin-golden-sun-tan-gorgeous-irresistible' and so on. In Lacanian terms desire never survives its satisfaction: it is necessary to constantly pursue new desires. Thus, when Norman succeeds in winning the attention of one woman, he is already thinking of another, while she, too, is thinking of other things. When he is at a holiday resort he is always already moving on. Norman represents the decentred subject of postmodernity, restlessly enjoying experimentation and play with fashion and stylisation, while constantly seeking new sensations and experiences ('seaside-ski-resort-paradise-world-castaway-exclusive [...] anywhere-but-here-theme-park') through the playful exploration of transitory experiences and surface aesthetic effects. The tenor of the text (*Riley*) accords with Featherstone's observation that obsessive consumption and seeking of sensation through 'the enjoyment of the immediate, sensory, "grotesque" bodily pleasures of the popular classes' (2007, p. 71) characteristic of the postmodern world, is not the answer. Instead, as Riley notes with old-fashioned common sense, 'the answer is very simple, really – you just have to be happy with a lot less'. This contention highlights the paradox of the postmodern/esque picturebook discussed in the Introduction. While these picturebooks undoubtedly bear traces, both stylistically and thematically, of the influence of postmodernism, they often revert to a liberal humanist position of conventional children's texts. This text, *The Short and Incredibly Happy Life of Riley*, privileges the stable, coherent identity that is Riley and interrogates the fragmented subject of postmodernity as represented by Norman.

Constructions of self through consumption

Flash Harry Hare of *The Race of the Century* also represents a postmodern subject. Rather than the restless experimentation and consumption exercised by Norman, Harry selects cultural resources which contribute to the construction of a particular subjectivity for a particular time and place. This accords with Goodman's (2007) assertion that within the context of consumer culture cultural elements represent an individual choice in a cultural supermarket to be mixed and matched to suit an individual style. This choosing from a cultural supermarket to construct an individual style is evident in Harry's preparation for the big race. Not only does he train for the physical demands of the race, he also carefully constructs a subjectivity through which to appeal to the anticipated global audience. This is similar to the actions of pop stars such as Madonna, for instance, who, according to Beynon and Dunkerley (2000, p. 31), is best regarded not as a person but rather as 'a carefully crafted, polysemic "text", composed of a set of signifiers to guarantee her appeal to a multi-segmented global audience [including ...] teenage girls, heterosexuals, gays, lesbians or ethnic audiences'. Harry constructs himself as a branded sports star like Beckham, for instance. Through the appropriation and adoption of consumer goods he constructs a subjectivity that is dialogic: it is formed through different cultural discourses of the global society in which he lives, and he hopes it will meet with approval. He adopts the logo, Flash Harry Hare (not unlike the red Coca-Cola logo), and emblazons it in red across the chest of his running gear. Other cultural signifiers adopted by Harry include designer, wraparound sunglasses and RbK runners (a subsidiary trademark of the popular Reebok brand). These contemporary cultural commodities contrast with references to the 1950s discussed earlier, yet form part of the pastiche of styles so typical of postmodernity and exploited by the text.

Harry also works on his body which becomes a site (and sight) of commodified perfection. The illustrative text shows a toned body with broad shoulders, narrow hips and well-developed 'pecs'. He stands posing with clenched fists and muscles flexed. While Harry is primarily pitching his appeal to the rabbits (or is it the bunnies?), like Madonna he seeks a broader audience. For instance, Mallan (2009, p. 168) points out that: 'Harry's pink T-shirt, tight-fitting blue pants and poses invoke a homoerotic aesthetic, despite his posturing as a heterosexual stud.' As noted above, Harry also courts the media in his efforts to win over his target audience. He poses for photographs, has signed posters to hand out to his fans and displays an ego to match. (The poster proclaims Harry as 'Critterville's Greatest Athlete'.) Goodman (2007) suggests that cultural resources and individual choices are connected in a global system of meaning that is created and reproduced through the practices of consumption. This trend could provide an explanation for Harry's decision to wear sunglasses; a decision not governed by their use value, but rather for their cultural cachet – why else would he be wearing them disco dancing in an already darkened room? Certainly, observation of the illustrative text, especially the audience response to Harry's particular choice of signifiers, suggests his efforts are successful. He attracts a crowd of cheering fans gathered specifically to see him, as opposed to the 'menagerie' at the start of the race that is there more for the spectacle than any outcome of the actual race. His defeat strips him of his subjectivity and his loss of status highlights the transience of sports commodities.

In this section, each of the three main texts examined with regards to consumer consumption offers different positions on the subject. *In the City* celebrates a consumer subjectivity that revels in the proliferation of choice of consumer goods, *The Race of the Century* reveals the rise and fall of a commodified subjectivity shaped by the media and advertising, while *The Short and Incredibly Happy Life of Riley* advocates a restrained consumption ('You just have to be content

with a lot less') and challenges its own postmodernesque procliv-
ity by endorsing a unified subject (Riley) – one that is essentially
unchanging. These latter points are not isolated examples as they
reflect earlier contentions that postmodern (and postmodernesque)
picturebooks often revert to a consensual, liberal humanist position
that is more aligned with the general tenor of children's literature
than with the postmodern condition.

In reviewing the selection of texts examined in this chapter (and the
preceding chapters), it must be remembered that, while there will
be cross-over texts which could be categorised in either group, the
essential difference between postmodern and postmodernesque picturebooks is that the former interrogate aspects of liberal humanism
while the latter engage with characteristics of postmodernity. Those
aspects of the postmodern world which particularly occupy the
postmodernesque texts under discussion in this chapter pertain to
globalisation and its associated domains of mass media and consumerism. Canclini (2001) argues that globalisation is not characterised
by homogenisation, but by fragmentation and recomposition into
hybrid cultural forms. *Il Libro piu corto del mondo*, with typical postmodern detachment, raises issues of both connectivity and global
consciousness, particularly through typographic experimentation
and repetition, with minor variations. *In the City* playfully examines
issues concerning the role of the postmodern city in a globalised
world, issues of place and space, and consumer consumption, including the consumption of diverse cultural experiences and spectacles.
The Short and Incredibly Happy Life of Riley addresses postmodernism's
obsession with consumerism and its effects on the construction of
identity and subjectivity, while *The Race of the Century* celebrates
consumption and the potential of the mass media to engage with
a global audience and construct a marketable subjectivity. These
diverse narrative responses to the complex concerns of postmodernity characterise the postmodernesque picturebook.

(In)Conclusion: Looking Forward

> The postmodern world may be more unsettling than the modern-
> ist world it replaced, but it is, at the very least, much more excit-
> ing. (Berger, 2003, p. 100)

Throughout this book I have considered how postmodernism offers a
way through which to observe the world and provides a lens through
which to view history, interpret reality and (re)consider unity. In
line with Berger's comment above, postmodern fiction may urge, or
even force, its readers and critics alike to reconsider previously fixed
notions of both fiction and the discourses usually represented within
that fiction. However, it also opens the possibilities to engage with
the texts in entirely new and exciting ways. My approach throughout this book has been to raise issues, draw attention to strategies,
acknowledge inconsistencies, but also to delight in the playfulness
and subversion within the texts under discussion. Whether it is
possible to arrive at any definite conclusions is another matter. In a
similar manner to the postmodern enterprise itself, rather than seek
conclusions I merely offer a number of observations.

Postmodern picturebooks

Children's writers and illustrators are very much a part of the cultural
and intellectual milieux that postmodernism has engendered so it
is hardly surprising that traces of postmodern influences would be
evident in their work. However, it was never the intention of this
book to provide a finite definition of the *postmodern picturebook*.

As noted in the Introduction, that is a rather futile exercise and one fraught with dangers. Rather, the intention has been to extend readers' understandings of the ways in which picturebooks have been influenced by postmodernism, both stylistically and ideologically. It should be apparent, from a reading of this book, that the postmodern picturebook is a complex and evolving genre which utilises the visual and verbal dynamic to create a multifaceted text that is playful and has a tendency towards resistance if not subversion of both narrative conventions and aspects of society. Postmodern picturebooks employ a pastiche of styles and generally defy categorisation. They are playful, parodic and ironic; they resist closure and offer multiple points of view through both the verbal and visual texts. Postmodern picturebooks blur boundaries between high and popular culture, promote the position of the marginalised, create uncertainty and generally provide a space for resistance. They achieve all, or some of this, by utilising postmodern literary strategies, including metafictive strategies, such as parody, intertextuality, metalepsis and polyphony. Further, postmodern picturebooks playfully exploit the interanimation between the visual and verbal codes of the picturebook genre to draw attention to the constructed nature of narrative and the naturalised values and attitudes embedded within these narratives. The influence of postmodernism on picturebooks has also given rise to a number of paradoxes.

A particular paradox of children's literature is that while the field is often marginalised as an area of creative endeavour and academic study, it is also often regarded as a 'sacred' site in that children's texts are subjected to far greater scrutiny than adult texts. This seems to have been particularly observed with regards to picturebooks suspected to have been influenced by postmodernism. This trend is evident as far back as 1963, with the publication of *Where the Wild Things Are* by Maurice Sendak. This picturebook received criticism and censure from a number of groups (such as parents, librarians, publishers) that felt that the text was not suitable for children. Ironically, it has since gone on to become one of the most popular picturebooks[1] of all time and recently was made into a film. Nodelman (2008, p. 157) argues that such (initial) criticism stems from an adult belief that children are 'innocent and inexperienced' and it is the adults' duty to teach children what they don't know while protecting them from 'things they ought not to know about'.

He goes on to suggest (p. 158) that adults commonly believe that children need protection from some knowledge and experience of the world; this extends to the literature offered to children and results in a genre which tends to be both exclusionary and didactic. The opposition to postmodern literature for children and young adults, which has been regularly expressed over the years, seems to stem from such attitudes towards children's literature.

And yet, children's texts have a tradition of being both compliant and resistant. Compliance is evident in their tendency to take a route around a truly radical or iconoclastic position. However, carnivalesque literature is one example of the more subversive routes that children's texts can take, but even these texts generally return to the status quo. This is another of the paradoxes of postmodern picturebooks. On the one hand, these texts show signs of postmodernism's attack on liberal humanism and modernism; on the other, they are often caught up in proposing aspects of a liberal humanist perspective and adopting modernist strategies. This contradictory position is evident in several of the picturebooks discussed in the preceding chapters, particularly *Voices in the Park* and *The Three Pigs* examined in Chapter 1. Therefore, while delighting in transgressive behaviour, the texts also attempt to foster socio-cultural values in order to enculturate children into the prevailing ways of the society in which they live. In doing so, however, the picturebooks may undermine the postmodernist influences otherwise evident in the texts. Thus, the texts are caught between the transgressive impulses of postmodernism and the didacticism of traditional (modern) children's literature. This 'in-between' or ambivalent status is most apparent in the emergence of the *postmodernesque* picturebook. My designation of the postmodernesque is based on my observation of the emergence of a number texts, published since the turn of the century, that draw attention to particular features of postmodernism and the conditions of postmodernity rather than to aspects of liberal humanism. Texts discussed in Chapter 6 include *Il Libro piu corto del mondo*, *The Empty City* and *The Race of the Century*.

Resistance to conventional approaches has made a space for the development of the postmodern/postmodernesque picturebook. While postmodern fiction typically disrupts the conventions of realist fiction, picturebooks already constitute a genre that is 'in-between': not strictly 'realist' fiction, but also not simply 'not realist'. Most of the picturebooks under discussion actively seek to draw readers' attention to the narrative processes that are common to realist texts and often employed in conventional picturebooks. This attention-seeking is achieved by making explicit the conventions and strategies of realist fiction through metafictive devices, playfully creating uncertainty, fragmentation and ambiguity within their narratives, rather than offering readers the certainty, coherence and resolution of more conventional, realist picturebooks. However, as Waugh (1984, p. 18) asserts, there is often a fine line between 'realistic' and 'postmodern' fiction: very often realistic conventions supply the 'control' in metafictional texts, the norm against which the experimental strategies can foreground themselves. This self-consciousness contributes to a paradox of postmodern fiction that Hutcheon (1988) notes: while seemingly subversive, postmodernism works from within the very systems it is challenging; it is both complicitous with and critical of prevailing norms. Postmodern and postmodernesque picturebooks contribute to this paradox in similar ways, and is most vividly illustrated in my discussion of frames and frame-breaking in Chapter 1, although reference is made to it throughout the book, particularly in relation to picturebooks such as *The Stinky Cheese Man and Other Fairly Stupid Tales*, *Black and White*, *Wolves*, *Wait! No Paint!* and *Il Libro piu corto del mondo*.

Ceci n'est pas une finale

Currently the influence of postmodernism on the picturebook is, as indicated throughout this book, undergoing a series of shifts and changes; the postmodernesque is one indication of how playfulness is becoming almost commonplace in many picturebooks, and, as such, risks losing the surprise and shock of the postmodern provocative style. Furthermore, announcements of the demise of postmodernism, at least within adult literature, have been broadcast for over a decade but its influence continues in one form or another (Hassan, 2001; Lewis, 2001; McLaughlin, 2004; Kirby, 2006). These same commentators mentioned here are looking to the future with predictions of post-postmodernist texts. Others believe that narratives will continue to be influenced by aspects of postmodernism while taking up issues surrounding the politics of identity under the umbrella term of postcolonialism[2] (Hassan, 2001). The discussion of

A Coyote Columbus Story is one example of a text that exhibits both postcolonial and postmodern influences. The cycle of influence of postmodernism on the picturebook may be slightly behind that experienced by the adult novel, but as some examples of postmodernesque picturebooks demonstrate, an interrogation of liberal humanist discourses is being replaced by a mocking of postmodernism itself, as witnessed in the discussion of such texts as *The Short and Incredibly Happy Life of Riley* and *In the City* in Chapter 6. Fittingly, perhaps, the direction of postmodernism's influence on the picturebook at the current time is similar to the postmodern phenomenon itself: it is ambiguous, fragmented and decentred, where the boundaries remain in constant flux creating not a homogeneous collection but a range of hybrid texts defying categorisation (despite attempts to categorise, such as 'postmodernesque'). Magritte's playful caption 'Ceci n'est pas une pipe' under his image of a pipe intended to point out that while we may come close to depicting something, we can never capture the real item itself. The same applies to the postmodern picturebook. There will no doubt be more playing with picturebooks ahead.

Play on!

Notes

Introduction: Looking Back

1. Bertens (2001, p. 7) indicates that the philosophical notions commonly referred to as liberal humanism are a cluster of ideas coming out of an Arnoldian tradition which is based on the autonomy and self-sufficiency of the individual (our legal system for instance is based on the premise of individual autonomy). This liberal humanist view characterises much of our contemporary literature, promoting notions of 'eternal' truths and presenting the ways of the world as 'natural' rather than constructed. Hutcheon (1988, pp. 13, 58) posits that the humanistic principles of value, order, meaning, control and identity are still operative in our culture but for many are no longer seen as eternal and unchallengeable. Postmodernism, including postmodern fiction, interrogates these once-accepted certainties of liberal humanism.
2. For further discussion on 'multiliteracies' and 'new literacies' see, for instance, Anstey (2002), Pantaleo (2010). Such terminology stems from recognition of the increasing 'multimodality' of the picturebook. Maria Nikolajeva (2008b) also offers the term 'intermediality' in this regard.
3. 'iPad generation' may be more applicable at the time of writing but will, no doubt, also become redundant or at least passé as technology continues to produce new products and capabilities.
4. Hassan (2001, pp. 6–7) attributes the early use of the term to, among others, Toynbee (although as early as 1939), Bernard Smith (1945) and, in the 1950s, Charles Olsen. He concludes with the comment that Irving Lowe (1959) and Harry Levin (1960) argue that postmodernism intimates a decline in high modernist culture. McHale (1987) argues that it is not so clear who should get the credit (or blame) for coining the term but suggests Toynbee, Olson and Jarrell as possible contenders.
5. Jameson (1991) further argues that at some point following World War II a new kind of society began to emerge in which new types of consumption, planned obsolescence, rapid fashion and styling changes, as well as the penetration of advertising, television and media unparalleled in their influence on society, all signalled a radical break with the older pre-war society in which high modernism was a force.
6. For further discussion on these points see Featherstone (2007, pp. 2–12), who writes of the 'family of terms' associated with postmodernism which can best be understood by contrasting them to those terms derived from 'the modern'. He contrasts modernity with postmodernity, modernism with postmodernism and so on.

7. For instance, the ontology of a fairy-tale world will be quite different in many respects from that of a science-fiction one although they may contain a number of general ontological characteristics shared by all literary worlds.

8. Historiography: the principles, theories and/or methodologies of scholarly historical research and presentation.

9. A number of writers from within a Marxist tradition, including Fredric Jameson (1991), Christopher Norris (1990, 1993) and Terry Eagleton (1997), have found fault with the theories and practices of postmodernism, particularly with postmodernism's pragmatism in the face of the utopian visions of both modernism and Marxism.

10. For further extensive discussion of this see Nodelman (2008).

11. With the exception perhaps of *The Stinky Cheese Man and Other Fairly Stupid Tales* which, Lewis concedes, could be labelled postmodern. Brian McHale (1987), however, argues that, while not all modes of contemporary writing should be labelled postmodern, neither should the definition be applied too narrowly. McHale uses the example of the declaration that Paul Celan is the only 'true' postmodern poet. McHale argues if that is the case there would be no need to discuss 'postmodern poetry' but rather the poetry of Paul Celan. Taken to extremes, Lewis' argument could see the establishment of a *Stinky Cheese Man* subgenre of picturebooks.

12. These early examples, like the later works of Joyce, Woolf et al., were not generally recognised as forerunners of postmodernism until much later.

13. This is similar to Jameson's (1991, p. 4) claim that the works of modernists such as Picasso and James were, by the 1950s, no longer regarded as 'ugly' as a result of canonisation and academic institutionalisation of the modern movement by that time.

14. Australian boorishness is known as Ockerism, from a slob-like character called Ocker in a television series. It is the embodiment of oafish, blinkered self-satisfaction.

15. Or 'late capitalism', which is Jameson's preference (1991).

16. Bret Easton Ellis, Jay McInerney, Tama Janowitz, Dennis Cooper and Douglas Coupland, for instance (see Woods, 1999; Nicol, 2009).

1 Looking Beneath the Surface

1. As Stephens and Watson (1994, p. 44) note, there are attempts to date metafictive application as far back as Chaucer. *Don Quixote* (1605) by Cervantes is generally recognised as the first metafictive novel while Sterne's *Tristram Shandy* (1759–67) is acclaimed as the most celebrated metafiction in the English language (Ommundsen, 1993, p. 59).

2. The introduction of self-reflexivity in the picturebook was initially driven by the work of author/illustrators such as John Burningham, Anthony Browne and Maurice Sendak, while more recent exponents include Chris Van Allsburg, David Macaulay, Lauren Child, David Wiesner, Shaun Tan and Tohby Riddle.

3. Widely known as Barthes' (1977) 'Death of the Author' statement.

4. Analepsis or flashbacks are often used to recount events that happened prior to the story's primary sequence of events or to fill in crucial details that occurred before the time of the narrative. Similarly, prolepsis, which is the strategy of flashforward, details events related to narrative which happen in the future.

5. McHale (1987) refers to such characters as 'transworld identities' who belong to different fictional worlds and bring with them intertextual and ontological traces of those worlds.

6. An extension of polyphony is evident in Bakhtin's notion of *heteroglossia*. Heteroglossia also presents multiple, often fragmented voices, yet differs from polyphony in that the multiple voices of heteroglossia are more likely to be antagonistic and competing (Morris, 1994, pp. 248–52). An example of this is offered in the adult fairy tale *Snow White* (Barthelme, 1967). Nicholas Sloboda (1997, pp. 117, 121) posits that Barthelme creates a heteroglossia which juxtaposes fragments of discourses, imagery and narratives without co-ordinating these pieces into an overall or predetermined design. Rather, ideas are presented, affirmed and challenged within a mosaic or textual collage which creates an open-ended text that rejects synthesis.

7. Kristeva's view accords with Barthes' proclamation on the 'Death of the Author' (1977) in which he argues that the 'Author' of a text can no longer be considered as the sole source of textual authority (p. 148).

8. The Soviet formalist scholar Vladimir Propp argued (in *Morphology of the Folktale*, 1928) that all fairy tales were constructed of certain plot elements, which he called functions, and that these elements consistently occurred in a uniform sequence.

2 Destabilising Modes of Representation

1. Baloney is an American slang word for nonsense thereby signalling that the tale *is* nonsense.

2. Interestingly, the picturebook *Previously* (Ahlberg and Ingman, 2007) also implies that Jack of Jack and the Beanstalk and Jack of 'Jack and Jill' fame are one and the same character.

3 Disturbing the Air of Reality

1. The original story by Robert Southey (1873) was in fact entitled *The Story of the Three Bears*, which makes Goldilocks' attitude in this text all the more outrageous.

2. Lehr (2008, p. 176) labels this Goldilocks 'the Paris Hilton of the story'.

4 Interrogating Representations of the Past

1. I also acknowledge that a number of postmodern picturebooks target an older audience.

2. The Moreton Bay Fig is a rainforest tree which can grow up to 50 metres in width so is an excellent shade tree for parks. It has large buttress roots.
3. Translated from the Latin, *terra nullius* means 'land that belongs to no one', www.mabonativetitle.com/tn_01.shtml
4. A billabong is a branch of a river made by water flowing from the main stream when the water level is high but which then becomes an isolated waterhole during drier times.
5. From an essay on Tan's website: see www.shauntan.net/essay2.html
6. The term 'Stolen Generations' is used for Aboriginal people who were forcefully taken away (stolen) from their families between the 1890s and 1970s, in many cases never to see their parents again. Because the period covers many decades we speak of 'generations' (plural) rather than 'generation', www.creativespirits. info/aboriginalculture/politics/stolen-generations.html#stolen-generations-guide. Read more: www.creativespirits.info/aboriginalculture/politics/stolen-generations.html#stolen-generations-guide#ixzz1kQoP35kF
7. See Tan's website: www.shauntan.net/essay2.html
8. The Penticton area was first inhabited by the Okanagan Natives, a branch of the Interior Salish. They were traditionally a hunting and gathering society. The name Penticton was derived from the native word 'pentktn', which means 'a place to stay forever'. Perhaps this symbolised a utopian space to which to escape from Columbus? www.learnforestry. com/lessons/grade3/2007/timeline_penticton.pdf
9. The Argentinians refer to the conflict as the Malvinas War, which also points to the ways in which history is told from different perspectives.
10. www.ppu.org.uk/falklands/falklands3.html
11. There is a more recent edition of this book called *The Discovery of Dragons: New Research Revealed* (2007) by Graeme Base. This second edition includes most of the material from the original edition along with the addition of an extra chapter on the discovery of dragons of the New World by Francisco de Nuevo. However, I felt that, for the purposes of this chapter, this new addition was less appropriate than the original.

5   Problematising Unity through Ex-centricity and Difference

1. Interview with Tohby Riddle, www.magpies.net.au/magpies/public/? Mlval=m_pages&pagename=MCI_E
2. www.tohby.com/Tohby_Riddle-Sunday_Age.html
3. Although, in a piece of playful intertextuality, the mother in *The Lost Thing* (Tan, 2000) is reading a newspaper which exhibits a headline 'Flamingo Recaptured'.
4. This assumption is based on a number of markers in the text, including the appropriation of paintings of Melbourne landmarks: John Brack's *Collins St., 5pm* (1955) and *Cahill Expressway* (1962) by Jeffrey Smart.

5. Both Dudek (2005) and Stephens (2008) label the city as industrial, while Mallan (2005) also sees it as post-industrial.
6. Another Tan picturebook, *The Arrival* (2006), deals directly with immigration and its attendant sense of defamiliarisation and alienation. However, the new Arrival in the text by the same name, unlike the lost thing, eventually becomes familiar with his new space and makes a place for himself and his family.
7. Well-known Australian cartoonist Michael Leunig, www.leunig.com.au/

6 Towards the Postmodernesque Picturebook

1. Robertson and White are noting the widespread usage of the term in academia rather than the existence of the phenomenon of globalisation.
2. *McDonaldization* was coined by Ritzer (1993) in response to the global rationalisation and commodification of goods and services in a similar manner to the operation of the McDonald's franchise. Barber (1995) however labels the thrusts of homogeneity *McWorld*, with its consumer freedom, and heterogeneity *Jihad*, representing tribal separatism with the two worlds feeding off each other.
3. Butler (2002, p. 117) describes the Internet as a typically postmodern phenomenon as it is (currently) a non-hierarchised, indeed disorganized, collage.
4. Such as McDonalds, CNN, Microsoft, Shell, MTV among others. See Kellner and Pierce (2007), for instance.
5. The Vietnam War was the first conflict to be brought into people's living rooms via television coverage.
6. Harry is depicted in a white suit in a scene that cites John Travolta's character of the disco-dancing stud in the film *Saturday Night Fever* (1977).
7. www.barrydownard.com/3.Bio.html
8. Sovereign Hill is a replica village near Ballarat, Victoria, Australia presenting the story of Australia's gold rush history. It is a living museum with a strong emphasis on working machinery and exhibits, costumed interpreters and visitor participation, www.sovereignhill.com.au/
9. For instance: 'Every aspect of the venue has been well thought out and planned to give the arena a truly unique and authentic Australian look and feel. From the fully themed Australian landscape with great iconic Australian natives and scenic backdrops, the Arena sand which evokes Australian outback, the corrugated iron roof and galvanised railings and heavy timbers that are used throughout the arena to the old fashioned wagon wheel light fittings, and the winding billabong located under the entrance bridge – the venue truly feels and looks like a traditional outback shearing shed located in the Outback. You will become truly immersed in the spirit and grandeur of the Australian Outback from the moment you step through the arena doors. You can pull up a stool at the Aussie pub and whet your whistle. Doors to the Aussie Pub open approximately one hour prior to show time for your opportunity to relax

and purchase beverages during the Pre-show entertainment.' http://outbackspectacular.myfun.

(In)Conclusion: Looking Forward

1. *Where the Wild Things Are* has been one of the most recognised and most popular of its genre since its publication in 1963. The book has sold an estimated 19 million copies and won the 1964 Caldecott Medal as the 'Most Distinguished Picture Book of the Year'. http://fantasyfilms.suite101.com/article.cfm/in_theaters_where_the_wild_things_are
2. Postcolonialism, in its widest possible application, to include not only texts dealing with the postcolonial experience of colonised peoples but also peoples colonised by any hegemonic discourse such as patriarchy, heterogeneity and so on.

Bibliography

Primary

Ahlberg, Janet and Ahlberg, Alan (1986) *The Jolly Postman and Other People's Letters*. Boston: Little, Brown.

Ahlberg, Alan and Ingman, Bruce (2007) *Previously*. London: Walker Books.

Banyai, Istvan (1995) *Zoom*. New York and London: Viking.

Barthelme, Donald (1967) *Snow White*. New York: Atheneum.

Base, Graeme (1996) *The Discovery of Dragons*. Melbourne: Penguin Books.

Base, Graeme (2007) *The Discovery of Dragons: New Research Revealed* (2nd edn). Camberwell, Victoria: Viking.

Briggs, Raymond (1984) *The Tin-Pot Foreign General and the Old Iron Woman*. London: Hamish Hamilton.

Browne, Anthony (1977) *A Walk in the Park*. London: Hamilton.

Browne, Anthony (1986) *Piggybook*. London: Walker Books.

Browne, Anthony (1998) *Voices in the Park*. London: Doubleday

Browne, Anthony (2001) *Willy's Pictures*. London: Walker Books.

Burningham, John (1977) *Come Away from the Water, Shirley*. London: Jonathan Cape.

Burningham, John (1984) *Granpa*. London: Jonathan Cape.

Champion, Tom and Singleton, Glen (2008) *Cindy-ella*. Sydney: Scholastic.

Child, Lauren (1999) *Clarice Bean, That's Me*. Cambridge, MA: Candlewick Press.

Child, Lauren (2000a) *I Will Not Ever NEVER Eat a Tomato*. London: Orchard Books.

Child, Lauren (2000b) *My Uncle is a Hunkle Says Clarice Bean*. London and Sydney: Orchard Books.

Child, Lauren (2000c) *Beware of the Storybook Wolves*. London: Hodder Children's Books.

Child, Lauren (2002) *That Pesky Rat*. London and Sydney: Orchard Books.

Child, Lauren (2003) *Who's Afraid of the Big Bad Book?* London: Orchard Books.

Cole, Babette (1986) *Princess Smartypants*. London: Hamilton.

Cole, Babette (1992) *Prince Cinders*. London: Picture Lions.

Cox, Paul (2002) *Il Libro piu corto del mondo* (*The Shortest Book in the World*). Rome: Corraini Editore.

Crew, Gary (1991) *Strange Objects*. Port Melbourne, Victoria: Mammoth Australia.

Crew, Gary and Tan, Shaun (1999) *Memorial*. Port Melbourne, Victoria: Lothian.

Downard, Barry (2008) *The Race of the Century*. New York: Simon & Schuster.

Felix, Monique (1988) *The Story of a Little Mouse Trapped in a Book*. London: Methuen.

Gravett, Emily (2006) *Wolves*. London: Macmillan Children's Books.

Gravett, Emily (2007) *Little Mouse's (Emily Gravett's) Big Book of Fears*. Oxford: Macmillan Children's Books.

Harvey, Roland (2007) *In the City: Our Scrapbook of Souvenirs*. Crows Nest, New South Wales: Allen & Unwin.

Hobbs, Leigh (2001) *Horrible Harriet*. Sydney: Allen & Unwin.

Kalman, Maira (1991) *Ooh-la-la (Max in Love)*. New York: Penguin/Viking.

King, Thomas and Monkman, William Kent (1992) *A Coyote Columbus Story*. Toronto: Groundwood Books.

Lendler, Ian and Martin, Whitney (2005) *An Undone Fairy Tale*. New York and London: Simon & Schuster Books for Young Readers.

Macaulay, David (1990) *Black and White*. Boston: Houghton Mifflin.

Marsden, John and Tan, Shaun (1998) *The Rabbits*. Melbourne: Lothian Books.

McMillan, Dawn and Kinnaird, Ross (2002) *Why do Dogs Sniff Bottoms?* Auckland: Reed (NZ) Publishers.

Megarrity, David and Oxlade, Jonathon (2007) *The Empty City*. Sydney: Hachette Livre Australia.

Muller, Jorg (2002) *El llibre dins el llibre dins el llibre (A Book in a Book in a Book)*, trans. Hilary Hughes. Barcelona: Ediciones Serres.

Muntean, Michaela and Lemaitre, Pascal (2006) *Do Not Open This Book!* New York: Scholastic Press.

Riddle, Tohby (1997) *The Great Escape from City Zoo*. Sydney: Angus & Robertson.

Riddle, Tohby (2000) *The Singing Hat*. Melbourne: Penguin.

Riddle, Tohby (2008) *Nobody Owns the Moon*. Melbourne: Penguin/Viking.

Scieszka, Jon and Johnson, Steve (1991) *The Frog Prince Continued*. New York: Viking

Scieszka, Jon and Smith, Lane (1989) *The True Story of the 3 Little Pigs!* London and New York: Puffin Books.

Scieszka, Jon and Smith, Lane (1992) *The Stinky Cheese Man and Other Fairly Stupid Tales*. New York: Viking Penguin.

Scieszka, Jon and Smith, Lane (2001) *Baloney (Henry P.)*. New York: Puffin Books.

Sendak, Maurice (1963) *Where the Wild Things Are*. New York: Harper & Row.

Snow, Alan (1993) *How Dogs Really Work*. London: HarperCollins.

Tan, Shaun (2000) *The Lost Thing*. Melbourne: Lothian Books.

Tan, Shaun (2001) *The Red Tree*. Melbourne: Lothian Books.

Tan, Shaun (2006) *The Arrival*. Melbourne: Lothian Books.

Thompson, Colin and Lissiat, Amy (2005) *The Short and Incredibly Happy Life of Riley*. Melbourne: Lothian Books.

Van Allsburg, Chris (1995) *Bad Day at Riverbend*. Boston: Houghton Mifflin.

Whatley, Bruce (2001) *Wait! No Paint!* Sydney: HarperCollins.

Wiesner, David (2001) *The Three Pigs*. New York: Clarion Books.

Secondary

Adams, Rachel (2007) The End of America, the Ends of Postmodernism. *Twentieth Century Literature*, 53(3), pp. 248–72.

Albrow, Mike (1997) *The Global Age: State and Society beyond Modernity.* Stanford University Press.

Allan, Cherie (2006) Stop All the Clocks: Time in Postmodern Picture Books. *Papers: Explorations into Children's Literature,* 16(2), pp. 77–81.

Allen, Graham (2000) *Intertextuality.* London and New York: Routledge.

Ang, Ien (1996) *Living Room Wars: Rethinking Media Audiences for a Postmodern World.* London and New York: Routledge.

Anstey, Michelle (2002) It's Not All Black and White: Postmodern Picture Books and New Literacies. *Journal of Adolescent and Adult Literacy,* 45(6), pp. 444–58.

Antonio, Robert (2007) The Cultural Construction of Neoliberal Globalization. In G. Ritzer (ed.) *The Blackwell Companion to Globalization.* Malden, MA and Oxford: Blackwell, pp. 67–83.

Appadurai, Arjun (ed.) (2001) *Globalization.* Durham, NC: Duke University Press.

Bacchilega, Cristina (1997) *Postmodern Fairy Tales: Gender and Narrative Strategies.* Philadelphia: University of Pennsylvania Press.

Bader, Barbara (1976) *American Picture Books from Noah's Ark to the Beast Within.* New York: Macmillan.

Bakhtin, Mikhail (1968) *Rabelais and His World,* trans. Helene Iswolsky. Bloomington: Indiana University Press.

Bakhtin, Mikhail (1981) *The Dialogic Imagination: Four Essays,* trans. C. Emerson and M. Holquist. Austin: University of Texas Press.

Bakhtin, Mikhail (1984) *Problems of Dostoevsky's Poetics,* ed. and trans. Caryl Emerson. Manchester University Press.

Bal, Mieke (1985) *Narratology: An Introduction to the Theory of Narrative,* trans. C. van Boheemen. University of Toronto Press.

Barber, Benjamin (1995) *Jihad vs McWorld.* New York: Times Books.

Barker, Chris (1999) *Television, Globalization and Cultural Identities.* Buckingham: Open University Press.

Barth, John (1984) Literature of Exhaustion. In *The Friday Book: Essays and Other Non-Fiction.* London: Johns Hopkins University Press, pp. 62–76.

Barthes, Roland (1972) *Mythologies,* trans. Annette Lavers. New York: Noonday Press.

Barthes, Roland (1976) *The Pleasures of the Text,* trans. Richard Miller. London: Cape.

Barthes, Roland (1977) The Death of the Author. In *Image-Music-Text,* trans. Stephen Heath. New York: Hill & Wang, pp. 142–8.

Barthes, Roland (1981) Theory of the Text. In Robert Young (ed.) *Untying the Text: A Post-structuralist Reader.* London: Routledge, pp. 31–47.

Baudrillard, Jean (1983) *Simulations.* New York: Semiotext(e).

Bauman, Zygmunt (1998) *Globalization: The Human Consequences.* Cambridge: Polity Press.

Beckett, Sandra (ed.) (1999) *Transcending Boundaries: Writing for a Dual Audience of Children and Adults.* New York: Garland Publishing.

Beere, Diana (2000) *Nurturing Ideology: Representations of Motherhood in Contemporary Australian Adolescent Fiction.* Brisbane: Griffith University.

Belsey, Catherine (2002) *Critical Practice*. London: Routledge.

Berger, Arthur (2003) *The Portable Postmodernist*. New York: Altamira Press.

Bernstein, Richard J. (1992) *The New Constellation: The Ethical-Political Horizons of Modernity/Postmodernity*. Cambridge, MA: MIT Press.

Bernstein, Richard (2006) An Allegory of Modernity/Postmodernity: Habermas and Derrida. In Lasse Thomassen (ed.) *The Derrida–Habermas Reader*. University of Chicago Press, pp. 71–97.

Bertens, Hans (1997a) The Debate on Postmodernism. In H. Bertens and D. Fokkema (eds) *International Postmodernism: Theory and Literary Practice*. Amsterdam and Philadelphia: John Benjamins, pp. 3–14.

Bertens, Hans (1997b) The Sociology of Postmodernity. In H. Bertens and D. Fokkema (eds) *International Postmodernism: Theory and Literary Practice*. Amsterdam and Philadelphia: John Benjamins, pp. 103–18.

Bertens, Hans (2001) *Literary Theory: The Basics*. London and New York: Routledge.

Best, Steven and Kellner, Douglas (1991) *Postmodern Theory: Critical Interrogations*. New York: Guilford.

Beynon, John and Dunkerley, David (eds) (2000) *Globalization: The Reader*. New York: Routledge.

Bhabha, Homi (1994) *The Location of Culture*. London and New York: Routledge.

Boli, John and Petrova, Velina (2007) Globalization Today. In George Ritzer (ed.) *The Blackwell Companion to Globalization*. Malden, MA and Oxford: Blackwell, pp. 103–24.

Bradford, Clare (1993) The Picture Book: Some Postmodern Tensions. *Papers: Explorations into Children's Literature*, 4(3), pp. 10–14.

Bradford, Clare (ed.) (1996) *Writing the Australian Child: Texts and Contexts in Fictions for Children*. Nedlands, WA: University of Western Australia Press.

Bradford, Clare (2001) *Reading Race: Aboriginality in Australian Children's Literature*. Carlton, Victoria: Melbourne University Press.

Bradford, Clare (2007) *Unsettling Narratives: Postcolonial Readings of Children's Literature*. Waterloo, Ontario: Wilfrid Laurier University Press.

Bradford, Clare, Mallan, Kerry, Stephens, John and McCallum, Robyn (2008) *New World Orders in Contemporary Children's Literature: Utopian Transformations*. New York: Palgrave Macmillan.

Brooker, Peter (ed.) (1992) *Modernism/Postmodernism*. London and New York: Longman.

Bullen, Elizabeth and Mallan, Kerry (2011) Local and Global: Cultural Globalization, Consumerism, and Children's Fiction. In Kerry Mallan and Clare Bradford (eds) *Contemporary Children's Literature and Film: Engaging with Theory*. Basingstoke: Palgrave Macmillan.

Butler, Christopher (2002) *Postmodernism: A Very Short Introduction*. Oxford University Press.

Caldwell, Melissa and Lozada, Eriberto (2007) The Fate of the Local. In George Ritzer (ed.) *The Blackwell Companion to Globalization*. Malden, MA and Oxford: Blackwell, pp. 498–515.

Canclini, Garcia (2001) From National Capital to Global Capital: Urban Change in Mexico City. In Arjun Appadurai (ed.) *Globalization*. Durham, NC: Duke University Press.

Cashmore, Ellis and Rojek, Chris (eds) (1999) *Dictionary of Cultural Theorists*. London: Arnold.

Certeau, Michel de (1975) *L'Ecriture de l'histoire*. Paris: Gallimard.

Cobley, Paul (2001) *Narrative*. London: Routledge.

Collins, Louise (2002) The Virtue of 'Stubborn Curiosity': Moral Literacy in *Black and White*. *The Lion and the Unicorn*, 26(1), pp. 31–49.

Connor, Steven (ed.) (2004) *The Cambridge Companion to Postmodernism*. Cambridge University Press.

Crismann, Christopher (2009) *Postmodern Space*. http://crisman.scripts.mit. edu/blog/?p=188

Crook, Stephen, Pukulski, Jan and Waters, Malcolm (1992) *Postmodernization: Change in Advanced Society*. London: Sage.

Culler, Jonathan (1975) *Structuralist Poetics: Structuralism, Linguistics and the Study of Literature*. London: Routledge & Kegan Paul.

Culler, Jonathan (1996) Fabula and Sjuzhet in the Analysis of Narrative: Some American Discussions. In S. Onega and J. Landa (eds) *Narratology: An Introduction*. New York: Longman.

Culler, Jonathan (1997) *Literary Theory: A Very Short Introduction*. Oxford University Press.

Culler, Jonathan (2007) *The Literary in Theory*. Stanford University Press.

Darby, David (2001) Form and Context: An Essay in the History of Narratology. *Poetics Today*, 22(4), pp. 829–52.

Davis, F. (1974) *Yearning for Yesterday: A Sociology of Nostalgia*. New York: Free Press.

Deleuze, Gilles and Guattari, Félix (1987) *A Thousand Plateaus: Capitalism and Schizophrenia*, trans. Brian Massumi. Minneapolis: University of Minnesota Press.

Derrida, Jacques (1976) *Of Grammatology*, trans. Gayatri Spivak. Baltimore: Johns Hopkins University Press.

Derrien, Marie (2005) Radical Trends in French Picturebooks. *The Lion and the Unicorn*, 29(2), pp. 171–89.

Doonan, Jane (1993) *Looking at Pictures in Picture Books*. Stroud: Thimble Press.

Doonan, Jane (1999) Drawing out Ideas: A Second Decade of the Work of Anthony Browne. *The Lion and the Unicorn*, 23(1), pp. 30–56.

Downard, Barry (2010) *Barry Downard – Photo Illustration*. www.barrydownard. com/

Dresang, Eliza (1999) *Radical Change: Books for Youth in a Digital Age*. New York: H. Wilson.

Dresang, Eliza (2008) Radical Change Theory, Postmodernism, and Contemporary Picturebooks. In L. Sipe and S. Pantaleo (eds) *Postmodern Picturebooks: Play, Parody, and Self-Referentiality*. New York and London: Routledge, pp. 41–54.

Dudek, Debra (2005) Desiring Perception: Finding Utopian Impulses in Shaun Tan's *The Lost Thing*. *Papers: Explorations into Children's Literature*, 15(2), pp. 58–66.

Eagleton, Terry (1986) *Against the Grain: Essays 1975–1985*. London: Verso.

Eagleton, Terry (1996) *Criticism and Ideology: A Study in Marxist Literary Theory* (2nd edn). London: Humanities Press.

Eagleton, Terry (1997) *The Illusions of Postmodernism*. Oxford: Blackwell.

Fantasy Films (2011) Where the Wild Things Are on *Fanstasy Films website*. http://fantasyfilms.suite101.com/article.cfm/in_theaters_where_the_wild_things_are

Featherstone, Mike (1995) *Undoing Culture: Globalisation, Postmodernism and Identity*. London: Sage.

Featherstone, Mike (2007) *Consumer Culture and Postmodernism*. Los Angeles and London: Sage.

Foucault, Michel (1973) *The Order of Things: An Archaeology of the Human Sciences*. New York: Vintage Books.

Freeman, Elizabeth (2005) Monsters, Inc.: Notes on the Neoliberal Arts Education. *New Literary History*, 36(1), pp. 83–96.

Frow, John (2002) The Literary Frame. In B. Richardson (ed.) *Narrative Dynamics: Essays on Time, Plot, Closure, and Frames*. Columbus: Ohio State University Press, pp. 333–8.

Fuery, Patrick and Mansfield, Nick (2000) *Cultural Studies and Critical Theory*. Oxford University Press.

Gardner, John (1978) *On Moral Fiction*. New York: Basic Books.

Genette, Gerard (1980) *Narrative Discourse*. Oxford: Blackwell.

Genette, Gerard (1997) *Paratexts: Thresholds of Interpretation*, trans. Jane E. Lewin. Cambridge University Press.

Geyh, Paula (2003) Assembling Postmodernism: Experience, Meaning, and the Space in Between. *College Literature*, 30(2), pp. 1–29.

Gilbert, Alan (2006) *Another Future: Poetry and Art in a Postmodern Twilight*. Middletown, CT: Wesleyan University Press.

Glesne, Corrine and Peshkin, Alan (1992) *Becoming Qualitative Researchers: An Introduction*. New York: Longman.

Goldstone, Bette (2001) Whaz up with our Books?: Changing Picture Book Codes and Teaching Implications. *The Reading Teacher*, 55(4), pp. 362–70.

Goldstone, Bette (2008) The Paradox of Space in Postmodern Picturebooks. In L. Sipe and S. Pantaleo (eds) *Postmodern Picturebooks: Play, Parody, and Self-Referentiality*. New York and London: Routledge, pp. 117–29.

Goodman, Douglas (2007) Globalization and Consumer Culture. In G. Ritzer (ed.) *The Blackwell Companion to Globalization*. Malden and Oxford: Blackwell, pp. 330–51.

Gottdiener, Mark (1995) *Postmodern Semiotics: Material Culture and the Forms of Postmodern Life*. Oxford: Blackwell.

Grieve, Ann (1993) Postmodernism in Picture Books. *Papers: Explorations into Children's Literature*, 4(3), pp. 15–25.

Grieve, Ann (1998) Metafictional Play in Children's Fiction. *Papers: Explorations into Children's Literature*, 8(3), pp. 5–15.

Hall, Christine (2008) Imagination and Multimodality: Reading, Picturebooks, and Anxieties about Childhood. In L. Sipe and S. Pantaleo (eds) *Postmodern Picturebooks: Play, Parody, and Self-Referentiality*, New York and London: Routledge, pp. 130–46.

Haraway, Donna (1985) A Cyborg Manifesto: Science, Technology, and Socialist-Feminism in the Late Twentieth Century. Reprinted in N. Spiller (ed.) (2002) *Cyber Reader: Critical Writings for the Digital Era*. London and New York: Phaidon.

Harvey, David (1990) *The Condition of Postmodernity: An Enquiry into the Origins of Cultural Change*. Oxford: Blackwell.

Hassan, Ihab (2001) From Postmodernism to Postmodernity: The Local/ Global Context. *Philosophy and Literature*, 25(1), pp. 1–13.

Hassan, Ihab (2003) Beyond Postmodernism: Towards an Aesthetics of Trust. In K. Stierstorfer (ed.) *Beyond Postmodernism: Reassessments in Literature, Theory, and Culture*. Berlin: Walter de Gruyter, pp. 199–212.

Heise, Ursula (1997) *Chronoschisms: Time, Narrative, and Postmodernism*. Cambridge University Press.

Held, David and Moore, Henrietta (eds) (2008) *Cultural Politics in a Global Age: Uncertainty, Solidarity and Innovation*. Oxford: Oneworld.

Hoberek, Andrew (2007) Introduction: After Postmodernism. *Twentieth Century Literature*, 53(3), pp. 233–47.

Hodge, Bob and Mishra, Vijay (1990) *Dark Side of the Dream: Australian Literature and the Post-Colonial Mind*. Sydney: Allen & Unwin.

hooks, bell (1990) Postmodern Blackness. *Postmodern Culture* 1(1), www.sas.upenn.edu/African_Studies/Articles_Gen/Postmodern_Blackness_18270.html

Hunt, Peter (ed.) (1992) *Literature for Children: Contemporary Criticism*. London and New York: Routledge.

Hutcheon, Linda (1984) *Narcissistic Narrative: The Metafictional Paradox*. New York: Methuen.

Hutcheon, Linda (1985) *A Theory of Parody*. New York and London: Methuen.

Hutcheon, Linda (1988) *A Poetics of Postmodernism: History, Theory, Fiction*. New York: Routledge.

Hutcheon, Linda (1989) *The Politics of Postmodernism*. London: Routledge.

Hutcheon, Linda (1995) Nostalgia, Irony, and the Postmodern. www.library.utoronto.ca/utel/criticism/hutchinp.html

Hutcheon, Linda (2002) *A Poetics of Postmodernism* (2nd edn). London: Routledge.

Iser, Wolfgang (1978) *The Act of Reading: A Theory of Aesthetic Response*. London: Routledge.

James, Kathryn (2002) Scatology, Taboo and the Carnivalesque. *Papers: Explorations into Children's Literature*, 12(3), pp. 19–27.

Jameson, Fredric (1983) Postmodernism and Consumer Society. In Hal Foster (ed.) *The Antiaesthetic: Essays on Postmodern Culture*. Port Townsend, WA: Bay Press.

Jameson, Fredric (1991) *Postmodernism, or The Logic of Late Capitalism*. London and New York: Verso.

Jencks, Charles (1991) Postmodernism versus Late Modernity. In Ingeborg Hoesterey (ed.) *Zeitgeist in Babel: The Postmodernist Controversy*. Bloomington: Indiana University Press, pp. 4–8.

Jenkins, Keith (1991) *Re-thinking History*. London and New York: Routledge Classics.

Jones, Kathryn (2006) Getting Rid of Children's Literature. *The Lion and the Unicorn*, 30(3), pp. 287–315.

Joseph, Sarah (1998) *Interrogating Culture: Critical Perspectives on Contemporary Social Theory*. New Delhi: Sage.

Kaplan, Deborah (2003) Read All Over: Resolution in Macaulay's *Black and White. Children's Literature Association Quarterly*, 28(1), pp. 37–41.

Keep, Christopher, McLaughlin, Tim and Parmar, Robin (2001) Postmodernism and the Postmodern Novel, www.iath.virginia.edu/elab/hfl0256.html

Kellner, Douglas and Pierce, Clayton (2007) Media and Globalization. In George Ritzer (ed.) *The Blackwell Companion to Globalization*. Malden, MA and Oxford: Blackwell, pp. 383–95.

Kirby, Alan (2006) The Death of Postmodernism and Beyond. *Philosophy Now* (February/March), www.philosophynow.org/issue58/58kirby.htm

Korff, Jens (2010) *Australia's Stolen Generations*. www.creativespirits.info/ aboriginalculture/politics/stolen-generations.html#stolen-generations-guide

Kort, Wesley (2004) *Place and Space in Modern Fiction*. Gainesville: University Press of Florida.

Kress, Gunter and van Leeuwen, Theo (2006) *Reading Images: The Grammar of Visual Design*. London: Routledge.

Kristeva, Julia (1969) *Sémèiôtikè. Recherches pour une sémanalyse*. Paris: Éditions du Seuil.

Kristeva, Julia (1986) Word, Dialogue, and the Novel. In T. Moi (ed.) *The Kristeva Reader*. New York: Columbia University Press, pp. 35–61.

Kummerling-Meibauer, Bettina (1999) Metalinguistic Awareness and the Child's Developing Concept of Irony: The Relationship between Pictures and Text in Ironic Picture Books. *The Lion and the Unicorn*, 23(2), pp. 157–83.

Lehr, Susan (2008) Lauren Child: Utterly and Absolutely Exceptionordinarily. In L. Sipe and S. Pantaleo (eds) *Postmodern Picturebooks: Play, Parody, and Self-Referentiality*. New York and London: Routledge, pp. 164–79.

Leunig, Michael (2009) *The Michael Leunig Website*. www.leunig.com.au/

Lewis, Barry (2005) Postmodernism and Fiction. In S. Sim (ed.) *The Routledge Companion to Postmodernism* (2nd edn). London and New York: Routledge, pp. 111–12.

Lewis, David (1990) The Constructedness of Texts: Picture Books and the Metafictive. *Signal*, 61–3, pp. 131–46.

Lewis, David (2001) *Reading Contemporary Picturebooks: Picturing Text*. London: Routledge Falmer.

Lowenthal, David (1985) *The Past is a Foreign Country*. Cambridge University Press.

Lucy, Niall (1997) *Postmodern Literary Theory: An Introduction*. Oxford and Malden, MA: Blackwell.

Lucy, Niall (ed.) (2000) *Postmodern Literary Theory: An Anthology*. Oxford: Blackwell.

Lyon, David (1999) *Postmodernity* (2nd edn). Buckingham: Open University Press.

Lyotard, Jean-François (1984) *The Postmodern Condition: A Report on Knowledge*, trans. G. Bennington and B. Massumi. Minneapolis: University of Minnesota Press.

Mackey, Margaret (2003) 'The Most Thinking Book': Attention, Performance and the Picturebook. In M. Styles and E. Bearne (eds) *Art, Narrative and Childhood*. Stoke-on-Trent: Trentham Books.

Mackey, Margaret (2008) Postmodern Picturebooks and the Material Condition of Reading. In L. Sipe and S. Pantaleo (eds) *Postmodern Picturebooks: Play, Parody, and Self-Referentiality*. New York and London: Routledge, pp. 103–16.

Mallan, Kerry (1999a) *In the Picture: Perspectives on Picture Book Art and Artists*. Wagga Wagga: Charles Sturt University.

Mallan, Kerry (1999b) Reading(s) Beneath the Surface: Using Picture Books to Develop a Critical Aesthetics. *Australian Journal of Language and Literacy*, 23(1), pp. 11–21.

Mallan, Kerry (2002a) Picture Books as Performative Texts: Or How to Do Things with Words and Pictures. *Papers: Explorations into Children's Literature*, 12(2), pp. 26–37.

Mallan, Kerry (2002b) Picturing the Male: Representations of Masculinity in Picture Books. In J. Stephens (ed.) *Ways of Being Male: Representing Masculinities in Children's Literature and Film*. New York and London: Routledge, pp. 15–37.

Mallan, Kerry (2005) Trash Aesthetics and Utopian Memory: *The Tip at the End of the Street* and *The Lost Thing*. *Bookbird*, 33(1), pp. 28–34.

Mallan, Kerry (2009) *Gender Dilemmas in Children's Literature*. Basingstoke and New York: Palgrave Macmillan.

Mallan, Kerry and Bradford, Clare (eds) (2011) *Contemporary Children's Literature and Film: Engaging with Theory*. Basingstoke: Palgrave Macmillan.

Mansfield, Nick (2000) *Subjectivity: Theories of the Self from Freud to Haraway*. Sydney: Allen & Unwin.

Marshall, Catherine and Rossman, Gretchen (1999) *Designing Qualitative Research* (3rd edn). London: Sage.

Martin, James (2006) Vernacular Deconstruction: Undermining Spin. *Journal of Documentary Studies in Theoretical and Applied Linguistics (DELTA)*, 22(1).

McCallum, Robyn (1996) Metafictions and Experimental Work. In P. Hunt (ed.) *International Companion Encyclopedia of Children's Literature*. London: Routledge, pp. 397–409.

McCallum, Robyn (1999) *Ideologies of Identity in Adolescent Fiction: The Dialogic Construction of Subjectivity*. New York: Garland Publishing.

McCallum, Robyn (2008) Would I Lie to You?: Metalepsis and Modal Disruption in Some 'True' Fairy Tales. In L. Sipe and S. Pantaleo (eds)

Postmodern Picturebooks: Play, Parody, and Self-Referentiality. New York and London: Routledge, pp. 180–92.

McHale, Brian (1987) *Postmodernist Fiction*. London and New York: Routledge.

McHale, Brian (1992) *Constructing Postmodernism*. London and New York: Routledge.

McKenzie, John (2005) Bums, Poos and Wees: Carnivalesque Spaces in the Picture Books of Early Childhood. Or has Literature Gone to the Dogs? *English Teaching: Practice and Critique*, 4(1), pp. 81–94, http://edlinked.soe.waikato.ac.nz/research/files/etpc/files/2005v4n1art6.pdf

McLaughlin, Robert (2004) Post-Postmodern Discontent: Contemporary Fiction and the Social World. *symploke*, 12(1–2), pp. 53–68.

McMillan, Cheryl (2000) Metafiction and Humour in *The Great Escape from City Zoo*. *Papers: Explorations into Children's Literature*, 10(2), pp. 5–11.

McMillan, Cheryl (2002) Re-Visions of Form: Utilising Postmodernist Perspectives in Children's Literature. Unpublished Doctor of Philosophy Thesis, Macquarie University, Sydney, New South Wales.

Meek, M. (1988) *How Texts Teach what Readers Learn*. Stroud: Thimble Press.

Meek, Margaret (1992) Children Reading – Now. In M. Styles, E. Bearne and V. Watson (eds) *After Alice*. London: Cassell.

Mendoza, Jean Paine (2007) Goodbye Columbus: Take Two. In D. Seale and B. Slapin (eds) *A Broken Flute: The Native Experience in Books for Children*. New York and Toronto: AltaMira Press and Oyate, pp. 196–200.

Moon, Brian (2001) *Literary Terms: A Practical Glossary* (2nd edn). Cottesloe, WA: Chalkface.

Moore, Henrietta (2008) The Problem of Culture. In D. Held and H. Moore (eds) *Cultural Politics in a Global Age: Uncertainty, Solidarity and Innovation*. Oxford: Oneworld, pp. 21–8.

Morley, David and Robins, Kevin (1995) *Global Media, Electronic Landscapes and Cultural Boundaries*. London and New York: Routledge.

Morris, Meaghan (2002) Feminism, Reading, Postmodernism. In Bran Nicol (ed.) *Postmodernism and the Contemporary Novel: A Reader*. Edinburgh University Press, pp. 390–5.

Morris, Pam (ed.) (1994) *The Bakhtin Reader: Selected Writings of Bakhtin, Mededev and Voloshinov*. London: Arnold.

Mortensen, Peter (2003) 'Civilization's Fear of Nature': Postmodernity, Culture, and Environment in *The God of Small Things*. In K. Stierstorfer (ed.) *Beyond Postmodernism: Reassessments in Literature, Theory, and Culture*. Berlin: Walter de Grutyer, pp. 179–95.

Moss, Geoff (1992) Metafiction, Illustration, and the Poetics of Children's Literature. In P. Hunt (ed.) *Literature for Children: Contemporary Criticism*. London and New York: Routledge, pp. 44–65.

Munslow, Alun (1997) *Deconstructing History*. London: Routledge.

Munslow, Alun (2003) *Preface to Routledge Classics Edition*. London and New York: Routledge.

Nelson, Claudia (2006) Writing the Reader: The Literary Child in and beyond the Book. *Children's Literature Association Quarterly*, 31(3), pp. 222–36.

Nicol, Bran (2009) *The Cambridge Introduction to Postmodern Fiction*. Cambridge University Press.

Nikolajeva, Maria (2003) Beyond the Grammar of Story, or How Can Children's Literature Benefit from Narrative Theory? *Children's Literature Association Quarterly*, 28(1), pp. 5–16.

Nikolajeva, Maria (2008a) Comparative Children's Literature: What is There to Compare? *Papers: Explorations into Children's Literature*, 18(1), pp. 30–40.

Nikolajeva, Maria (2008b) Play and Playfulness in Postmodern Picturebooks. In L. Sipe and S. Pantaleo (eds) *Postmodern Picturebooks: Play, Parody, and Self-Referentiality*. New York and London: Routledge, pp. 55–74.

Nikolajeva, Maria and Scott, Carole (2000) The Dynamics of Picturebook Communication. *Children's Literature in Education*, 31(4), pp. 225–39.

Nikolajeva, Maria and Scott, Carole (2006) *How Picturebooks Work*. New York: Routledge.

Nodelman, Perry (1988) *Words about Pictures: The Narrative Art of Children's Picture Books*. Athens: University of Georgia Press.

Nodelman, Perry (1992) *The Pleasures of Children's Literature*. New York: Longman.

Nodelman, Perry (2008) *The Hidden Adult: Defining Children's Literature*. Baltimore: Johns Hopkins University Press.

Norris, Christopher (1990) *What's Wrong with Postmodernism: Critical Theory and the Ends of Philosophy*. Baltimore: Johns Hopkins University Press.

Norris, Christopher (1993) *The Truth about Postmodernism*. Oxford: Blackwell.

O'Connor, Juliet (2004) *The Gingerbread Man Meets Dali: Postmodernism and the Picture Book*. State Library of Victoria, www.statelibrary.vic.gov.au/slv/children/postmodernism/

Ommundsen, Wenche (1993) *Metafictions?: Reflexivity in Contemporary Texts*. Carlton, Victoria: Melbourne University Press.

O'Sullivan, Suzanne (2008) Playfulness in Lauren Child's Picture Books. *Papers: Explorations into Children's Literature*, 18(1), pp. 48–54.

Paley, Nicholas (1992) Postmodernist Impulses and the Contemporary Picture Book: Are There any Stories to these Meanings? *Journal of Youth Services in Libraries*, 5, pp. 151–61.

Pantaleo, Sylvia (2010) Mutinous Fiction: Narrative and Illustrative Metalepsis in Three Postmodern Picturebooks. *Children's Literature in Education*, 41(1), pp. 12–27.

Peace Pledge Union (2010) *Remembering the Victims of the Falklands War*, www.ppu.org.uk/falklands/falklands3.html

Pennell, Beverley (1996) Ideological Drift in Children's Picture Books. *Papers: Explorations into Children's Literature*, 6(2), pp. 5–13.

Penticton (2011) *History of Penticton*, www.learnforestry.com/lessons/grade3/2007/timeline_penticton.pdf

Pleasants, K. (2006) Does Environmental Education Need a Thneed?: Displacing *The Lorax* as Environmental Text. *Canadian Journal of Environmental Education*, 11, pp. 179–94.

Reynolds, Kimberley (2008) *Radical Children's Literature: Future Visions and Aesthetic Transformations in Juvenile Fiction*. London and New York: Palgrave.

Richardson, Brian (ed.) (2002) *Narrative Dynamics: Essays on Time, Plot, Closure and Frames*. Columbus: Ohio State University Press.

Ricoeur, Paul (1985) *Time and Narrative*, vol. 2, trans. K. McLaughlin and D. Pellauer. University of Chicago Press.

Riddle, Tohby (2010) Every Picture Tells a Story, from *Sunday Age* (3 December 2000), www.tohby.com/Tohby_Riddle-Sunday_Age.html

Ritzer, George (1993) *The McDonaldization of Society: An Investigation into the Changing Character of Contemporary Social Life*. Thousand Oaks, CA: Pine Forge Press.

Ritzer, George (ed.) (2007) *The Blackwell Companion to Globalization*. Malden, MA and Oxford: Blackwell.

Robertson, Roland (1992) *Globalization: Social Theory and Global Culture*. London: Sage.

Robertson, Roland and White, Kathleen (2007) What is Globalization? In G. Ritzer (ed.) *The Blackwell Companion to Globalization*. Malden, MA and Oxford: Blackwell, pp. 54–66.

Robinson, William I. (2007) Theories of Globalization. In George Ritzer (ed.) *The Blackwell Companion to Globalization*. Malden, MA and Oxford: Blackwell, pp. 125–43.

Rose, Gillian (2007) *Visual Methodologies: An Introduction to the Interpretation of Visual Materials* (2nd edn). London and New Delhi: Sage.

Rose, Jacqueline (1984) *The Case of Peter Pan: or, The Impossibility of Children's Fiction*. London: Macmillan.

Ryan, Marie-Laure (1999) Immersion vs Interactivity: Virtual Reality and Literary Theory. *SubStance*, 28(2), pp. 110–37.

Ryan, Mark (1999) *Literary Theory: A Practical Introduction*. Oxford: Blackwell.

Saussure, Ferdinand de (1959) *Course in General Linguistics*, trans. Wade Baskin. New York: Philosophical Library.

Schwenke-Wyile, Andrea (2006) The Drama of Potentiality in Metafictive Picture Books: Engaging in Pictorialization in *Shortcut*, *Ooh-la-la*, and *Voices in the Park* (with occasional assistance from A. Wolf's *True Story*). *Children's Literature Association Quarterly*, 31(2), pp. 176–96.

Screen Australia Digital Learning (2008) *Mabo: The Native Title Revolution*, www.mabonativetitle.com/tn_01.shtml

Selden, Raman and Widdowson, Peter (1993) *A Reader's Guide to Contemporary Literary Theory*. New York: Harvester Wheatsheaf.

Serafini, Frank (2005) Voices in the Park, Voices in the Classroom: Readers Responding to Postmodern Picture Books. *Reading Research and Instruction*, 44(3), pp. 47–64.

Silvey, Anita (2001) Pigs in Space. *School Library Journal*, 27(11), pp. 48–50.

Sim, Stuart (ed.) (1999) *The Routledge Critical Dictionary of Postmodern Thought*. New York: Routledge.

Sim, Stuart (2005) Postmodernism and Philosophy. In S. Sim (ed.) *The Routledge Companion to Postmodernism* (2nd edn). London and New York: Routledge, pp. 3–12.

Sipe, Lawrence (1998) How Picture Books Work: A Semiotically Framed Theory of Text–Picture Relationships. *Children's Literature in Education,* 29(2), pp. 97–107.

Sipe, Lawrence and Pantaleo, Sylvia (eds) (2008) *Postmodern Picturebooks: Play, Parody, and Self-Referentiality.* New York and London: Routledge.

Sloboda, Nicholas (1997) Heteroglossia and Collage: Donald Barthelme's *Snow White. Mosaic,* 30(4), pp. 109–23.

Smethurst, Paul (2000) *Postmodern Chronotope: Reading Space and Time in Contemporary Fiction.* Amsterdam and Atlanta, GA: Rodopi.

Solomon, M.R., Bamossy, G. and Askegaard, S. (2002) *Consumer Behaviour: A European Perspective* (2nd edn). Harlow: Prentice Hall.

Sovereign Hill (2010) *Sovereign Hill Home page,* www.sovereignhill.com.au/

Spencer, Lloyd (2005) Postmodernism, Modernity, and the Tradition of Dissent. In S. Sim (ed.) *The Routledge Companion to Postmodernism* (2nd edn). London and New York: Routledge, pp. 158–69.

Stephens, John (1992) *Language and Ideology in Children's Fiction.* Harlow: Longman.

Stephens, John (1996) Children's Literature, Interdisciplinarity and Cultural Studies. In Clare Bradford (ed.) *Writing the Australian Child: Texts and Contexts in Fictions for Children.* Nedlands, WA: University of Western Australia Press, pp. 161–79.

Stephens, John (2008) They are Always Surprised at What People Throw Away: Glocal Postmodernism in Australian Picturebooks. In L. Sipe and S. Pantaleo (eds) *Postmodern Picturebooks: Play, Parody, and Self-Referentiality.* New York and London: Routledge, pp. 89–102.

Stephens, John and Watson, Ken (eds) (1994) *From Picture Book to Literary Theory.* Sydney: St. Clair Press.

Stevenson, Deborah (1994) 'If you Read this Last Sentence, It Won't Tell You Anything': Postmodernism, Self-Referentiality, and *The Stinky Cheese Man. Children's Literature Association Quarterly,* 19(1), pp. 32–4.

Stierstorfer, Klaus (2003) Introduction: Beyond Postmodernism – Contingent Referentiality? In K. Stierstorfer (ed.) *Beyond Postmodernism: Reassessments in Literature, Theory, and Culture.* Berlin: Walter de Gruyter, pp. 1–10.

Styles, Morag and Bearne, Eve (eds) (2003) *Art, Narrative and Childhood.* Stoke-on-Trent: Trentham Books.

Tan, Shaun (2008) *Essay: Originality and Creativity,* www.shauntan.net/essay2.html

Thacker, Deborah and Webb, Jean (2002) *Introducing Children's Literature: From Romanticism to Postmodernism.* New York: Routledge.

Todorov, Tzvetan (1973) *The Fantastic: A Structural Approach to a Literary Genre,* trans. Richard Howard. Cleveland, OH: Press of Case Western Reserve University.

Tomlinson, John (1991) *Cultural Imperialism.* London: Pinter Publishers.

Tomlinson, John (2007) Cultural Globalization. In George Ritzer (ed.) *The Blackwell Companion to Globalization*. Malden, MA and Oxford: Blackwell, pp. 352–66.

Travis, Molly (1998) *Reading Cultures: The Constructions of Readers in the Twentieth Century.* Carbondale: Southern Illinois University Press.

Tumber, Howard and Webster, Frank (2007) Globalization and Information and Communication Technologies: The Case of War. In George Ritzer (ed.) *The Blackwell Companion to Globalization*. Malden, MA and Oxford: Blackwell, pp. 396–413.

Turner, Bryan (1991) *Theories of Modernity and Postmodernity.* London: Sage.

Turner, Bryan (2000) Globalization and the Postmodernization of Culture. In John Beynon and David Dunkerley (eds) *Globalization: The Reader.* New York: Routledge, pp. 110–12.

Virilio, Paul (1991) *The Lost Dimension*, trans. Daniel Moshenberg. New York: Semio-text(e).

Virilio, Paul (2000) *Polar Inertia.* London: Sage.

Waters, Malcolm (1995) *Globalization.* London: Routledge.

Watson, Nigel (2005) Postmodernism and Lifestyles. In S. Sim (ed.) *The Routledge Companion to Postmodernism* (2nd edn). London and New York: Routledge, pp. 35–44.

Waugh, Patricia (1984) *Metafiction: The Theory and Practice of Self-conscious Fiction.* London: Routledge.

White, Hayden (1976) The Fictions of Factual Representation. In Angus Fletcher (ed.) *The Literature of Fact.* New York: Columbia University Press.

White, Hayden (1978) *Tropics of Discourse: Essays in Cultural Criticism.* Baltimore, MD: Johns Hopkins University Press.

Wilkie-Stibbs, Christine (1996) Intertextuality. In P. Hunt (ed.) *International Companion Encyclopedia of Children's Literature.* London: Routledge, pp. 131–7.

Woods, Tim (1999) *Beginning Postmodernism.* Manchester University Press.

Zurbrugg, Nicholas (2000) *Critical Vices: The Myths of Postmodern Theory.* Amsterdam: G+B Arts International.

Index

Aboriginal peoples, 102–4
absences, 99, 101, 111
absolutism, 19, 70
Adams, Rachel, 20–2, 126
aesthetic, 7, 21, 48–9, 63, 133, 166, 168
agency, 42, 77, 91, 104
Ahlberg, Alan, 3, 18, 177
Ahlberg, Janet, 3, 18
Albrow, Mike, 143
alienation, 126, 154, 179
Allan, Cherie, 34, 146, 157
ambiguity, 6, 11, 29, 33, 48, 51, 68–70, 75, 80
Americas, the, 105–6, 109–10
anachronism, 90, 97, 103, 110, 114–15, 159
anagram, 60, 113
Ang, Ien, 143
An Undone Fairy Tale, 21
arbitrary, 9, 14, 58–9, 62–5
artefact (text as), 15, 22, 30, 36, 80, 84–5, 88–90, 97, 113, 145
atrium, 153
audience, 3–4, 56, 75, 85, 126, 162
  dual, 82
  implied, 51, 98
  primary, 15, 19, 98, 145, 146
authenticity, 86, 97, 100, 114, 120, 159, 164

Bad Day at Riverbend, 71, 88
Bakhtin, Mikhail, 24, 31, 34–5, 40–2, 48, 151, 163, 177
Baloney (Henry P.), 59, 62, 177
Banyai, Istvan, 70
Barker, Chris, 143, 144
Barth, John, 19, 21, 140
Barthes, Roland, 31, 35, 72, 176, 177
Base, Graeme, 98, 110, 113

Baudrillard, Jean, 57, 73, 158
Bauman, Zygmunt, 125, 142–4, 160–2
Belsey, Catherine, 38, 41
Berger, Arthur, 5, 6, 57, 164, 166, 170
Bernstein, Richard, 14
Bertens, Hans, 14, 60, 70, 74, 75, 175
Best, Steven, 5
Beware of the Storybook Wolves, 32, 64, 91–2
Beynon, John, 140, 147, 167
Bhabha, Homi, 13, 138
Black and White, 16, 18, 33, 36, 66–70, 74–5, 124, 141, 173
blogs, 151, 162
Boli, John, 147
boundaries, 3, 9, 11–12, 45, 57–8, 68, 73–4, 80, 129–30, 139, 158–64, 171, 174
  violation of, 11, 81–93
Bradford, Clare, 15, 18, 29, 100–8
Briggs, Raymond, 98, 110
Browne, Anthony, 3, 10, 18, 39–40, 176
Burningham, John, 11, 18, 33, 176
Butler, Christopher, 5, 6, 10, 19, 74, 79, 123, 157, 179

Caldwell, Melissa, 144
Canclini, Garcia, 144, 148, 169
Carnivalesque, 24, 48–9, 91, 116, 150–1, 163, 165, 172
Carter, Angela, 124
Ceci n'est pas une pipe (Magritte), 70, 174
Certeau, Michel de, 12, 95
characters, 12, 29, 33, 39, 41, 44–6, 50–1, 54, 74–6, 80, 84, 87–9, 90–3, 128, 132, 138, 177
  ontological status of 74–6, 84–94

Child, Lauren, 3, 18, 28, 32, 57, 67, 72–3, 77, 89, 91, 156, 176
children's literature, 2–3, 10–12, 15–23
Chinese-box structure, 89
chronotope, 35
    postmodern chronotope, 35–6, 41, 66, 134, 147
Cindy-ella, 21
city (or cities), 3, 142, 152, 162
cityscape, 128, 133–4, 137, 148–9, 151, 153
clichés, 126
closure, 10, 19, 33, 64, 70, 145, 165, 171
Cobley, Paul, 14, 35
Cole, Babette, 10, 32
collage, 48, 72–4, 86, 118
    photo, 131, 133
colonists, 100–3
Columbus, Christopher, 105–10
Columbus Day, 108
Come Away from the Water, Shirley, 11
conclusions (endings), 64, 86, 104, 170
connectivity, 143–8, 169
Connor, Stephen, 20–3, 141
consciousness, 133, 140, 147
    global, 143–4, 147, 169
constructions, 17, 74–6, 84, 96, 112, 113, 167
consumer, 3, 23, 33, 142–3, 147, 154–5, 160–8
    consumer goods, *see* goods: consumer
consumerism, 3, 24, 134, 139, 142, 165–6, 169
consumption, 3, 23, 37, 141–3, 160–9
contradiction, 30, 49, 128
covers (of book), 18, 63, 145, 178
Cox, Paul, 24, 64, 142, 145
Coyote Columbus Story, A, 98, 105, 107, 110, 174
Crook, Stephen, 10
cultural norms, 15, 106, 128

demand acts, 51, 85, 117
Derrien, Marie, 30, 157
dialogic, 34, 40–1, 167
diegetic, 11, 34, 49, 69, 74, 82–3, 88–90; *see also* hypodiegetic
différance, 59
direct address, 21, 43, 84, 115, 120
discourse, 12, 16, 20–1, 25, 31, 35, 37–8, 40, 47–8, 78–80, 96, 103–5, 123, 174
Discovery of Dragons, The, 98, 110, 113–14, 122, 178
diversity, 122–4, 142, 148
Do Not Open This Book!, 21
Downard, Barry, 42, 98, 142, 158–9, 179
dramatis personae, 91
Dudek, Debra, 134–8, 179
Dunkerley, David, 140, 147, 167
durée (or duration), 146

Eagleton, Terry, 5, 9, 80
El llibre dins el llibre dins el llibre, 70
embodiment, 76, 135, 176
Empty City, The, 24, 142, 145, 147–9, 172
endpapers, 37, 62, 71, 84, 86, 102, 131, 135, 148, 152–4
Enlightenment, 7, 8, 75, 126
epistemological issues, 11–12, 69
ex-centrics, 20, 124–32
excess, 18, 54, 101, 134, 137, 145, 152, 165
extraliterary discourses, 97

fairy tale, 3, 10, 21, 31, 43, 47–8, 64–5, 76, 85, 89–93, 116, 120, 176–7
Falkland Islands, 111
fantastic, 98, 110, 153
Featherstone, Mike, 3, 57, 154, 157, 159–66, 175
First Nation, 105–9
focaliser, 12, 38, 40, 43, 55, 76
folk tale, 48, 81, 116–17

fragmentation, 4, 11, 21, 29, 48, 51, 144, 148, 152, 162, 169, 173
frame-breaking, 33, 40, 44, 46, 63, 64, 121, 173
frames, 25, 33, 44, 53, 63, 66, 68, 75, 83, 96, 173
Freeman, Elizabeth, 4
Frog Prince Continued, The, 32, 65
Frow, John, 63
Fuery, Patrick, 31, 61, 138
future, 102, 145, 146, 149, 153, 173, 177

Galtieri, General Leopoldo (President of Argentina), 111
gamescape, 149–51
gaze, the, 125, 127, 129, 149
Genette, Gerard, 34, 37, 45, 72, 146
gentrification, 154
Geyh, Paula, 1, 4, 22, 23, 29
global, 142–4, 147, 149–51
    cities, 147, 150–4
globalisation, 7, 23–4, 139–47, 161, 163, 169, 179
glocalisation, 142, 144
Goldstone, Bette, 35, 51, 71
goods, 151, 160–2, 165, 166, 179
    consumer, 148–9, 167–8
    cultural, 141–2, 148, 160
Granpa, 33–4, 156
Great Escape from City Zoo, The, 32, 118, 125, 130, 132, 138
Grieve, Ann, 11, 18, 23, 26, 37, 47, 72

Harvey, Roland, 24, 142, 151
Hassan, Ihab, 5, 7, 8, 17, 20–2, 141, 173, 175
Heise, Ursula, 8, 9, 22, 145
heterogeneity, 25, 123, 133, 143, 153, 179–80
heteroglossia, 40, 44, 47, 50–1, 177
hierarchy of voices, 38–9, 50–1
historiographic metafiction, 13, 94, 96–122
historiography, 12–13, 95–7, 100, 105, 110–11, 115–16, 120, 122, 176

history, 12–13, 17, 95–122, 164, 170, 178, 179
Hoberek, Andrew, 21, 22, 95, 141
homogeneity, 123, 133, 144, 148, 153, 179
hooks, bell, 124
humour, 61, 70, 110, 126, 154
Hutcheon, Linda, 6, 7, 12–13, 16, 20, 25, 27, 30–3, 44, 47, 56–8, 79, 81, 84, 93–7, 106, 112–13, 118, 124–6, 133, 141, 173, 175
hybrid, 9, 100, 102, 104, 110, 135, 137, 144, 152, 169, 174
hybridity, 110, 152–3
hyperreality, 3, 6, 57–8, 73, 163
hypodiegetic, 11, 69, 74, 82–3, 90–2

iconography, 85, 131, 133, 151
identity, 8, 20, 74–9, 87, 99, 124, 133, 135, 139, 142–3, 151, 161, 167–9, 175
identity politics, 20, 139, 178
ideological drift, 53, 103
ideology, 53, 82, 97, 103, 124
Il Libro piu corto del mondo, 24, 64, 142, 145–7, 169, 172–3
immediatization, 23
indeterminacy, 6, 10–11, 18, 33, 53, 57, 68, 75, 80, 127
Indigenous peoples, 100–1, 104
    systems of narrative, 105
instantaneity, 145, 147
Internet, 22–3, 145, 147–8, 155, 157, 179
intertextuality, 4, 14, 29, 31–3, 36, 40, 47, 57, 63, 81, 89, 97, 122, 171, 178
In the City, 24, 142, 145, 147, 151–3, 160–9, 174
irony, 9, 14, 18, 19, 22, 30, 62, 63, 70, 86, 90, 108, 109, 112, 115, 117, 122, 145, 153, 154, 156, 158, 163, 166
I Will Not Ever NEVER Eat a Tomato, 57

Jameson, Fredric, 4, 7, 13, 14, 61, 160, 175, 176
Jencks, Charles, 7, 21
Jolly Postman, The, 3

Keep, Christopher, 5, 10
Kellner, Douglas, 5, 149, 179
Kent Monkman, William, 105, 107
King, Thomas, 105, 107
Kirby, Alan, 20, 22, 141, 173
knowability of the past, 114
Kress, Gunter, 50, 51, 71, 117, 148
Kristeva, Julia, 31, 41, 177

language, 8, 12, 31, 35, 38, 58–63, 77, 79–80, 82, 98, 115–16, 126, 153, 162–3, 176
  invented, 59, 62
Lehr, Susan, 73, 177
leisure, 3, 146, 160–2
Lewis, Barry, 20, 141, 173
Lewis, David, 1, 15, 18, 19, 29, 30, 33, 54, 65, 176
liberal humanist, 2, 5, 20, 23, 25, 53, 54, 122, 123, 125, 138, 141, 167, 169, 172, 174, 175
linguistic, 27, 59, 61, 62, 76, 120, 126, 161
  games, 29, 58, 151
  modifiers, 120
  subterfuge, 121
Lissiat, Amy, 142, 165
'Literature of Exhaustion' (Barth), 19, 21
Little Mouse's (Emily Gravett's) Big Book of Fears, 36
Lost Thing, The, 24, 125, 133–8, 178
Lowenthal, David, 150
Lozada, Eriberto, 144
Lucy, Niall, 14
Lyon, David, 7, 9
Lyotard, Jean-François, 5, 14

Macaulay, David, 16, 66, 67, 75, 176
Mackey, Margaret, 54, 71, 72, 82, 85
Magritte, René, 70, 77, 126, 174
Mallan, Kerry, 29, 101, 110, 134, 143, 145, 168, 179

Mansfield, Nick, 32, 61, 138
marginalisation, 123, 125, 127, 128
Marsden, John, 98, 100, 104, 152
Martin, James, 111
mass media, 22–4, 74, 139, 141–4, 155–6, 169
McCallum, Robyn, 28, 29, 35, 39, 88, 89, 96–109, 117, 121
McDonaldization, 144, 149, 179
McHale, Brian, 10–12, 44, 66, 68, 74, 80–91, 102, 105, 110–11, 131, 175–7
McLaughlin, Robert, 20, 22, 141, 173
McMillan, Cheryl, 11, 15, 126
McWorld, 144, 179
mediatisation, 155
Megarrity, David, 24, 147
Memorial, 98–9, 112
Mendoza, Jean Paine, 108–10
metadiegetic, 88
metafiction, 13, 27, 28, 37, 80, 176
  metafictional strategies, 13, 28, 96, 173
metalepsis, 34, 40, 44–51, 81, 171
metanarratives, 3–7, 14, 79, 101, 103, 126, 134
metaphor, 29, 73, 100, 132
mise-en-abyme, 71, 81, 89, 159
modality, 52, 58, 72–3, 86, 88, 99
modernism, 5–8, 12, 19, 21, 36, 74, 143, 172, 175, 176
modernist, 5, 7, 11, 19, 134, 137, 160, 170, 172, 175, 176
modernity, 7, 143, 161, 175
Moon, Brian, 56, 57
Morris, Meaghan, 13
motif, 42, 48, 102, 146, 162
multiliteracies, 4, 175
mythical time, 120
My Uncle is a Hunkle Says Clarice Bean, 73, 156

narration, 34, 38, 40, 43–4, 48–9, 50, 55, 74, 78, 101, 120
  first person, 40
  third person, 49, 52, 96–7, 120, 122
narrative, 1–3, 9, 12, 13, 16, 17, 25, 27–31, 33–6, 42–3, 44, 46–8,

50–2, 55–8, 64–6, 68–70, 74, 78,
    80–6, 87–9, 92, 96–7, 100, 109,
    115, 120, 126, 134, 141, 169,
    171, 173, 177
  disruption, 23, 33
  gaps, 18
  polyphonic, 51
narrator, 1, 9, 19, 28, 34, 37–41,
    43–50, 55, 75–6, 101, 106, 134,
    138, 146
  intrusive, 44, 86
  unreliable, 52
Nelson, Claudia, 72
Nicol, Bran, 7, 12, 23, 96, 176
Nikolajeva, Maria, 29, 39, 175
Nobody Owns the Moon, 125, 128–30,
    138
Nodelman, Perry, 2, 16, 34, 79, 171,
    176
nonconformity, 48, 132, 137
non-linear, 4, 157
nostalgia, 82, 97, 109, 150, 159, 164
  collective, 154, 159, 165
  ironic, 112

O'Connor, Juliet, 18
Ommundsen, Wenche, 56, 176
ontology/ontological, 10–12, 17–18,
    46, 48, 51, 53, 63, 69, 76–8,
    80–91, 145, 176, 177
Ooh-la-la (Max in Love), 59–60, 156
originality, 18, 31, 47, 72
otherness, 58, 123–5, 134, 137
Oxlade, Jonathan, 24, 142, 147

Pantaleo, Sylvia, 2, 4, 15–16, 83, 84,
    175
paradox, 16–17, 30, 95, 97, 106, 124–
    5, 130, 154, 157, 167, 171–3
parody, 10, 18, 29, 31–3, 40, 43, 48,
    50–1, 63, 66, 72, 87, 97, 106,
    109–10, 122–3, 158, 161, 165,
    171
past (the), 12–13, 34, 95–103,
    109–18, 131, 141, 145–6, 150,
    153–4, 159, 163–4
pastiche, 4, 9, 18, 48, 72, 99, 126,
    148, 159, 165, 168, 171

Pennell, Beverley, 53, 103
peritext, 36–8, 69
permanent present, 145
Petrova, Velina, 147
photographs, 58, 72–4, 99, 112, 151,
    159, 168
photo illustration, 159
picturebook, 1, 4, 8, 29–30, 32–4,
    38, 46, 75, 76, 80, 97, 98, 146,
    172–3
  conventional, 2, 12, 18, 19, 66
Pierce, Clayton, 149, 179
place, 41, 66, 100, 133, 135–8, 152
  placelessness, 134, 152–4, 161,
    ˙167, 169, 179
playfulness, 3, 4, 9, 19, 21, 29, 30,
    39, 43, 59–63, 83–4, 86, 115,
    122, 126, 142, 153, 155, 158,
    161–3, 170, 173
Pleasants, Kathleen, 101, 104
point of view, 35, 38–40, 43–4, 46,
    49, 50–1, 55, 100, 111, 116–17,
    119
polyphony, 40–1, 50–1, 57, 171, 177
popular culture, 2–4, 91, 109,
    129–30, 159, 171
post-industrial society, 23, 133
postliterate strategies, 4
postmodern art, 48, 58, 129
postmodernesque, 5, 23–6, 139,
    140–5, 147, 149, 151–2, 155–6,
    158, 161, 164–5, 169, 172–4,
    179
postmodernism, 1–2, 4, 6, 10–12,
    17, 24, 30, 61, 70–2, 80, 95,
    112, 124, 130, 147, 160, 170–1,
    174–5
  changing nature of, 22–3
  criticism of, 13–15, 176
  decline of, 19–21
  influence on children's literature,
    17–18
  meaning of, 6–9
  origins of, 5–6, 7
  representative (particular), 15, 16,
    54, 97, 167
postmodernist ontological
  confrontation, 84

postmodernity, 7–8, 23–5, 57, 139,
    141, 143, 147, 149, 153, 161,
    163, 165–6, 168–9, 172, 175
postmodern picturebook, 2–5, 8,
    15–19, 22–31, 33, 36, 40–1, 54,
    56, 59, 63, 74, 78, 80, 86, 93,
    97, 122, 124, 141, 147, 170–3,
    177
  audience, 4, 15, 19, 51, 56, 76, 82,
    98, 145, 146, 177
post-postmodernism, 20, 141, 173
present (time), 11, 34, 46, 97, 99,
    100, 110, 114, 115, 118, 145–6,
    150, 164
  timeless present, 157
Princess Smartypants, 10, 32
proliferation of choice, 148, 161,
    168
Propp, Vladimir, 48, 177
pseudo places, 152–3
puns, 59, 154, 159

Rabbits, The, 98, 100–3, 105
Race of the Century, The, 24, 142,
    158, 160, 167–9, 172
realism, 30, 38, 40–1, 81, 84
realist fiction, 9–11, 27–30, 39, 86,
    172–3
reality, 8, 10, 25, 27–8, 33, 36, 40,
    44, 55–8
referent, 58, 60, 97, 158
register, 48, 52, 82, 87, 90, 110, 112,
    117, 120, 121
repetition, 28, 42, 75, 131, 135, 146,
    157, 169
representation, 4, 9, 12, 23, 25, 28,
    35–6, 55–9, 63, 66, 73, 78, 80,
    124, 132, 151, 164, 174
  linguistic, 58–63
  of the past, 95–6, 100–12
  visual, 70–3, 77, 86
resistance, 19, 28, 43, 104, 108, 136,
    140, 171, 172
resolution, 10, 18–19, 24, 29, 35, 54,
    64–5, 69, 75–6, 79–80, 173
rhizome, 144

Riddle, Tohby, 32, 125, 128, 131–3,
    176, 178
Robertson, Roland, 142, 143, 144,
    154, 159, 179

Schwenke-Wyile, Andrea, 51, 53, 59
Scieszka, Jon, 1, 32, 43–5, 59, 65, 75,
    98, 116, 117
self-reflexivity, 18, 21, 27, 31, 157,
    176
semiotics, 61
Sendak, Maurice, 28, 85, 148, 176
*Short and Incredibly Happy Life of
    Riley, The*, 24, 142, 160, 168–9,
    174
Shortest Book in the World, The, see *Il
    Libro piu corto del mondo*
signifier, 48, 58–62, 76, 85, 102,
    121, 128, 132, 167–8
signifying systems, 13, 96
signs, 3, 35, 57, 58, 62, 76, 127–8,
    130–4, 137, 141, 148, 151–2,
    159, 160–2
Sim, Stuart, 8
simulacrum/simulacra, 157, 164
simultaneity, 145–6
Singing Hat, The, 125, 131–2, 138
Sipe, Lawrence, 2, 15–16
Smethurst, Paul, 35, 140, 152, 153
Smith, Lane, 1, 32, 43–5, 59, 75, 98,
    116
space, 3, 4, 33, 35–6, 45–6, 48, 51,
    68, 80–1, 83, 93, 100, 123, 130,
    137–8, 145–7, 149, 153, 157,
    169, 171–2, 178, 179
  cyberspace, 36
  ontological, 81, 83, 85, 145
  postmodern, 131, 152–3, 160
  story, 49, 50, 68, 87
  urban, 131, 151
spatio-temporality, 33, 36
spectacle, 23, 90, 153, 158, 161, 164,
    168, 169
Spencer, Lloyd, 14, 163
spiral, 64, 145, 147, 157
split text, 66

Stephens, John, 2, 15, 28, 29, 38, 39, 40, 49, 50, 51, 65, 126, 127, 134, 144, 176, 179
Stevenson, Deborah, 4, 54, 66
Stierstorfer, Klaus, 6, 20
Stinky Cheese Man and Other Fairly Stupid Tales, The, 1, 4, 9, 18, 19, 26, 32–3, 37, 40, 43, 45, 47–8, 54, 64–5, 69, 74–6, 125, 141, 173, 176
Story of a Little Mouse Trapped in a Book, The, 33, 34, 49
subject, 38, 51, 71, 77, 111, 123, 124, 135, 151, 166, 167, 169
subversion, 22, 30, 46, 170, 171

Tan, Shaun, 26, 59, 98, 104, 178
technology, 17, 23, 36, 142, 145, 147, 148, 175
television, 3, 4, 22–3, 73–4, 112, 145, 147–8, 155–60, 175, 176, 179
Thatcher, Margaret, 111
That Pesky Rat, 77
Thompson, Colin, 24, 142, 165
Three Pigs, The, 18, 32–4, 40, 48–51, 53–4, 59, 116, 141, 172
time, 11, 20, 33, 34, 35–6, 41, 66, 68, 101, 120, 122, 130, 134, 135, 145–7, 150, 153–4, 155, 157, 167, 174, 177
time–space dynamics, 145
Tin Pot Foreign General and the Old Iron Woman, The, 98, 110–11
Tomlinson, John, 143, 147, 155
Toynbee, Arnold, 5, 175
transglobal corporations, 144, 152
transgression, 34, 81, 83–4, 92, 97, 148, 150
transmigratory figures, 91, 131
Travis, Molly, 27
True Story of the 3 Little Pigs, The, 98, 116–17, 120, 122
truth, 10, 12, 28, 38, 40, 48, 52, 79–81, 84, 93, 96, 99, 114, 116, 118, 121–2, 141

typographic experimentation, 169
uncertainty, 9, 14, 29, 48, 51, 70, 75–6, 86, 90, 93–4, 97, 99, 122, 127, 131, 171, 173
unity, 12, 25, 35, 79, 122, 123–5, 127, 130, 132–3, 138, 144, 170

Van Allsburg, Chris, 71, 176
van Leeuwen, Theo, 50–1, 71, 117, 148
vector
   non-transactional, 102
   transactional, 42, 156, 159
Virilio, Paul, 145
Virtual Reality technology, 147
virtuous disobedience, 132
Voices in the Park, 18, 33, 36, 40–1, 43, 51–4

Wait! No Paint!, 32, 34, 81, 86–7, 173
Walk in the Park, A, 39–40, 141, 156
Watson, Nigel, 153, 161, 164
Waugh, Patricia, 27–30, 47, 56–7, 63, 65, 76, 79, 173
West, the (Western), 5, 8, 13, 20, 25, 46, 57, 64, 75, 108, 110, 126, 143, 144, 147, 160, 165
Where the Wild Things Are, 17, 28, 33, 36, 85, 148, 150–1, 171, 180
White, Hayden, 12, 95, 109, 116, 120
White, Kathleen, 142
Who's Afraid of the Big Bad Book?, 3, 18, 28, 32–3, 89, 92
Wiesner, David, 18, 32, 48, 59, 116, 176
Willy's Pictures, 3, 18
Wolves, 81, 83–6, 173
Woods, Tim, 6, 8, 17, 23–4, 141, 153, 176

Zoom, 70

CPSIA information can be obtained at www.ICGtesting.com
Printed in the USA
LVOW10*0700270414

383332LV00002B/28/P